THE OTHER SIDE OF
MIDDLETOWN

THE OTHER SIDE OF MIDDLETOWN

Exploring Muncie's African American Community

Edited by Luke Eric Lassiter,
Hurley Goodall, Elizabeth Campbell,
and Michelle Natasya Johnson

Photos by Danny Gawlowski

ALTAMIRA
PRESS

A Division of Rowman & Littlefield Publishers, Inc.
Walnut Creek • Lanham • New York • Toronto • Oxford

ALTAMIRA PRESS
A division of Rowman & Littlefield Publishers, Inc.
1630 North Main Street, #367
Walnut Creek, CA 94596
www.altamirapress.com

Rowman & Littlefield Publishers, Inc.
A wholly owned subsidary of
The Rowman & Littlefield Publishing Group, Inc.
4501 Forbes Boulevard, Suite 200
Lanham, MD 20706

PO Box 317
Oxford
OX2 9RU, UK

Photos by Danny Gawlowski

British Library Cataloguing in Publication Information Available

Library of Congress Cataloging-in-Publication Data

The other side of Middletown : exploring Muncie's African American
community / edited by Luke Eric Lassiter . . . [et al.].
    p. cm.
Includes bibliographical references (p. 281) and index.
  ISBN 0-7591-0483-2 (hardcover : alk. paper) — ISBN 0-7591-0484-0
(pbk. : alk. paper)
  1. African Americans—Indiana—Muncie—Social conditions. 2. African
Americans—Indiana—Muncie—Social life and customs. 3. Muncie
(Ind.)—Social conditions. 4. Muncie (Ind.)—Social life and customs.
I. Lassiter, Luke E.

  F534.M9O84 2004
  305.896'073077265—dc22
                                2003024699

Printed in the United States of America

For the good people of Muncie, Indiana,

in whose honor
all royalties will be donated to
the Vivian Conley Memorial Scholarship Fund,

a Ball State University scholarship for nontraditional, part-time students who
demonstrate a commitment to the betterment of our community.

*The late Vivian V. Conley (1922–1993), community activist for children and seniors.
Courtesy of Ball State University.*

We must study, we must investigate, we must attempt to solve; and the utmost that the world can demand is, not lack of human interest and moral conviction, but rather the heart-quality of fairness, and an earnest desire for the truth.

—W. E. B. DuBois

Contents

Foreword

When I was a first-year sociology major at San Jose State University in California in 1964, the 1929 sociology classic *Middletown: A Study of a Modern American Culture* was required reading. As a young African American undergraduate student, I read the book, not knowing that Muncie, Indiana, had an actively engaged African American population. As a matter of fact, very few of the texts that I read during my undergraduate experience in the late 1960s had references to African Americans and their positive contributions to their families, communities, neighborhoods, or society. Most of those texts I read in sociology portrayed the lives of African Americans as marginal or deviant. So, in some sense, the original Middletown study was a metaphor for the invisibility of people of color in the social science literature during the twentieth century.

This book begins to expand the study that should have been expanded in 1929 to include the African American community. It is important in that it involves anthropologists, students from a variety of disciplines and African American collaborators of black Muncie in an unprecedented partnership and collaborative effort. Under the leadership of anthropologist Luke Eric Lassiter and Muncie native Hurley Goodall, this book is the end result of multiple projects that led up to its publication, including a museum exhibit, an innovative course sponsored by the Virginia B. Ball Center for Creative Inquiry at Ball State University, and ethnographic fieldwork by a group of interdisciplinary undergraduate students and their community partners. This project is also a collaboration among students and faculty. Students worked with faculty to design and carry out their own fieldwork, as well as to contribute to the larger collective ethnography.

In a larger context, this project should also be seen as part of two very important national trends: one in higher education and one in the discipline of anthropology. The first is known as the "engaged university" and the second is the reemerging field called public interest anthropology.

Public universities have long had as a part of their missions to be of service to and engaged with the external community. This engagement can take many forms, from economic development to service learning. The premise for this work is that higher education is a public good, and that universities, by extension, are vehicles for the distribution of those goods or resources. The work done by this project is clearly done for the good of the city of Muncie at large. It is also done on behalf of and in partnership with the African American community of Muncie. A campus that is engaged is one that articulates the larger social purposes of education and uses its resources on behalf of its surrounding community, often in partnership with the community. In this case, the resources are the faculty and students of Ball State University and the partnership is with the people in the black community of Muncie, who finally have an opportunity to tell their stories about their contributions to the city in their own voices. They are setting the record straight. But, more than that, they are contributing to the richness of the legacy of a city that excluded them and their contributions in the past. At the same time, they are laying the foundation to help Muncie move toward a more inclusive future, as difficult as that may be.

The other growing field of inquiry and action is that of public interest anthropology (PIA). Researchers, ethnographers, and practitioners in this field represent a wide range of theoretical and methodological approaches, and all four fields of anthropology. What they have in common is that they are socially engaged and passionate about working on behalf of the interest of their publics.

The goals of public interest anthropology are summarized by anthropologist Peggy Sanday (personal communication) as follows:

1. This approach is motivated by the conviction that anthropology's effectiveness has been diluted by the unwillingness of its academic arm to insert itself into the public sphere of debate and action.
2. Public interest anthropology seeks to merge research and theory development with action and practice in the interest of social change. The research process merges theory development and practice by studying, acting on, and publicly debating particular interests connected to definable publics.

3. The practical aim of public interest anthropology research and action is to mold public opinion and change culturally bound ways of seeing as a way of shaping a political climate and public policies that are sensitive to local needs and global issues.

While PIA is still taking shape in the theory building and in the empirical ethnographic work of anthropologists and other social scientists, it is clear that this publication embodies the major goals of this approach in its focus on collaboration. From the conceptualization of the project, to the collection of the data, to the writing of the book, Lassiter and his colleagues have made every effort to authentically involve the voices of their advisors and the black community of Muncie in their own ethnography. They are involved not as subjects, but as empowered actors, who actually helped to shape and to write the text of this book. This was no easy task, but as Lassiter points out in his introduction: "In that ethnographers work with local communities to construct their texts, the approach to ethnography, as a method, is essentially collaborative. But what makes ethnographic *writing* collaborative is closely involving consultants in the actual writing of the text. For this project, that meant taking the developing chapters back to community advisors and other consultants for corrections, clarifications, and commentary."

I am also struck by the authentic way in which the undergraduate students were involved as collaborators from the very beginning of the project. First, these students worked with the researchers to develop an impressive code of ethics to guide their work in a mutual partnership with the community consultants. How incredibly valuable it is for these young students to have such an experience as a part of their undergraduate careers! Even if many of these students do not go on to be social science researchers, they have already had a life-changing experience. I certainly had no such opportunity as an undergraduate; nor, for that matter, as a graduate student. Second, the students were responsible for writing whole chapters of the book along with their community advisors. While the end result, a published essay, is an achievement to be proud of, the process of growth and development from reluctant ethnographers to accomplished chroniclers of the lives and stories of the people on the "other side of Middletown" is priceless.

Finally, it is only fitting that social scientists in the opening decade of the twenty-first century set out to bring full circle, and in the process improve upon, the seminal study of a typical Midwest community that was done in the early part of the twentieth century. The original *Middletown* set out to show a more "typical" or "stylized" community, by depersonalizing the people who were interviewed and ignoring whole groups of people, including African Americans. This study does just the opposite. Its goals, according to Lassiter, are to "fully embrace the experiences of our consultants, their memories, and their stories, and to use our coexperience (as engendered by our relationships with one another, particularly between the students and their community collaborators) as the foundation for creating our collaborative ethnographic text." This book has achieved those goals. And so much more.

> Yolanda T. Moses,
> past president of the American Anthropological
> Association and president of the American
> Association for Higher Education, July 2003

Acknowledgments

This book would have never come to fruition without the support and guidance of the good people of Muncie, Indiana. Our deepest gratitude goes out to our community advisors who, in addition to Hurley and Fredine Goodall, guided this project: Renzie Abram Jr., Julius Anderson, Phyllis Bartleson, Geraldine Burns, Edgar Faulkner, Eric Johnson, Edward McNeary, Delores Pryor, Carl Rhinehart, Dolores Rhinehart, Phyllis Joanne White, and John Young-El. These community advisors led us to several others who willingly gave of their time so that we might understand more deeply the experience that serves as the foundation for what follows. They are (all of whom are not cited in the text): Sam F. Abram, Belinda Anderson, Brenton Anderson, Stefan S. Anderson, Mamie Barker, Viola Jeanne Boyd, Vida Burton, Jayné Carey, Anthony Conley, Wilma Cooper, B. J. Crumes, Kelli A. Daugherty, Emma Sue Davis, Rosemary Edwards, Deja Gauldin, Bill Harrell, Dorothy Harris, Denise Hill, Josh Hughes, Willie James Jackson, Denise Jones, Robert L. Jones III, Robert L. Jones IV, Yolanda E. Jones, Bessie Jordan, Lonnie Jordan, Charlotte Levi, Erica Rena Long, Samuel L. Long, Catrice Marks, Gary D. Mason, S. Michael Millben, Richard Miller, TaNesha Moore, Monte Murphy, Ella McNeary, Jessica McNeary, Wondreia Nevings, Gwynne Orcutt, Ron Orcutt, Daidra Pryor, Erika Quarles, Ruth E. Redd, Ruth Robinson, Mallie V. Ross, Q. L. Stevens, Willa Mae Stevens, Fronia M. Stigler, Jasmine Taylor, Robert Vance, Ralph Vaughn, Ren-á Wagner, Rhonda Ward, Nicole Watson, Kimberly Williams, Shelia A. Williams, Evelyn Wilson, Frank W. Wilson, and Kellie Woods.

A good number of these folks attend the historic Shaffer Chapel A.M.E. Church, where we were graciously welcomed to meet for class, interviews, or community forums. The church's "Golden Girls" often cooked meals or served refreshments when we gathered, and for this we are especially grateful!

Several people at Ball State University worked with us during different stages in this work, helping us to more fully understand the Muncie community, introducing us to resources, or guiding our writing. They include Michael Doyle, Department of History; E. Bruce Geelhoed, Center for Middletown Studies; Melinda Messineo, Department of Sociology; Robert Nowatzki, Department of English; and John Straw, Archives and Special Collections.

A very special thanks to AltaMira Press for believing so strongly in this project and for extending their support at every stage in its development. Thanks especially to Rosalie Robertson, editor-in-chief at AltaMira, who showed her enthusiasm by first reading the classic *Middletown*, then conducting a conference call with the students during the second week of class, and then, at midsemester, taking the time to fly out to Muncie from California to help us conceptualize the book's trajectory. Thanks also to Detta Penna of Penna Design and Production, who carefully edited the final manuscript, and, like Rosalie, flew out from California to meet with the research team before we sent the book to AltaMira for review.

We especially commend the dedicated staff at the Virginia B. Ball Center—Director Joseph Trimmer, Assistant Director Donna Ferguson, and technical genius James Miles—who, while working to make so many projects like this one a reality, carefully attended to our particular vision with encouragement and enthusiasm when an overabundance of naysayers doubted we could actually pull it off.

In addition to the Virginia B. Ball Center, our other sponsors included the Center for Middletown Studies, the Muncie Commission on the Social Status of Black Males, and the Community Foundation of Muncie and Delaware County, Inc. We are grateful to them as well, and to all of the many not named here who rooted for us.

This project would have never happened without Virginia B. Ball, who, through funding the Virginia B. Ball Center for Creative Inquiry, has made many exceptional educational experiences like this one possible. A great believer in *The Other Side of Middletown*, Virginia eagerly anticipated its publication. Sadly, she passed away just as this book went to press. We, and many others in our community, deeply regret that she will never see this publication, the end product of a project she so faithfully supported. In a way, though, her absence now heightens the importance of an idea embedded in all VBC projects: as important as the center's community-based products are, in the end, these projects are as much about process as they are about products. Though we cannot share this product of *The Other Side of Middletown* with Virginia, we are deeply grateful that she was with us to share in its process.

Introduction

The Story of a Collaborative Project

Luke Eric Lassiter

On a cold afternoon in early January 2003, a group of Ball State University faculty and students gathered at the Virginia B. Ball Center for Creative Inquiry to talk about beginning the collaborative ethnography that lies before you—the brainchild of retired seventy-seven-year-old Indiana state legislator Hurley Goodall. After making some introductions, I asked Hurley to talk about the work that lay ahead: "I wondered if Hurley could talk a little about his vision for this project and how it is we're here now. . . ."

"Okay, I'm Hurley Goodall," he began. "I'm a native of Muncie, and that's one of the reasons I'm extremely interested in what you're doing. On behalf of the community, I'd like to thank you. . . ." Hurley pulled out a piece of paper from a folder that sat on the table in front of him. It was a selection from his own writing. "I would just like to read you part of the original Lynd plan—to tell you why this project is being done."

Hurley began reading: "In 1929, Robert S. Lynd and Helen Merrell Lynd [published] . . . what they called an 'objective study' of American society. The method they used was to come and live in that American community, observe the people, the institutions, and forces that made the community work. The effort was also designed to show how communities change over time, but also how certain things did not change. The choice of the Muncie community was determined, in part, by population. . . ."

Hurley looked up from his reading. "And this is the part I'm interested in," he said, ". . . a homogeneous native born population, a small foreign-born and Negro population that could basically be ignored."

"That was the standard the Lynds set," said Hurley after a short pause. "So, in essence, the African American community here . . . was

1

completely ignored by that study. And, hopefully, some of the things you'll be doing will fill that void."[1]

When Robert S. and Helen Merrell Lynd first published *Middletown: A Study in Modern American Culture* in 1929, it was immediately heralded for its unprecedented survey of a "typical" American city. With few exceptions, social scientists had never attempted an American-based study so broad in its scope.[2] Influenced by anthropologists such as Clark Wissler (who wrote the book's foreword), the Lynds used anthropological research methods to organize their fieldwork (long-term participation and observation in one locality).[3] The Lynds also used the theoretical approaches to culture in use among the day's social anthropologists to organize their writing: they split their study into six broad cultural categories (with each receiving treatment in individual chapters)—Getting a Living, Making a Home, Training the Young, Using Leisure, Engaging in Religious Practices, and Engaging in Community Activities—categories that social anthropologists used as guiding categories to explain human behavior cross-culturally.[4] Wrote the Lynds:

> Whether in an Arunta village in Central Australia, or in our own seemingly intricate institutional life of corporations, dividends, coming-out parties, prayer meetings, freshmen, and Congress, human behavior appears to consist in variations upon a few major lines of activity: getting the material necessities of food, clothing, shelter; mating; initiating the young into the group habits of thought and behavior; and so on. This study, accordingly, proceeds on the assumption that all the things people do in this American city may be viewed as falling under one or another of [these] . . . six main-truck activities.[5]

At a time when anthropology had its sights set on non-Western tribal peoples, *Middletown* became a sociology classic, and remains so today. It has never gone out of print.

The Lynds chose Muncie because they perceived it to be a relatively homogeneous community. In many ways it was. In the 1920s, Muncie was a medium-sized city "large enough to have put on long trousers and to take itself seriously, and yet small enough to be studied from many aspects as a unit"; was relatively self-contained and not "a satellite city" of a larger metropolis; and had "a small Negro and foreign-born population."[6] Although Muncie's black population was indeed a small percentage of the overall Muncie population, importantly, the Lynds missed that Muncie's black community was growing at a faster rate, and was indeed larger, "as a proportion of overall population" in Muncie, than in such major cities as Chicago, New York, or Detroit.[7]

One can almost excuse the Lynds for missing this, especially because, in recognizing their omissions of "racial change" in lieu of their focus on the larger "base-line group," they acknowledged that they were ignoring significant heterogeneities such as race, and thus encouraged that "racial backgrounds may be studied by future workers."[8] Several researchers took up the Lynds' call, focusing on different minority groups in Muncie, including its African American population.[9] But even so, when one reads the corpus of Middletown literature—for this literature is much larger for Muncie than for any other town of its size—one still may be struck by how the contributions of African Americans to the larger Muncie community are so often categorically ignored, even dismissed. The most recent study of Middletown, *Back to Middletown: Three Generations of Sociological Reflections*, does just this, for example. The author, Rita Caccamo, writes that "[o]nly a small group of intellectuals associated with the college is active in the fight for civil rights."[10] As we argue in the following chapters, black Muncie has been at the heart of a vibrant civil rights movement in the city for the past several decades, continuing to this day (albeit in different forms). To place that civil rights activity solely in the hands of college professors is to seriously—to inexcusably—miss the role of Muncie's African American community here. For civil rights activists like Hurley Goodall, who, with many others, has spent nearly his entire adult life organizing the African American community around civil rights issues, such omissions of the African American community and their contributions forcefully echo "the standard the Lynds set."

From Idea to Project: Some Background

This book is thus an attempt to fill the void about which Hurley Goodall spoke on that January afternoon. It is, however, only a *small* part of a much larger effort to document the history and contributions of the African American community to Muncie—a *small* part because Hurley, for one, has collected community photographs, church histories, newspaper clippings, and individual narratives for well over three decades. In addition to this, he has written extensively about Muncie and the African American experience here; much of these writings remain archived in Ball State's Archives and Special Collections.

Hurley and Fredine Goodall. Photo by Danny Gawlowski.

In 2001, Hurley and I began to discuss combining his own research and writing with an ethnographic perspective. But the roots of this conversation had begun much earlier—specifically during a museum exhibit on early African American pioneers and farmers in Indiana, an exhibit organized for Muncie's Minnetrista Cultural Center (a local museum) by folklorist and ethnographer Elizabeth (Beth) Campbell. Both Hurley and I served as consultants for the project, and through Beth, Hurley and I first met. Soon after this time, all three of us were also involved in a project sponsored by Ball State's Virginia B. Ball Center for Creative Inquiry—a unique and innovative educational program privately funded by Virginia B. Ball that allows Ball State faculty and students to design a collaborative and community-based project on which both the students and faculty focus solely for one semester (with no other course commitments for both faculty and students). The project, entitled "Transformations" and headed by Ball State English professor Lee Papa, brought together students, faculty, and community members to explore their memories of Muncie's 1967 race riots, on which they focused to build an ethnographically and collaboratively based play.[11] Beth and I were hired as consultants for the ethnographic part of the project; Hurley as a consultant on Muncie's black community. It was during this time that I learned of Hurley's extensive collec-

The Virginia B. Ball Center for Creative Inquiry is currently located in the Kitselman Mansion, owned by Ball State University. Photo by Danny Gawlowski.

tions and writings on Muncie's African American community, a collection that served as the basis for a third project in which Beth and Hurley, in particular, put together for a photo exhibit entitled "The Other Middletown."

With all of this in mind, Hurley, Beth, and I began to envision an extension of the "The Other Middletown" project: a Ball State University seminar that would bring a student-based and ethnographic perspective to Hurley's work. In collaboration with Hurley and Beth, I proposed the project to the Virginia B. Ball Center, and with their generous support (in cooperation with the Muncie Commission on the Social Status of Black Males, the Center for Middletown Studies, and the Community Foundation of Muncie and Delaware County, Inc.), we designed a collaboratively based project to involve local experts, ethnographers, and Ball State students to add to and complete this part of Goodall's work for publication.

The work would be the quintessential collaborative project—between faculty, students, and community consultants. We split the work into two parts, which are now represented by the two parts of this book. Ball State history professor (and director of the Center for Middletown Studies) Bruce Geelhoed, Beth, and Hurley would conduct the research for and write part I of the book; the students would conduct the research for and write part II of the book. In particular, the role of the students would be twofold. First, they would conduct ethnographic research in the community for a semester: that is, they would participate in Muncie's African American community by attending, for example, community meetings, church services, or family events; taking photographs; observing social landscapes; and, most importantly, conducting interviews. Second, the students—in teams, advised by community advisors—would combine their own ethnographic research with Goodall's and other historic materials archived in Ball State's Bracken Library (which includes an unpublished 1986 University of Virginia and Virginia Commonwealth University study of Muncie's African American community) to write their ethnographic contributions for the larger book project. Throughout this phase the students would work closely with the community and with faculty and independent researchers to learn and participate in the process of publishing an actual ethnographic manuscript.

Recognizing this unique opportunity for a "quintessential" collaboration between faculty, students, and community members, I also wanted someone to closely study the collaborative process itself, to understand more deeply just how collaboration works and how we (and others) could learn from it. With the Department of Anthropology and the Virginia B. Ball Center's combined financial support, I put out a national call for a graduate student to do just this. Several students from all over the country applied but one stood out: Michelle Natasya Johnson, whose intense interest in African American studies and collaborative models made her an ideal addition to the project. She joined us in August 2002, took up the project's collaborative process as the topic of her master's thesis, closely studied our collaborative approach throughout its development, and provided some preliminary reflections for the book (see appendix A).

Our Collaborative Methodology
from Beginning to End

The collaborative methodology for this project began in the months before the Virginia B. Ball Center seminar began (January 2003). Hurley, Beth, and I—now along with Michelle—called two community meetings to outline our plans for the project. Our main purpose at these meetings was to find community advisors who could serve as both mentors and facilitators—that is, key consultants who could lead students to further contacts within their subject area. We asked community members to volunteer for those subject areas in which they felt they could make the best contributions. For example, business owners volunteered to assist the Making a Living student research team; ministers volunteered to assist the Engaging in Religious Practices team; current and former political leaders volunteered to assist the Engaging in Community Activities team; and so forth.

Thanks mostly to Hurley and his wife Fredine, who spread the word throughout Muncie, the enthusiasm showed us by the African American community was extraordinary. Numerous people agreed to help the students in any way they could; after our second community meeting, in addition to Hurley and Fredine, twelve community advisors eagerly agreed to work with the students full time throughout the seminar: Renzie Abram Jr., Julius Anderson, Phyllis Bartleson, Geraldine Burns, Edgar Faulkner, Eric Johnson, Edward McNeary, Delores Pryor, Carl Rhinehart, Dolores Rhinehart, Phyllis Joanne White, and John Young-El.

Meanwhile, I set about finding students who would be interested in the work, and who could, for an entire semester, focus *solely* on the project.[12] The team had to be interdisciplinary as a requirement of the Virginia B. Ball Center, so, in addition to a core of anthropology students, I sought out students from disciplines that were closely related to anthropology—especially disciplines that counted "culture" and/or "ethnography" as among their key concepts. The obvious choices were sociology and history. But I also drew students from philosophy, journalism, English, education, urban planning, and telecommunications, believing such an interdisciplinary group would only help enhance the project. (Indeed it did.)

After interviewing each student, and after much thinking about the class's composition (which included its racial diversity), by early January we had our student team: Michelle Anderson (anthropology), Jessica Booth (journalism), Brandy Bounds (urban planning and sociology), Sarah Bricker (anthropology and Spanish), Carla Burke (English and education), Abigail Delpha (sociology and Spanish), Jarrod Dortch (history), Eric Efaw (anthropology and history), Mia Fields (English), Danny Gawlowski (anthropology and photojournalism), Carrie Kissel (anthropology), Anne Kraemer (anthropology and history), Ashley Moore (telecommunications), and Cari Peterson (organization communication and philosophy).

With the students' individual interests in mind (for example, in education or family life or religion), we organized the students into six teams, teams that would focus their research and writing on the subject areas set out in the original Lynd study: again, Getting a Living, Making a Home, Training the Young, Using Leisure, Engaging in Religious Practices, and Engaging in Community Activities. (One student, Danny Gawlowski, an award-winning photographer, was assigned an auxilary member of each group and worked with teams to illustrate their chapters with his photographs). These teams paralleled the teams of community advisors that had been already organized along similar lines. The next step was to bring these two groups together.[13]

The Student–Community Advisor Teams

On that January afternoon—the first day of spring semester 2003 classes—when Hurley reminded us why we had come together in the first place, the faculty and students met first to learn about what lay ahead of us. That evening we met at Shaffer Chapel, a place, as we'll learn in the forthcoming chapters, that is steeped in history and meaning. There the students and community advisors met each other for the first time and ate dinner together. After introductions, they split up into their respective groups and by the end of the evening our collaborative project had officially begun.

Sarah Bricker (left) and John Young-El (right) at the first Student-Community Advisor team meeting. Photo by Danny Gawlowski.

These six teams served as the foundation for writing the six chapters of part II. We (Hurley, Beth, Michelle, and I) recognized early on that having the students research and write fully exhaustive chapters of Muncie's African American experience (including all of its social, economic, and political dimensions) was not only theoretically suspect, but pragmatically, an impossible task for one semester's work. Recognizing that the groups' composition was established along lines of common interest, we instead wanted the teams to define their own subjects for study: they were to focus, within their respective topic areas, on those parts of Muncie's black experience that interested them the most (more on this later).

This was a particularly difficult challenge for the students at first. Several, for example, wanted clear guidelines for what they were supposed to look for and write about. A collaborative ethnographic methodology, we explained, centered on defining the questions of study *with* our community advisors; not imposing research questions on them from the outside.[14] It was to be an inductive process, not a reductive one. Although we had indeed chosen to stick with the Lynds' original six categories to remain consistent with the classic study, these six categories would serve only as a loose guide—a springboard to the larger issues that mattered to the people with whom we were working. To illustrate this, and to initiate talk between the students and community advisors about the topics and issues that would direct their writing, the students read *Middletown*, with each student research team focusing on their respective chapters and making notes of the subject areas within those chapters that the Lynds had originally explored. After discussing these at length as a group, the students took their reading of *Middletown* back to their community advisors, asking them to what extent the Lynds' discussion represented their own experience in Muncie. In some cases, the Lynds' focus was similar to that of our community advisors; in others, however, they were quite different. For example, the Getting a Living student team learned that while the Lynds had made much of the divisions between the business and working class in their original study, the divisions were never as pronounced in Muncie's black community, especially because the city's wealthy business class was (and remains) almost entirely made up of white Munsonians. The community advisors, as we'll see, thought the students should focus instead, among several other things, on the businesses that had a particular significance to the black community, past and present.

Interviews/Conversations

Through this exercise and subsequent conversations, the student-advisor teams began to define the issues that they thought were most important to explore. This was no easy task, however. The community advisors led the students to other consultants, who, like the community advisors, had topics and issues of their own that they thought were important to the study. For example, the community advisors for the Making a Home team encouraged the students to focus on single mothers, who, in turn, led the students to other single parents, including single fathers. Many of these consultants encouraged the students to focus, as well, on dual-parent homes lest the students stereotype the community in their writings and forego the actual diversity of families.

We encouraged students to begin identifying themes (as well as important exceptions to those themes) so that they might develop more directed research questions about the topics and issues that were emerging in their field conversations. These they took back to their community advisors, who helped them further develop their questions. These questions were regularly revamped and revised as the research progressed, however. The Engaging in Religious Practices student team, for example, began with a long list of questions the students had first hammered out on their own, and then with their community advisors during their first meeting. Many of these questions were very general in their scope and served as a guide in their earliest field conversations, but as the students learned more about the role of the church in Muncie's African American community (such as in the civil rights movement) their questions became much more refined, centering around specific topics and issues (such as the ministers who were also civil rights activists).

The students' interviewing methods, then, were simple but time-consuming: the students asked community advisors about the topics they thought were most important for them to explore; they developed research questions along these lines; they structured interviews around these research questions. These interviews led to new topics and issues to explore, which in turn led to new questions upon which to structure interviews. These interviews, actually, were more like conversations in that they were much more free flowing than structured interviews often are. On many occasions, the community advisors and students met to talk—sometimes for hours—about the project, about their respective interests, or just to visit. And each time,

Jessica Booth interviews Pastor Martel Winburn Sr. inside Shaffer Chapel. Photo by Danny Gawlowski.

the students learned a little more about what it was like to live in African American Muncie.

The students recorded most of their conversations either as field notes or, most often, on analog tape, using a Marantz PMD-201 professional field recorder with an external microphone (important for canceling out internal motor noise from the recording). The Virginia B. Ball Center provided each student research team with their own field recorder "kit" (which included a laptop computer) so competition for equipment between groups would be kept to a minimum. After each interview/conversation was complete, the students labeled their tapes (with a numbering system that we developed for archiving), and meticulously logged their recorded conversation. We did not ask the students to transcribe their conversations for several reasons. Most importantly, we wanted the students to regularly return to the original recordings—especially as they began to write (more on this below). Moreover, because we wanted the students to focus on *listening*, we wanted them to forego a dependency on written transcripts—that is, a prolonged focus on written transcriptions begins to yield a more narrowed focus on the *content* of speech (especially when the interview/conversation is long over) at the expense of its *intent*—such as its veiled, often more subtle meanings.

Regularly returning to the original recording forces one to listen for
both content *and* intent. Thus student logs generally looked like this
excerpt from a taped log entry by the Training the Young team:

Tape #:	M03TY14-I-02/27 (tape 1 of 2)
What:	Conversation with Phyllis Bartleson
Who:	Phyllis Bartleson
Where:	Human Rights Commission, City Hall, Muncie, Indiana
Time:	10:30 A.M.
Recorded by:	Carla Burke, Carrie Kissel
Specs:	Marantz, external mic
Notes:	Done in Phyllis's office; logged by Carrie

Side A

(000)   Discussion of training the young. Carla asks for definition.
Phyllis says it takes a strong fortitude due to really adverse
outside influences in society today. Sons twenty-eight, twenty-
two; daughter thirty-five.

(027)   Phyllis gets out picture of her first grade class at Garfield Elementary (over fifty years ago). Remembers the teacher—
seemed tall, must have been about 5 foot, 10 inches, but
seemed like a giant to first graders. Carla asks if we can get a
copy of it later, when we start getting pictures together.

(072)   A lot more difficult in raising youngsters than it was when my
children were small. Single parent, worked with young people
a good portion of her life. When she was going full time to Ball
State, worked at Youth Detention Center (now the Youth Opportunity Center). Children went to Burris then, probably
about first grade, sixth grade. Worked nights, best for education, but sometimes got to work with the kids—got her interested in working with young people.

(102)   Was director of a summer youth work program for ages fourteen through twenty-one: Partnership for Progress, mid-late
1980s. Taught adult responsibilities, good work ethic, also
other problems, job training.

(122)   Been Human Rights Commission Director for about fifteen
years, has worked with other groups who serve youth. . . .[15]

In the end, the students conducted more than 150 hours of interviews/
conversations with well over sixty people, including their community advisors and other consultants (about two-thirds of these interviews/con-
versations were tape recorded, logged, and archived). That the students

completed this many interviews in one semester's time is an amazing feat in and of itself. But conversing was not all they were doing.

Participant-Observation/Observant Participation

The students' intensive interview agenda was heavily subsidized with participant-observation, that staple of all ethnography: intensive participation and observation in a particular locality. At the beginning of the semester, we required the students to attend at least one community event (broadly defined) each week, but after the first few weeks, their community advisors were inviting and taking them to numerous family gatherings, school meetings, sporting events, church services, political rallies—you name it. Indeed, after the first month, many of the students had become a regular part of the "Muncie scene."

The purpose of this intensive participation was for the students to observe the larger social context in which their consultants lived their lives. But, as our students came to understand, a significant by-product of this intensive participation is recognizing how the "observer" is similar to and different from the people with whom she or he works: as we learn about others, we learn about ourselves; and as we learn about ourselves, we learn about others. This is extremely important for the serious fieldworker. One must recognize where Self leaves off and Other picks up. But, more importantly, one must also recognize how one's experience shapes one's interpretation of others. We thus encouraged the students to be, more precisely, "observant participants," to observe their own participation just as closely as they were observing others; to fully embrace fieldwork's "intersubjectivities" (put simply, the "co-experiences" and "co-understandings" that developed between and among the students and their Muncie collaborators); and to recognize the points when deeper understandings of Muncie's African American community began to emerge within this experiential context.[16]

With this in mind, we required the students to keep detailed field notes (a journal of sorts) of all of their activities and experiences; we also expected them to reflect openly in this writing about what they were learning about themselves and how this was shaping what they were discovering about Muncie's black community. This would be extremely important, we explained, for writing an honest and responsible ethnography. As we'll see in the coming chapters, they often used this material (excerpted straight from their field notes) to situate their discussions of their individual topic areas. Field notes thus took an open-ended form, much like these excerpts from the notes of Sarah Bricker (of the Using Leisure team):

Researcher's name:	Sarah Bricker
Date of visit:	2/9/03
Date recorded field notes:	2/9/03
Event:	Sunday Morning Worship
Place:	Shaffer Chapel A.M.E. Church
Documentation materials:	Notepad and pen; service bulletin and calendar of events

On the way to the service I felt some anxiety. I've been to more Christian services lately than usual, and in some ways feel like an outsider. . . . I wondered if there was a parking lot somewhere behind the church? I always park at the annex for class—but how can everyone fit on the streets on Sunday? As I neared the church there was plenty of space. I was surprised that there weren't more cars. I arrived close to 11 A.M. and as I walked toward the church, Eric Efaw pulled in. I waited for him and we walked together, passing the African Methodist Episcopal Church sign and walking up the few steps. Two people greeted us at the door, with bulletins, and "good morning." The woman asked for my coat which took me by surprise I guess— felt like being a guest at someone's home. We took a seat in one of the pews on the right side, closer to the back than the front. I noticed the windows right away—letting the sunlight into the church. Then I saw Carl and Dolores Rhinehart further back on the left side. It was great to see them, as I thought Eric Johnson would be the only person I'd know—I didn't see him yet. And Hurley and Fredine were sitting in front of us, and soon Geraldine was behind us! I loved it, so many people were here that I recognized, it made me a lot more comfortable. Everyone waved or said hello.

One of the choir members comes to the pulpit and brings praise. Talks about the Spirit. The choir begins in song, the drums, the piano, the song's upbeat. . . . Then a praise song, "Jesus in Heaven" and tambourines start in, the drums, the voices, the piano. Some claps from the congregation—about twenty-five people in the pews, mostly women, a couple of kids, a few men. Some voices say "Jesus." A woman comes in and sits behind Phyllis and the kids. She leans over the pew and hugs the young girl, and kisses her on the cheek, her lipstick stays and the girl tries to rub it off with the help of Phyllis. Later she moves back to sit by the woman. In the fourth pew from the front, a woman sits alone, she often sways from side to side in her seat, and claps moving her shoulders. . . . Eric Johnson comes to the podium, his Bible looks well-read, the papers scraggly coming out of it. He talks about the Middletown project, about Hurley's work in the community, about needing to document history, about working with the leisure group. He encourages people to stay after, and says my name, that I'll be staying after to do interviews, and if anyone can stay, especially women, please stay. . . . I felt connected to him there, how much he wants these stories written down, even though he works in Indianapolis, commuting every day to take care of his mom and brother, he's taking time to do this project. That's what it means.[17]

Students turned in field notes like these at the start of each week, adding exponentially to their growing corpus of fieldwork materials. In order to help the students' recognize their emergent understandings, these field notes were, during the project's earliest stages, discussed among the group at large or in smaller consultations between the individual research teams and either Beth, Michelle, or myself.

Reading and Researching Texts

In addition to the texts produced by the students as a result of their interviews and observant participation, they also read and researched extensive background materials on Muncie's African American community. Much of their historical research, in particular, had already been done for them by Hurley (and is further explored in depth in chapter 2). Before the seminar began, Hurley compiled a summation of his research to date for each category (Getting a Living, Making a Home, etc.), which he placed in individually labeled folders for use by each team (these folders also included original photographs). These materials provided direction to the much larger collection on Muncie's African American community held in Ball State University's Archives and Special Collections, which housed a plethora of materials. Of particular note were two manuscript collections, both in which Hurley was closely involved: the "Black Muncie History Project Records," which included newspaper clippings, pamphlets, and interviews collected by Hurley in the 1970s; and the "Black Middletown Project Records," interview transcripts from a 1981–1982 University of Virginia and Virginia Commonwealth University study of the black community (which was never published).[18]

Some student research teams depended more on this archived material than others, mainly because the student teams focusing on areas that had formal institutional histories (such as churches, schools, and businesses as studied by the Engaging in Religious Practices, Training the Young, and Getting a Living research teams, respectively) found more materials at their disposal; the student teams focusing on areas with less formal institutional histories (such as family, recreation, and public events as studied by the Making a Home, Using Leisure, and Engaging in Community Activities research teams, respectively) depended more on oral histories through their conversations with their community advisors and consultants to establish their historical understandings in this regard. Perhaps the largest formal institutional history was church history, which is reflected in the "Engaging in Religious Practices" chapter. Early on in their research, the Engaging in Religious Practices student research team found the archived materials particularly helpful to their growing understandings of how the role of present-day churches had emerged from its previous role in the civil rights movements of earlier eras.

Added to *this* reading was the students' reading of newspaper articles, pamphlets, and other community materials that they collected. They also read a number of texts to help them contextualize their work within larger currents. In addition to reading *Middletown*, the students read various excerpts from the larger Middletown literature (e.g., the Lynds' *Middletown in Transition*); general anthropological texts such as my own *Invitation to Anthropology* (to help them more fully understand the role of ethnography in larger discussions of culture and society); books on doing fieldwork such as Bonnie Stone Sunstein and Elizabeth Chiseri-Strater's *Fieldworking: Reading and Writing Research* (to provide models for specific research strategies); ethnographies that we sought to emulate (such as Glenn Hinson's *Fire in My Bones: Transcendence and the Holy Spirit in African American Gospel*); and, most especially, our guide for writing nonfiction to general audiences, William Zinsser's *On Writing Well*.[19]

Writing Ethnography

Simply put, ethnography is the description of culture; but it also implies both a field method and a method for writing. In this case, the students were practicing ethnography as a method as they sought to understand the culture of Muncie's African American community through their conversations with their community advisors and other consultants, through their observant participation, and through their intensive reading of historical and contemporary texts. Perhaps the biggest challenge was translating this work into an actual written ethnography.

Throughout the project, each student team compiled all of their research (particularly tape logs, field notes, archival and other materials) into portfolios, upon which they based their writing.[20] Early on, however, we encouraged the students to de-emphasize the separations between "collecting data" and "writing up the results"—indeed, such divisions have very little use and meaning to contemporary ethnography (especially in doing collaborative ethnography, which I will discuss below). Throughout the semester, then, we also conducted writing exercises (in addition to their instruction on writing field notes) so that students would be better prepared to translate their emergent understandings into an ethnographic text when the most intensive writing came. For example, during the third week of the seminar, we all attended a Martin Luther King Jr. celebration at Christ Temple Apostolic Church. I recorded the entire service, excerpted a few minutes from the sermon, and asked each research team to translate the excerpt as poetic transcription—a writing method developed by sociolinguists to more closely represent both the intent and content of speech in the final written ethnography.[21] One of these was eventually chosen for (and now appears in) the "Engaging in Community Activities" chapter. As we'll see in what follows, student teams chose to use poetic transcription (which is also called "ethnopoetics") where it was most appropriate for translating and writing particular types of speech that did not translate easily to the written page.

Soon after the first month of the seminar, we asked students to construct rough outlines for their chapters based on the themes they had discovered so far. These they shared with one another as a group. Much of their material overlapped, as expected, so they spent some time discussing which team would write about what, as well as how to best create transitions between chapters. While in the process of continuing their ethnographic research, they shared these outlines with their community advisors, which created further discussion about the direction the students' writing would take. These collaborative discussions thus distinguished gaps in the students' understandings and defined new trajectories for further research.

Near midsemester, the students began writing their first drafts, all the while continuing with their interviews and other research. Discussing their writing with their community advisors, each student team began to forge their chapters. They spent long days and nights at the Virginia B. Ball Center (some groups worked as much as eighteen hours per day), and within a week they had their first drafts completed. These we discussed as a group, and with the groups' suggestions, the student teams began their writing and rewriting anew. By the time they left for their well-deserved Spring Break, the students had

Carrie Kissel (left) and Carla Burke (right) work on their chapter, "Training the Young." Photo by Danny Gawlowski.

submitted their final "first drafts." While they vacationed (or should I say, slept), Beth, Michelle, and I (along with Ball State English professor Robert Nowatzki), heavily edited these drafts and made suggestions for rewriting. When we finished, we sent these drafts to Rosalie Robertson, editor-in-chief at AltaMira Press, who then flew out to Muncie to meet with the students after they returned from Spring Break—she added still more suggestions.

This initial editing process was perhaps the hardest part of the seminar for the students. We wanted big changes, *really big changes*; indeed, we were a long way from completing our ethnography. Some of the students, as expected, were angry and hurt; they had never had their writing critiqued like this before. But they had also never been part of an actual publishing process. This project was becoming a much larger group effort, we explained, which now included the book's publisher. Our sights had to be set accordingly.

After a few days, the students' anger subsided (in fact, I encouraged them to be mad at us—particularly me—this was part of the publishing process); and the group was back to intensive writing and rewriting. Our next step would be to present our chapter drafts to our community advisors and other consultants.

Michelle Anderson (left) and Dolores Rhinehart (right) review the "Getting a Living" chapter during a community meeting at Shaffer Chapel. Photo by Danny Gawlowski.

Writing Collaborative Ethnography

In that ethnographers work with local communities to construct their texts, the approach to ethnography, as a method, is essentially collaborative. But what makes ethnographic *writing* collaborative is closely involving consultants in the actual writing of the text. For this project, that meant taking the developing chapters back to community advisors and other consultants for corrections, clarifications, and commentary.

Within a few weeks after Rosalie Robertson had visited the seminar, the students had written new drafts and distributed them among all of their community collaborators (that is, both the community advisors and other consultants), all the while continuing to conduct interviews and other research. At the end of March, we met for a light dinner and an open forum to discuss the chapter drafts. The gathering was largely celebratory, with our collaborators praising the students for all of their hard work. But it also initiated the serious work of integrating consultant commentary into the chapter drafts. During the meeting, for example, community advisors voiced, in addition to corrections, that they wanted material reintegrated back into chapters that had been deleted through the editing process or that they wanted the students to elaborate certain points even more than they had.

This forum was only the beginning, however, of writing our collaborative ethnography. The more directed and intense discussions came after our public forum as the students met with their community advisors and other consultants individually, and in private, to talk about their developing chapters. Importantly, talk about the students' text spawned deeper co-interpretations of each chapter's content—a discussion that lasted until the students finished their final chapter drafts and continues with me even now.

Ultimately, writing a collaborative ethnography is built upon a trust relationship between ethnographer(s) and consultant(s), a moral and ethical "cocommitment" to one another as "cointellectuals." To keep this cocommitment in the forefront of our collaborative ethnography, early in the semester the students reviewed several different professional ethical codes (such as that of the American Anthropological Association), and from these, designed their own "statement of ethics" that reflected the particular contours of this specific project.[22] That statement is as follows:

1. Our primary responsibility is to the community consultants with whom we work.
2. We shall maintain academic integrity by creating faithful representations.
3. We shall establish good rapport with the community so that future collaborative studies can be undertaken. This project is not just about our book.
4. All project participants should be aware of the study's products. Materials are only archived with the participants' consent. Participants have rights to have copies of their own interviews.
5. We shall willingly and openly communicate intentions, plans, goals, and collaborative processes of the project.
6. We shall remain open to our consultants' experiences and perspectives, even when their views are different from ours.
7. We have a responsibility to the community, our respective disciplines, and our future audience to fulfill our commitment to finish what we have started: the book, *The Other Side of Middletown*.

This statement of ethics was specific to our particular collaborative ethnography in several different ways, but a couple of these points need clarification. Point 7, for instance, emerged from our discussions with our community advisors—especially Hurley—who had worked with teams of researchers before and had been extremely disappointed that they had never produced their results for neither Muncie's black community nor the general public. I, for one, had promised Hurley when the project began that I would do everything in my power to get our work published. And the students agreed.

Perhaps the most important part of this statement—"our primary responsibility"—is point 1. Being committed to our community collaborators first and foremost meant several things, but most prominent among these included (1) fully recognizing the contributions of our consultants, unless they preferred otherwise (that is, fully attributing knowledge to them as community experts, not as anonymous contributors); (2) representing our consultants the way they wanted to be represented (that is, as authors, we work very hard to present ourselves in the best possible light; our consultants should have that right also); and (3) allowing our consultants, as collaborative coauthors, to review, comment on, or change their contributions (quotations, for example) as they saw fit—all of which are indeed central to writing a collaborative ethnography.

On the Book's Goals and Purposes

From the very beginning, our goal for this project was, simply, to build our research upon a set of mutual relationships (framed by moral and ethical responsibilities to one another), and, in turn, to build our counderstandings around these relationships. We never asserted—and we still do not assert—that we were researching and writing an "exhaustive" or "objective" study (ours is indeed a humanistic effort, not a scientific one). Our purpose was to fully embrace the experiences of our consultants, their memories, and their stories, and to use our coexperience (as engendered by our relationships with one another, particularly between the students and their community collaborators) as the foundation for creating our collaborative ethnographic text.

Being Honest about Our Ethnography's
Potentials and Limitations

Building our collaborative ethnography around these relationships provided definite and clear potentials for in-depth counderstandings of our collaborators' experiences, memories, and stories. Our particular relationships, to be sure, engendered a very particular dialogue about the Muncie community. Had those relationships taken any other form, a very different dialogue would have emerged, and our collaborative ethnography would have thus looked very different. But, in the end, it would still point us to a deeper understanding of Muncie's African American community (as we believe this ethnography does in its current form).

As such, what follows is not so much an ethnography *of* Muncie's African American community as it is a dialogue *about* Muncie's African American community. Of course, all dialogues, and thus all ethnographies, have their boundaries, and ours is no exception. In that we base this ethnography on information collected in a very short amount of time (about four months) and that we primarily, although not exclusively, worked with older (often retired) middle-class collaborators (who had the time to work intensively with us within this short timeframe), our ethnography also has very clear limitations. Hence, we view this book not as a conclusive statement, but rather as a beginning to new study and new conversation.

How This Book Is Unique

This book is unique in two key ways. First, this book is among the very few widely published, full-length ethnographies written mostly by undergraduate college students.[23] Several anthropologists, in particular, have written books with their students (most posed as instruction manuals for doing ethnography).[24] These, however, feature student essays on disparate "subcultures" rather than on a single, local community. Second, and more obvious, we believe that this book is a significant contribution to the overall Middletown literature. In addition to the few works that take up the experiences, memories, and stories of Muncie's African American community, this book seeks to add to the growing Middletown literature that gives a "face" to the people who live here; that situates this place in real people's *experience*.[25] The Lynds' *Middletown*, for example, was a product of its time. It offered a "distanced" and "normalized" description of Muncie (the people and their quotations, for example, were nameless). We wanted to write a very different kind of ethnography. And that we did.

Notes

1. Class conversation, Virginia B. Ball Center for Creative Inquiry seminar. "The Other Side of Middletown," Ball State University, Muncie, Indiana, January 6, 2003.
2. An important exception is W. E. B. DuBois's *The Philadelphia Negro: A Social Study* (Philadelphia: University of Pennsylvania Press, 1899).
3. In fact, when the study's sponsors questioned the validity of the study (the Lynds had been charged to study religion in Muncie, not the entire com-

munity) and threatened to terminate its publication, Wissler convinced them otherwise and agreed to write the book's foreword (Theodore Caplow, personal communication, May 3, 2003).

4. On this point, the Lynds were primarily influenced by W. H. R. Rivers's *Social Organization* (New York: Knopf, 1924) and Clark Wissler's *Man and Culture* (New York: Crowell, 1923). See Robert S. Lynd and Helen Merrell Lynd, *Middletown* (New York: Harcourt Brace & Company, 1929), 4.

5. Lynd and Lynd, *Middletown*, 4.

6. Ibid., 8.

7. Jack S. Blocker, "Black Migration to Muncie, 1860–1930," *Indiana Magazine of History* 92 (1996): 297–320.

8. Lynd and Lynd, *Middletown*, 8.

9. See, for example, Dan Rottenberg, ed., *Middletown Jews: The Tenuous Survival of an American Jewish Community* (Bloomington: Indiana University Press, 1997) and Xiaozhao Huang, *A Study of African-American Vernacular English in America's "Middletown": Evidence of Linguistic Convergence* (Lewiston, N.Y.: E. Mellen Press, 2000).

10. Rita Caccamo, *Back to Middletown: Three Generations of Sociological Reflections* (Stanford, Calif.: Stanford University Press, 2000), 121.

11. This project is documented in Lee Papa and Luke Eric Lassiter, "The Muncie Race Riots of 1967, Representing Community Memory through Public Performance, and Collaborative Ethnography between Faculty, Students, and the Local Community," *Journal of Contemporary Ethnography* 32 (2003): 147–66.

12. As I've already mentioned, Virginia B. Ball Center seminars provide the resources for Ball State University faculty to teach the seminar, and only the seminar, for an entire semester. Students, too, take the seminar as their only course. But in order for students to take the course without losing credit for their majors and/or core curriculum, the center arranges for seminar credit to replace needed classes that are closely related. For example, students enrolled in "The Other Side of Middletown" seminar substituted courses such as ethnographic methods, race and ethnicity, cultural anthropology, sociology, Middletown studies, or African American studies.

13. The composition of these teams generally remained the same through the semester, with one exception. Due to medical problems, Brandy Bounds had to pull out of the class after about a month into the seminar. Several students stepped forward to help Jarrod Dortch complete the research and writing for the chapter (hence this chapter's large number of contributors). Elizabeth Campbell, in particular, volunteered to take a leadership role in this effort, and helped to define the chapter's trajectory.

14. See Luke Eric Lassiter, "From 'Reading Over the Shoulders of Natives' to 'Reading Alongside Natives,' Literally: Toward a Collaborative and Reciprocal Ethnography," *Journal of Anthropological Research* 57 (2001): 137–49.

15. The numbers to the left represent the recorder's tape counter. No standard exists for tape counters, but Marantz field recorders are very common, still in use among fieldworkers and archivists (hence the importance of the

"specs" line at the beginning of the log). Generally, students made note of the tape counter with a change in conversation topic.

16. See Barbara Tedlock, "From Participant Observation to the Observation of Participation: The Emergence of Narrative Ethnography," *Journal of Anthropological Research* 47 (1991): 69–94.

17. Generally, we asked the students, if possible, to make short notes during their visits to community events and then to expand on these brief notes in longer form as soon as possible after attending the event.

18. As Hurley was closely involved in this study (called the "Black Middletown Project"), he is, to this day, extremely disappointed that the research team never published their results as promised. They "came to Muncie in the middle 1980s with a sizeable federal grant and spent one year here in our city," he writes. "I, among others, spent many hours helping to open doors in homes, places of business, churches, clubs, and other venues. One of the persons interviewed at the time was my mother, who was in her late eighties. No product of any kind was produced by this team. Frustrated, I wrote to the president of the University of Virginia and expressed my feelings, especially after I found through research that they had expended $250,000 while here. I felt sure that no other study of the African American community in Muncie would be possible." (Hurley Goodall, comments at "Writing Muncie's African American Community: How We Wrote the Other Side of Middletown," Union Baptist Church, Muncie, Indiana, April 17, 2003.)

19. See Robert S. Lynd and Helen Merrell Lynd, *Middletown in Transition: A Study in Cultural Conflicts* (New York: Harcourt Brace & Company, 1937); Luke Eric Lassiter, *Invitation to Anthropology* (Walnut Creek, Calif.: AltaMira Press, 2002); Bonnie Stone Sunstein and Elizabeth Chiseri-Strater, *Fieldworking: Reading and Writing Research*, 2nd ed. (Boston: Bedford/St. Martin's, 2002); Glenn Hinson, *Fire in My Bones: Transcendence and the Holy Spirit in African American Gospel* (Philadelphia: University of Pennsylvania Press, 2000); and William Zinsser *On Writing Well: The Classic Guide to Writing Nonfiction*, 25th ed. (New York: Quill, 2001), respectively.

20. See Sunstein and Chiseri-Strater, *Fieldworking*, in which building a research portfolio is a major component of their approach.

21. See, for example, Dennis Tedlock, *The Spoken Word and the Work of Interpretation* (Philadelphia: University of Pennsylvania Press, 1983). This exercise is also featured in Sunstein and Chiseri-Strater, *Fieldworking*, 300–301.

22. This exercise we pulled from Sunstein and Chiseri-Strater, *Fieldworking*, 116–18.

23. See, for example, Mary LaLone, ed., *Appalachian Coal Mining Memories: Life in the Coal Fields of Virginia's New River Valley* (Blacksburg, Va.: Pocahontas Press, 1997).

24. See, for example, James P. Spradley and David McCurdy, *The Cultural Experience: Ethnography in Complex Society* (Prospect Heights, Ill.: Waveland Press, 1972).

25. See, for example, Dan Rottenberg, *Middletown Jews*.

PART I

MIDDLETOWN AND MUNCIE'S AFRICAN AMERICAN COMMUNITY

1

The Enduring Legacy of Muncie as Middletown

E. Bruce Geelhoed

At first glance, Muncie, Indiana, hardly appears to be the kind of community that would attract the attention of social scientists, journalists, and film producers. A small city with a population slightly less than 70,000, located in the flatlands of east central Indiana, devoid of any natural beauty, Muncie resembles many Midwestern communities that grew from infancy in the nineteenth century to maturity in the twentieth century. Now, in the early years of the twenty-first century, Muncie still retains many of the noticeable characteristics that have defined its existence for at least the past seventy-five years. In their book, *In Search of America*, Peter Jennings and Todd Brewster describe Muncie, accurately, as a "town of wide streets flanked by stolid brick houses, a place compact enough that you can drive from one end of town to the other in under twenty minutes and where people embrace their typical 'Americaness.'"[1] Likewise, journalist Ed Field has suggested that there "is something ineffably average about Muncie, Indiana. . . . [Its] 70,000 residents continue to ooze middle America. They work in factories, banks, and grain elevators. There are lots of bowling tournaments. A few months ago, a sign reading 'Welcome to America's Hometown' greeted a convention of makers of model aeroplanes."[2]

Despite such sentiments, this spectacularly undistinguished community catapulted to national fame and attention in the 1920s and 1930s after the publication of two books, *Middletown: A Study in Contemporary Culture*, and *Middletown in Transition: A Study in Cultural Conflict*, written by social researchers Robert S. Lynd and Helen Merrell Lynd.[3] The Lynds first came to Muncie in 1924 with the support of the Institute for Social and Religious Research, one of the many nonprofit organizations established by the wealthy philanthropist John D. Rockefeller Jr. With

Traffic flows across Jackson Street down Walnut Avenue in downtown Muncie, May 2003. Photo by Danny Gawlowski.

the institute's support, the Lynds were expected to conduct a "small city" study, one designed to document the patterns of religious behavior in a contemporary urban setting.

Rockefeller's interest in the project stemmed from his anxiety about the tensions that existed in America between capital and labor. A devout churchman, Rockefeller wanted to fund a study that would reveal how the influence of religion might help to alleviate economic, social, and cultural tensions.[4]

Robert Lynd was not initially involved in the institute's plan for the small city study. In 1923, the institute chose sociologist William Louis Bailey of Northwestern University to direct the project but abruptly removed him within months after he began his work. The institute then turned to Robert S. Lynd, who was doing editorial work in New York. Lynd was a curious choice to succeed Bailey as project director. He was not a professionally trained social scientist and some of his writings criticized John D. Rockefeller Jr. and the business practices of the Standard Oil Company, the enterprise that had provided much of the Rockefeller family's immense fortune.[5]

Furthermore, Lynd had ambitions for the small city study that went well beyond the fairly limited objective outlined by the institute.

Even though Lynd held a degree in theology, by this point in his life he had become a religious skeptic. He wanted to conduct a more inclusive, urban anthropological study instead of a narrowly defined investigation of religious practices in a small city. As a result, Lynd was working at cross-purposes with his sponsors at the institute almost from the beginning of his tenure as principal investigator. Under these circumstances, one might argue that the prospects for the success of the small city study were meager.

Nevertheless, after examining a number of Midwestern cities, Lynd eventually settled on Muncie as his subject. Muncie met his criteria for "Middletown." It was a medium-sized community with mostly native-born citizens instead of immigrants; it had a mixed profile of business and industry; minorities comprised only a small percentage of the total population; and no single family, institution, or business appeared to dominate local life. As sociologist Theodore Caplow observed, Lynd wanted to study a city "which had nothing particularly outstanding about it, and this remains true of Middletown (Muncie) to this very day."[6]

In conducting their study, Lynd and his team of researchers focused on six areas of community life: getting a living (business, commerce, and labor); making a home (family life); training the young (schools and the local educational system); using leisure (recreation and social life); engaging in religious practices (the church life of the community); and engaging in community activities (the political world and the volunteer sector).[7] More important than their examinations of these various areas of human activity, however, was the Lynds' conclusion that Muncie essentially was divided into two classes: the "business class" and the "working class." To quote Jennings and Brewster: "*Middletown* showed that, despite Americans' egalitarian ideals, the city was divided by an entrenched class system. Residents belonged to either the small 'business' class or far larger 'working class.' The two camps had their own values and expectations and rarely mingled."[8]

According to the Lynds, the "business class" consisted of the occupational range of those who worked "with people," including not only businessmen, but also lawyers, physicians, educators, clergymen, and others who required education and professional training to perform their work. By contrast, the "working class" consisted of those who worked "with things" and provided the labor for Muncie's ever-growing number of factories and shops.[9] The characteristic that differentiated the membership of the "business class" from the membership of the "working class" was not necessarily social status or even size of income. Rather, as historian David Kennedy has observed, it was stability of employment, or employment security, that separated the two classes. Members of the business class were less likely either to lose their jobs or suffer an interruption in their employment than members of the working class.[10]

The Lynds finished their study in 1927 but then encountered some difficulty finding a publisher for it. Eventually, the publishing company of Harcourt, Brace, and World agreed to publish *Middletown* and, to considerable surprise, the book became a bestseller. In many respects, *Middletown* became one of the seminal works of American sociology in the twentieth century. The book remains in print and is still studied extensively in college courses.

With *Middletown* enjoying such commercial success, Robert Lynd's publisher encouraged him to write a sequel. In 1935, Lynd returned to Muncie to begin his follow-up to *Middletown*, but Helen Lynd remained behind in New York. Lynd stayed in Muncie for only six months in 1935, and he witnessed a community that was in the midst of the Great Depression. Lynd also discovered (and later admitted) that, on his first visit to Muncie, he had underestimated the importance both of the Ball family, and of the Ball State Teachers College, in the life of the community. *Middletown in Transition*, the Lynds' second book on Muncie, was published in 1937.[11] While *Middletown in Transition* did not enjoy either the critical acclaim or commercial success of *Middletown*, it did present a compelling, poignant portrait of a community bewildered by the economic calamity that had befallen it. The success of the Middletown studies also culminated in an appointment for Robert S. Lynd to the faculty of Columbia University, where he became acknowledged as one of America's leading sociologists.

Three weeks after the publication of *Middletown in Transition* in late April 1937, the celebrated photojournalist Margaret Bourke-White published a photo essay of Muncie/Middletown in *Life* magazine. In her essay, "Muncie Ind. Is the Great US Middletown," Bourke-White identified Muncie as the subject of the Lynd studies. Moreover, her essay showed various groups of people, from the affluent to the poverty-stricken, going about their daily lives. With a circulation in the hundreds of thousands, *Life* may have done more to popularize "Muncie as Middletown" in the public imagination than the Lynd studies. Bourke-White certainly succeeded in giving American readers a visual impression of Muncie, something that the Lynd studies intentionally failed to do. Muncie, enthused Bourke-White, "is every small city [in the United States] from Maine to California."[12]

By the end of the 1930s, the Lynd studies, combined with Bourke-White's photo essay, had identified Muncie as a worthy subject of social and cultural investigation. In the ensuing seven decades, other researchers would pick up where the Lynds had left off and attempt to prove, disprove, or modify the belief that Muncie was "Middletown," the representative American community. Muncie was on its way to becoming the most studied, mid-size community in the United States, "the barometer of the average American life."[13] In fact, Munsonians have grown accustomed to being studied, surveyed, sampled, and investigated by outsiders. "Here, it's something of a way of life," remarked Larry Lough, editor of *The Star Press*, the community's daily newspaper.[14] Other Munsonians even saw some humor in the periodic efforts of outsiders to describe them as average Americans. "We're so ordinary; we're unique," they joked.[15]

Muncie's Double History

This chapter explores why Muncie has managed to endure in the public imagination as the "representative" small city as well as "one of the most studied communities in the United States."[16] Before venturing too far into that exercise, however, let me make an important observation. In reality, two Muncies tend to exist virtually side-by-side. First, there is the Muncie that is a geographic, cultural, social, political, and economic fact of history. Second, there is the Muncie that has been recorded as "Middletown" in popular and academic literature, as well as in contemporary media. Neither exists to the exclusion of the other. In fact, the Muncie that is a fact of history often provides the raw data and primary source material that eventually finds expression in the Middletown of the academic journal, the published monograph, or the film.

The Muncie of historical fact began during the American pioneer period and has since undergone three stages: the preindustrial stage, which lasted from the late 1820s until the discovery of natural gas in the mid-1880s; the industrial stage, which lasted for a century from the mid-1880s to the mid-1980s; and the deindustrial stage, which began in the mid-1980s and continues to the present. As sociologist Rita Caccamo observed in her book, *Back to Middletown*, "Middletown is a corner of America like any other, which has undergone a massive transformation from the industrial town of the past to a place where most jobs today are in the service sector. For all that, it is a sleepy place which still retains the vestiges of material well-being. Its normality is recompensed; it is proud of itself and of still representing some part of the industrialized north of the United States."[17]

Settlement in the area today known as east central Indiana began in the late eighteenth century. Indians belonging to the Delaware tribe moved into an area around the White River and established two villages. One clan, known as the Munsee or "Wolf" clan, established a village around the northern bend of the White River. Another clan settled to the southeast in a village first called Buckongahelastown. White settlement into the region after the Revolution and the War of 1812 created a rivalry between the Americans and the Delawares until, following the defeat of the Indians at the Battle of Tippecanoe and the Treaty of St. Mary's in 1818, Indian migration ceased and the resettlement of Indians to the west began.

After the departure of the Indians, the white settlers who migrated to Indiana focused mainly on farming and set about to clear a land that was primarily a wilderness. The region was heavily forested, inhabited by wild animals including wolves and bears, and a challenge for even the hardiest pioneer. Nevertheless, a small agricultural community had taken hold in east central Indiana by the end of the 1820s.[18]

The preindustrial stage of Muncie's history spanned almost sixty years, from the founding of the community in the late 1820s until industrialization gained a foothold in the mid-1880s. In the pre–Civil War period, Muncie was mostly a rural and semirural town whose economic livelihood was tied to the local agricultural community. Muncie was also the seat of Delaware County and acquired some regional status and geographic advantage by virtue of that designation. Even so, Muncie remained small, and its population was no more than three thousand residents when it was incorporated as a city in 1865.[19]

To understand the routine of life in Muncie and Delaware County during the preindustrial period, one can examine the lives of one of its founding families, the Gallihers. The Gallihers emigrated to Indiana from Pennsylvania and Ohio in the 1830s. Martin Galliher, the first member of the family to settle in Muncie, visited the area in 1836 on a business trip for his employer in Cincinnati. Galliher purchased eighty acres of land in Perry Township in the southern part of Delaware County and thereby laid the initial foundation for becoming one of the community's largest landowners. In 1837, Galliher married Rhoda Ann Ogden of Cincinnati and the couple lived in Ohio for the next three years. In 1840, Martin and Rhoda Ogden Galliher moved to Muncie where they established the family home at the corner of Kirby Avenue and Hackley Street, slightly south of the town center.[20]

Once established in Muncie, Martin Galliher continued to acquire property, eventually accumulating more than 340 acres in the southeast end of the city. In 1840, he opened a general store where he traded in a variety of hardware items, dry goods, and groceries. An advertisement for the store in 1841 read: "The subscriber just received, in addition to his former stock, a general assortment of GROCERIES, which he now offers for sale on the most reasonable terms, consisting in part of: Rio coffee, chocolate, young hysen and imperial teas, molasses, sugar, whisky, brandy, and wine, mackerel, sugar and snuff, powder and lead, salt, iron, nails, window glass, crackers, raisins, cheese, liquorices, ball, indigo, madder, capperas, blue vitrol, white card, Spanish brown, copal varnish, and spirits."[21] In 1847, Martin Galliher formed a partnership with Ralph Burt, another Muncie entrepreneur, and expanded the general store.

In addition to the store, Martin Galliher operated two other enterprises. First, he maintained a meatpacking and processing facility for pork on east Jackson Street in Muncie. The pork products were then transported by wagon to Cincinnati for distribution from that point. Second, he continued his development of a large farm on his property south of Muncie and, in 1852, retired from his other business pursuits in order to concentrate on his agricultural interests.

As Martin Galliher's businesses grew, so too did his family and his influence in the larger activities of the community. Between 1847 and 1854, four children were born to Martin and Rhoda Galliher: Martin Jerome (1847), Susan Zonetta (1850), Ida (1856), and Charles (1854).[22] The Gallihers were also actively involved in the establishment of Muncie's First Baptist Church in 1859 and Rhoda, in particular, played an influential role in the life of the church. Martin Galliher also figured prominently in the local Democratic Party and was a frequent delegate to the county and state political conventions.

Unquestionably, Martin and Rhoda Ogden Galliher lived productive lives as one of Muncie's pioneer families. Martin lived in Muncie until his death on June 29, 1887. Rhoda Ogden Galliher passed away on July 3, 1893. Frank Haimbaugh, editor of one of Muncie's local newspapers, wrote that Martin "entered upon life a poor boy but by an energy rarely equaled . . . accumulated quite a fortune."[23] Unlike many of Muncie's other pioneer families, the Gallihers have remained in Muncie and are prominent citizens to this day. The descendants of Martin and Rhoda Galliher continue to be active business owners and have managed successful enterprises as varied as a pharmacy, a medical practice, an insurance agency, a retail trade store, and a printing and publishing company.

Martin Galliher's death in 1887 coincided with the onset of the industrial stage of Muncie's history. Muncie's emergence as a factory city began on September 15, 1886, when a large vein of natural gas was discovered near Eaton, Indiana, twelve miles north of the city.[24] Within months, more gas wells were discovered throughout central Indiana, stretching from Portland in the east to Kokomo in the west. Referred to as the Trenton Field, this gas field covered five thousand square miles and included seventeen counties in Indiana and still more in Ohio. The availability of natural gas inevitably led to aggressive efforts to promote Muncie and attract numerous new enterprises to the city. Advertisements from that time described Muncie as the "Magic City," the "Birmingham of the North," and the "Young Giant of Indiana."[25]

By the mid-1890s, the industrial face of Muncie had changed dramatically. The city boasted seven glass plants, fourteen fabricators of steel or iron, two carriage works, four washing machine factories, two

Workers on the Warner Gear Company floor, circa 1918. Courtesy of Archives and Special Collections, Ball State University.

hub-and-spoke factories, a pulp company, and numerous other facilities. Several local banks and financial institutions had also been established.[26] By 1900, Muncie had become a working-class community, boasting that it was a place where "people made things" that contributed to a better life for everyone.

During the twentieth century, Muncie's industrial profile expanded while its population grew to 75,000 residents in the city, with another 50,000 living outside the city limits in unincorporated areas generally labeled as "the county." Between 1890 and 1920, the major contributions to local industry came from two families: the Ball family, manufacturers of glass for home canning and commercial packaging; and the Kitselmans, manufacturers of woven wire fencing and other wire-related products.

After 1920, industrialization took a different turn in Muncie. General Motors Corporation built two manufacturing facilities in Muncie during the 1920s, one for making transmissions and the other for making automobile batteries. These two enterprises complemented other locally owned auto parts makers, especially the Warner Gear Company (later to become part of the Borg-Warner corporation), which began in 1902. By World War II, Muncie's industrial profile could justifiably be identified with "jars and cars."

Between 1920 and 1945, Muncie's profile on the state and regional level also expanded, largely due to the efforts of the Ball family. In 1918, two of the family's five brothers, Edmund B. Ball and Frank C. Ball, along with their wives Bertha Crosley Ball and Elizabeth Brady Ball, acquired the assets of a defunct normal school and donated the property to the state for the establishment of a branch campus in Muncie of the Indiana Normal College in Terre Haute. By 1929, the small college in Muncie had grown sufficiently to be granted its independence and established as the Ball State Teachers College. In 1965, having surpassed an enrollment of 10,000 students, the school became Ball State University.[27]

Also in the mid-1920s, following the death of Edmund B. Ball, the family donated $2.5 million for the construction of Ball Memorial Hospital on a site near the Teachers College.[28] Ball Memorial Hospital was an impressive addition to the community and a valuable facility for the advancement of medical practice in Indiana. As one physician commented at the time: "Aside from Indianapolis, [Muncie] had Indiana's outstanding medical community. Credit Ball Hospital . . . certainly Marion, Kokomo, Lafayette, (and) Richmond had nothing to compare with Muncie. Nor did Fort Wayne or South Bend. Muncie was unique."[29]

A rally of Muncie's Ku Klux Klan, circa 1922. Courtesy of Archives and Special Collections, Ball State University.

Throughout the twentieth century, Muncie also became known for some other facts of its existence, some flattering and some not. During the 1920s, for example, it was common knowledge that members of the Ku Klux Klan controlled the city's government and political system. The Klan's anti-Catholic and anti-Jewish prejudices led to boycotts of businesses owned by its targets, as well as discriminatory provisions in neighborhood housing covenants in the fashionable neighborhoods on the city's northwest side.[30]

In a more positive vein, Muncie became a hotbed of enthusiasm for high school basketball during the 1920s, with a special fanaticism reserved for the Muncie Central Bearcats. In 1928, the Bearcats won their first Indiana state high school basketball championship and followed with seven other championships, the latest in 1988. After the 1928 state tournament, Munsonians rallied to support the Bearcats by raising sufficient funds to build the Muncie Fieldhouse on north Walnut Street, the largest arena for high school basketball in the United States for the next sixty years. The Muncie Fieldhouse opened the first week of December 1928. Even the Lynds were forced to admit that the Muncie Central Bearcats unified the various elements of the community. As sportswriter Alexander Wolff observed recently in Sports Illustrated: "The obsession [for basketball] extended beyond the small towns into the cities. In Middletown, their classic study of Muncie in the 1920s, sociologists Robert and Helen Lynd declared the Bearcats of Muncie Central to be 'an agency of group cohesion' that 'sweeps all before it. . . . No distinctions divide the crowds which pack the school gymnasium . . . Northside and Southside, Catholic and Kluxer, banker and machinist—their one shout is 'Eat 'em, Beat 'em, Bearcats!'"[31]

In the annals of Indiana high school basketball, Muncie became the Goliath, the unstoppable force. When tiny Milan High School managed an upset victory over the Bearcats in the 1954 state championship game, it seemed that the impossible had occurred. So incredible was the Milan victory, or the Bearcat defeat, that it later served as the inspiration for the film *Hoosiers*, directed by Indiana natives Angelo Pizzo and David Anspaugh, and starring Gene Hackman, Barbara Hershey, and Dennis Hopper.

After World War II, Muncie continued its pattern of industrial growth. The Westinghouse Corporation built a massive factory for the construction of transformers in 1954. The auto plants and the other related companies continued to expand their production. In 1962, however, Muncie received its first indication that industrialization had reached its crest when the Ball Brothers Manufacturing Company (later Ball Corporation in 1967) announced that it was closing its glass-making operations in Muncie. The company's action resulted in the loss of several hundred jobs, even though Ball maintained its headquarters in Muncie as well as a sizable portion of its home canning operations. Then, two major recessions, one from 1974 to 1975 and the other from 1981 to 1982, resulted in massive layoffs in the local auto plants and the loss of thousands of jobs which never returned. Muncie's population began to decline as unemployed autoworkers and their families left the city to look elsewhere for work. Muncie's century-long experience with industrial growth had ended. The city was about to experience the devastating effects of two double-whammies: the shift in economic power in America from the northeast and midwest to the south, southwest, and west, and by the end of the century, the effects of a globalized, world economy.

Muncie's third historical stage, beginning in 1984 and continuing to the present, is one of deindustrialization. In the mid-1980s, Muncie's community leaders began searching for a new economic model. Obviously, the community needed to diversify its local economy in the direction of the service sector. In fact, by 1985, the service sector had already surpassed the manufacturing sector in terms of total employment in the community.[32] Two obvious assets in the service sector were Ball State University and Ball Memorial Hospital which, by the mid-1990s, had become the community's largest employers. Increasing emphasis was also placed on expanding retail shopping outlets through the expansion of the local mall and the attraction of "big-box" retailers, such as Wal-Mart, Meijer, Menard's, and the national electronics companies. Such efforts were essential to Muncie's economic health as the process of deindustrialization continued to make its presence felt.

The Ball Corporation Factory, once the major employer in Muncie, is now simply an empty building behind chain-link fences. Photo by Daniel Gawlowski.

In the mid-1990s, deindustrialization reaccelerated. In 1996, Borg-Warner sold half of its transmission business to a company that manufactured a large share of its products in Mexico. In 1998, General Motors closed its modern Delco Battery manufacturing facility. Even Ball Corporation, the community's corporate mainstay, announced its decision to relocate the company headquarters to Colorado in 1998.[33] As local historian W. W. Spurgeon commented in the summer of 2000, "The industrial economy didn't collapse a couple of years ago. It took thirty years. But only in the last three to four years did we finally admit it."[34]

As mentioned previously, these facts of history have provided the raw data and the source material for the body of literature that has identified Muncie as Middletown. In the decades after the Lynds completed their studies, others joined the parade of commentators on the city. Between 1940 and 1975, however, this literature was limited to an occasional article, such as John Bartlow Martin's two pieces, "Is Muncie Still Middletown?" written for *Harper's* magazine in 1944, and his "Middletown Revisited," written for the same magazine in 1946.[35] But, as historian Dwight W. Hoover has pointed out, both *Middletown* and *Middletown in Transition* were cited extensively in the works of other notable scholars during this period, including Nelson Polsby, C. Wright Mills, and Stephan Thernstrom.[36]

A second renaissance in Middletown research and publication began in the late 1970s, given its impetus by sociologist Theodore Caplow from the University of Virginia. A former student of Robert Lynd's at Columbia University, Caplow assembled a team of researchers that included sociologists Howard Bahr and Bruce Chadwick of Brigham Young University. Supported with a major grant from the National Science Foundation, Caplow and his research team set out to replicate the original Middletown studies of the 1920s. Like the Lynds, Caplow and his researchers moved to Muncie and resided in the community where, Lynd-style, they met people from the city and carried out an extensive regimen of surveys, questionnaires, interviews, and research in newspapers and periodical sources. The Caplow-led project became known as Middletown III.

Using the voluminous data acquired by the Middletown III research team, Caplow eventually published two books, *Middletown Families* and *All Faithful People*.[37] As their titles suggest, the books dealt with contemporary family life in Muncie and the religious practices of the community. In both of these studies, Caplow and the scholars who assisted him emphasized that continuity with the past, instead of change, prevailed in Middletown. If anything, the importance of family ties and family relationships were closer in Muncie in the late 1970s than they were in the 1920s. In *All Faithful People*, Caplow reported that religious practices had changed in Muncie but that Munsonians were at least as religious as they had been in the 1920s. As Dwight Hoover wrote about *All Faithful People*: "Religious life and practice [in Muncie] has become less harsh. Munsonians were less conscious of denominational lines, less puritanical, more eager to attend church, and more tolerant of those who had struggled from the way."[38]

The Middletown III project occurred almost simultaneously with another major initiative, the Middletown Film Series. The two projects were essentially unrelated although, by virtue of the fact that they occurred almost simultaneously, outsiders came to the conclusion that Middletown III and the Middletown Film Series were part of a new, ambitious Middletown study. The film series began as an idea pursued by three Ball State professors: historians Dwight Hoover and Warren Vander Hill, and English professor Joseph Trimmer. The three humanists conceived of the idea for a film after they had completed a previous Middletown study relating to the work experience in Muncie and were encouraged to submit a proposal to the National Endowment for the Humanities in cooperation with the local Public Broadcasting Service (PBS) affiliate.[39] Concurrent with the plans of the three Ball State humanists, Vander Hill was introduced to Peter Davis, the award-winning documentary producer, and Davis eventually became the lead producer for the series. Davis and the three Ball State professors managed to acquire significant funding for the series from the National Endowment for the Humanities as well as from corporate sources. It was shown on the PBS in the spring of 1982.

The series consisted of six films: "The Campaign," which dealt with Muncie's mayoral election of 1979; "The Big Game," which showcased the daily lives of two high school basketball players, one in Muncie and the other in nearby Anderson, Indiana; "The Second Time Around," which dealt with the issue of divorce and remarriage; "Family Business," which chronicled the struggles of a Muncie entrepreneur; "Community of Praise," which dealt with one family's religious experience; and finally, "Seventeen," a look into the local youth culture against the backdrop of a city high school.

Each film was designed to correspond to one of the six subject categories identified by the Lynds. By far, the most controversial of the films was "Seventeen," a depiction of teenage life in the community. Vander Hill attributed the controversial nature of the film to its depiction of "pot smoking, drinking, interracial dating, and teenage pregnancy" within Muncie's youth culture.[40] A group of Muncie's community leaders threatened legal action against both PBS and the producers of "Seventeen" were the film to be shown in Muncie. Davis chose to withdraw "Seventeen" from the series rather than make the production changes demanded by the Muncie contingent.

The resurgence of interest in Muncie as Middletown, from the academic perspective, also galvanized the attention of Ball State University. Perhaps to complement Caplow and his research team, the Sociology Department at Ball State began conducting its own Middletown area survey in 1978. These studies, focused mainly on the religious and political activity in the community, succeeded largely through the efforts of professors Stephen Johnson and Joseph Tamney. In 1984, Ball State established its Center for Middletown Studies, a research unit dedicated to the study of the history of Muncie. Dwight W. Hoover, a participant in both the Middletown III project and the Middletown Film series, became the center's founding director. The author of several studies relating to Muncie as Middletown, Hoover's most notable contribution to scholarship in this field was his publication of *Middletown: The Making of a Documentary Film Series* in 1992.[41] Along with James V. Koch, Ball

State's provost at the time, Warren Vander Hill provided much of the administrative impetus for the creation of the center.

The popularity of Muncie as Middletown created further scholarly inquiry in the 1990s. Interestingly enough, the focus of this renewed inquiry centered on Muncie's minority community. In 1995, Gregory Howard Williams, currently president of the City College of New York and former dean of the law school at Ohio State University, published *Life on the Color Line*, his autobiographical account of his youth in Muncie during the 1950s. A child of mixed ancestry, Williams wrote a compelling narrative that examined the challenges confronting a young person who was identified with the city's African American community. The Muncie described by Williams lived by its "rules," a strict separation of the races in terms of social interaction. Williams painted a devastating picture of a city that he regarded as immersed in racism and unwilling to overcome its effects. Not until Williams enrolled at Ball State Teachers College, and was befriended by several helpful professors, including the historian Everett Ferrill and the psychologist Carson Bennett, was he able to overcome the racist traditions of Muncie.[42]

Another view of race relations in Muncie has been offered by Jack S. Blocker Jr., professor of history at Huron College of the University of Western Ontario. In his article, "Black Migration to Muncie, 1860–1930," written for the *Indiana Magazine of History* in December 1996, Blocker shows how Muncie was a more hospitable place for African Americans than originally assumed. Using census data and other demographic information, as well as oral history interviews gathered by researchers for the Black Muncie History Project, overseen by Hurley Goodall, Blocker demonstrated how African Americans were able to find employment and establish a family structure in Muncie during the early years of the twentieth century. According to Blocker, life in Muncie for African Americans never approached the promised land but it may not have been as negative as previously assumed, either.[43]

In 1997, Dan Rottenberg published his edited work, *Middletown Jews*, based on a series of interviews with Jewish residents of Muncie, conducted by Warren Vander Hill and Dwight Hoover in the late 1970s. In this study, Rottenberg enabled numerous Jewish Munsonians to tell their stories about life as a part of a very small minority, one which was forced to deal with a host of discriminatory practices. In his introduction to the book, Hoover wrote that "To be a Jew in Muncie was to live in a community of flux . . . where opportunities to participate in community life had shrunk and where anti-Semitism was openly articulated by the Ku Klux Klan."[44]

The studies by Williams, Blocker, Hoover, and Rottenberg in the 1990s demonstrated that Muncie/Middletown remained a lively subject of literary pursuit. These studies were worthy additions to the literature initially created by the Lynds and by Theodore Caplow.

Conclusion

In conclusion, one must address the question of Muncie's contemporary "representativeness" and the extent to which the community still typifies American beliefs, customs, and traditions. Perhaps even more important, does Muncie, a "stand-alone" city in the midst of a predominantly agricultural region, still represent the typical small city during the age of suburbanization and urban sprawl when large metropolises appear to be gobbling up their neighboring small cities?[45] Some voices will still testify that Muncie remains Middletown, or at least a close approximation to it. "Over the years, we faced the question, and we ducked and weaved, sometimes admitting [that] one place can typify the United States," Ted Caplow observed at the second annual Small Cities Conference at Ball State in November 2002. Statistically, Upper Sandusky, Ohio, appears to be the best indicator of American typicality, according to Caplow. But, he adds, "Muncie was second, out of thousands of communities. It is sometimes weird. If you look at the divorce rate, the robbery rate, the number of books taken from the public library, whatever, Muncie does come out very close to the national average."[46]

Likewise, two other writers, John Hendren and Ed Field, have discovered more support for the notion of Muncie as Middletown. An economics writer for the Associated Press, Hendren discovered that, in the decade between 1989 and 1999, Muncie's economic performance mirrored that of the nation as a whole. In his article, "Changes in Middletown," Hendren revealed that the cost-of-living in Muncie was 99.5 percent of the national average and that per-family income "paced both the state and the nation," rising by 13 percent.[47]

In his article, "The Lawnmower Vote," written for *The Economist* in November 1996, Field described Muncie as "the quintessential home of the swing voter. And because it has been flexible in choosing sides, it has gone for every winning president bar [John F.] Kennedy for the past sixty years."[48] Using research generated by Ball State sociologist Stephen Johnson and historian Bruce Geelhoed, the successor to Dwight Hoover as director of the Center for Middletown Studies, Field showed how the voting in Muncie for presidential candidates was a predictor of the national result. Two facets of this phenomenon were especially significant. First, not only did Muncie tend to vote for the winning presidential candidate, it also showed the capacity to swing from one party affiliation to the other as the issues in the campaign dictated. Second, sometimes the voting percentages in Muncie were virtually identical to the national vote. For example, in both 1976 and 1988, presidential candidates Jimmy Carter, Gerald Ford, George H. W. Bush, and Michael Dukakis, respectively, recorded the same percentage of the vote in Muncie as they did nationwide.[49]

Muncie/Middletown has also reflected national trends in congressional races. In 1974, Muncie helped to elect Philip Sharp, a Democrat, to the House of Representatives, thereby ousting David Dennis, a three-term Republican incumbent who had come to Congress after Richard Nixon's presidential victory in 1968. Phil Sharp was a member of the so-called Watergate class of Democratic congressmen and he served in the House for the next twenty years, retiring in 1994. In 1994, Republican David McIntosh, a conservative associated with the Newt Gingrich faction of the GOP, won the seat vacated by Phil Sharp.[50] McIntosh thereby became associated with the class of "Ditto-head Republicans," identified with Rush Limbaugh, the conservative talk-show host, when the GOP took control of the House of Representatives for the first time since 1952. The seat has remained in Republican hands ever since, although the current incumbent is Mike Pence, who won the seat in 2000 after McIntosh decided to run, unsuccessfully, for governor of Indiana.

So, does Muncie still represent Middletown? Academics will debate the point, probably indefinitely. Nevertheless, one may predict that they will eventually return to the observation made by Theodore Caplow at the Small Cities Conference in 2002: "You see, we're stuck with Muncie."[51]

Notes

1. Peter Jennings and Todd Brewster, *In Search of America* (New York: Hyperion, 2002), xvii–xviii.

2. Ed Field, "The Lawnmower Vote," *The Economist*, vol. 341, no. 7990 (November 2, 1996), 29. Rita Caccamo, an Italian sociologist who spent a summer as a visiting scholar at the Center for Middletown Studies at Ball State University, likewise noticed the distinctiveness of Muncie's caricature as "America's

Hometown." See Caccamo's *Back to Middletown* (Stanford, Calif.: Stanford University Press, 2000), 121–22.

3. Robert S. Lynd and Helen Merrell Lynd, *Middletown: A Study in Contemporary Culture* (New York: Harcourt, Brace, and World, 1929) and Robert S. Lynd and Helen Merrell Lynd, *Middletown in Transition: A Study in Cultural Conflict* (New York: Harcourt, Brace, and World, 1937).

4. Dwight W. Hoover, *Middletown Revisited* (Muncie, Ind.: Ball State University Monograph 34, 1991), 1.

5. Ibid., 2–3.

6. Theodore Caplow, quoted in *The First Measured Century*, documentary directed by Ben J. Wattenberg, produced by the Public Broadcasting Service (PBS), broadcast December 1999.

7. Lynd and Lynd, *Middletown*, 1–4.

8. Jennings and Brewster, *In Search of America*, xvii.

9. Anthony O. Edmonds and E. Bruce Geelhoed, *Ball State University: An Interpretive History* (Bloomington, Ind.: Indiana University Press, 2001), 42–43.

10. David Kennedy, quoted in *The First Measured Century*; see also David M. Kennedy, *Freedom from Fear: The American People in Depression and War, 1930–1945* (New York: Oxford University Press, 1998), 264.

11. Lynd and Lynd, *Middletown in Transition*.

12. Margaret Bourke-White, "Muncie Ind. Is the Great US Middletown," *Life*, vol. 2, no. 19 (May 10, 1937), 15–26.

13. Jennings and Brewster, *In Search of America*, xviii.

14. Ibid.

15. Ibid.

16. Hoover, *Middletown Revisited*, 1.

17. Caccamo, *Back to Middletown*, 121–22. Readers who wish to find a comprehensive listing of the literature of Muncie as Middletown should consult the bibliography of Caccamo's *Back to Middletown*, 134–43.

18. Wiley W. Spurgeon Jr., *Muncie and Delaware County: An Illustrated Retrospective* (Woodland Hills, Calif.: Windsor Publications, 1984), 11–15.

19. Edmonds and Geelhoed, *Ball State University*, 43. For another examination of Muncie's multidimensional history, see Martha Banta, "Natural Resources. The Three Muncies: Buckongahelastown, Munseytown, Middletown," Center for Middletown Studies, Ball State University, unpublished, 2002

20. E. Bruce Geelhoed, *Boyce Forms Systems: A Centennial History, 1889–1999* (Muncie, Ind.: privately published, 1999), 10–13.

21. Ibid., 12.

22. Ibid., 11.

23. Ibid., 13.

24. Edmonds and Geelhoed, *Ball State University*, 44–45.

25. Ibid. See also Dwight W. Hoover, "Becoming an Industrial City" in "Automobility in Muncie," manuscript, Center for Middletown Studies, Ball State University, unpublished, 1991, 2–3; and James A. Glass, "The Indiana Gas

Boom and Its Legacies," *Traces of Indiana and Midwestern History*, vol. 12, no. 3 (Summer 2000), 20–29.

26. Edmonds and Geelhoed, *Ball State University*, 46.

27. Ibid., 60–65.

28. Ibid., 87–90.

29. Ibid., 90.

30. See Dwight W. Hoover, "To Be a Jew in Middletown," in Dan Rottenberg, ed., *Middletown Jews* (Bloomington, Ind.: Indiana University Press, 1997), viii–x.

31. Alexander Wolff, "Class Struggle," *Sports Illustrated* (December 2, 2002), 50.

32. Mary Williams Walsh, "'New Economy' Deepens the Wealth Divide," *Los Angeles Times*, April 19, 2000; also Seth Slabaugh, "A Town Famous for Being Ordinary," *The Star Press* (Muncie, Ind.), August 24, 1998.

33. Slabaugh, "A Town Famous for Being Ordinary," *The Star Press*, August 24, 1998; see also David Penticuff, "Borg-Warner Business Sold," *The Star Press*, October 23, 1996; and "Good-bye Smokestack," *The Star Press*, December 27, 1998.

34. Gregg Fields, "How the New Economy Rocked the Rust Belt," *Miami Herald*, September 3, 2000.

35. John Bartlow Martin, "Is Muncie Still Middletown?" *Harper's*, vol. 189, no. 1130 (July 1944), 97–109; John Bartlow Martin, "Middletown Revisited," *Harper's*, vol. 193, no. 1155 (August 1946), 111–19.

36. Hoover, *Middletown Revisited*, 20–22.

37. Theodore Caplow, *Middletown Families* (Minneapolis: University of Minnesota Press, 1982); Theodore Caplow, *All Faithful People* (Minneapolis: University of Minnesota Press, 1983).

38. Hoover, *Middletown Revisited*, 28.

39. C. Warren Vander Hill, "The Middletown Film Project: One Year Later," address to the Friends of the Bracken Library, April 30, 1983, (Muncie, Ind.: Ball State University, 1983), 2–3.

40. Ibid., 18–20.

41. Dwight W. Hoover, *Middletown: The Making of a Documentary Film Series* (Philadelphia: Harwood Academic Publishers, 1992).

42. Gregory H. Williams, *Life on the Color Line* (New York: Dutton, 1995), 181–84, 267–68, 284–85.

43. Jack S. Blocker Jr., "Black Migration to Muncie, 1860–1930," *Indiana Magazine of History*, vol. 92, no. 4 (December 1996), 297–310.

44. Hoover, "To Be a Jew in Middletown," in Rottenberg, ed., *Middletown Jews*, viii–x.

45. See, for example, Seth Slabaugh, "Will Indianapolis Grow into Muncie?" *The Star Press*, November 3, 2002.

46. Seth Slabaugh, "Sociologists Find Muncie Really Is 'Middletown,'" *The Star Press*, November 8, 2002.

47. John Hendren, "Changes in Middletown," *Evansville Courier-Press*, October 17, 1999.

48. Field, "The Lawnmower Vote," *The Economist*, November 2, 1996, 29.

49. Ibid.

50. Ibid., see also Graham Fraser, "Bellwether City Leans toward Clinton," *Toronto Globe and Mail*, September 24, 1996.

51. Caplow, observation at the Small Cities Conference, November 2, 2002.

2

A City Apart

Hurley Goodall and Elizabeth Campbell

Yes, this is a harsh land, Mary, and I pray that after enduring the hard-ships of our journey to this place, that I have the strength to endure the loneliness and isolation which seems to lie ahead for me. Still, I feel hopeful. The woods are rich with game for food and the land is rich for planting. The many trees will be cut to provide shelter. Our task won't be easy, but when has it ever been? We will survive and we will thrive. Zango and I will raise our family here and, hopefully, live in peace. So wish us god speed and pray for us.[1]

Hannah Elliott wrote this letter shortly after she and fifty-four others finished the long journey from North Carolina to the Indiana frontier. The challenges that Hannah confronted were like the challenges con-fronted by all pioneers. She and her companions met with wilderness and rough roads, hard times, loneliness, and isolation. But her hopes also express something different, something most pioneers would never know. Hannah was a free woman of color, whose task had never been easy and whose great desire had always been to live in peace. We don't often think of nineteenth-century blacks as pioneers. But Hannah was one of thousands of black pioneers who came to Indiana in the first decades after statehood.

Black pioneers came west for many reasons. In part, of course, they were moving away from the slaveholding south, where laws designed to protect the property of slaveholders endangered all people of color—whether free or slave. With the first few decades of the 1800s had come deterioration in the legal status of free blacks; hence, many looked to the newly created free states of Indiana, Ohio, and Illinois as potentially safer places. But African Americans also moved, proac-tively, toward the fresh lands of the northwest, embracing the dream of

Well before the first African Americans came to Muncie, black farming communities dotted the surrounding countryside. Courtesy Archives and Special Collections, Ball State University.

all pioneers, regardless of color. They sought "woods rich with game" and "land rich for planting," the opportunity to "survive and thrive." Although pioneers of color faced challenges unknown to their white brothers and sisters, all pioneers shared at least part of the same dream: to carve out better and more prosperous lives for themselves and their families.[2]

Well before the first African Americans came to Muncie, black farming communities dotted the surrounding countryside.[3] Like Hannah and her companions, many of Indiana's first black farmers had come from long-free southern families. Others were the sons and daughters of those who had been recently manumitted, or freed. Still others had been recently freed themselves. Termed "people of color" in the parlance of the day, east central Indiana's first black farmers were people of color indeed whose ancestors included people from Europe, Africa, and and the tribes of American.[4]

African Americans in Indiana

Although it had been established as a free state in 1816, Indiana did not welcome its colored pioneers. The state's first constitution prohibited

"Negros" (and Indians) from serving in the militia and denied all men of color many of the privileges of citizenship, including the right to vote. In 1818, the Indiana General Assembly forbade intermarriage between whites and blacks and declared that no person with one-fourth or more Negro blood could testify in cases involving a white person. In 1831, fifteen years after statehood, Indiana's state legislature placed serious restrictions on the ability of free people of color to migrate to Indiana, as this act clearly demonstrates:

An Act Concerning Free Negroes and
Mulattos, Servants, and Slaves

(APPROVED, FEBRUARY 10, 1831)

Sec. 1. Be it enacted by the General Assembly of the state of Indiana, That from and after the first day of September next, no black or mulatto person coming or brought into this state, shall be permitted to reside therein unless bond with good and sufficient security be given on behalf of such person of color, to be approved of by the overseers of the poor of some township in this state, payable to the state of Indiana, in the penal sum of five-hundred dollars.[5]

The 1831 Constitution also established the state's "Negro Registers," which required all of Indiana's blacks to register at their county courthouses.[6] Interestingly, the provisions of the 1831 Constitution were enforced differently from place to place. In the case of the Negro Registers, for example, more than one hundred of Orange County, Indiana's black residents complied with the new law. But in Randolph County, home to hundreds of black settlers, only eight ever complied. Indiana was still a young state in 1831, and these differences in enforcement probably reflect its frontier nature. A statewide economy had not yet taken hold, nor had statewide transportation or trade infrastructures been established. Many places had not even been settled, and those that had been settled were ruled much more by local custom than by state law. East central Indiana, home to prosperous blacks and relatively friendly Quakers, was clearly more accepting of its black residents than were other places in the state.[7]

As the nineteenth century wore on, and Indiana became more settled and connected, the state's people of color began to see their legal status deteriorate even further. Topping off half a century of dwindling rights and freedoms, the 1850 United States Fugitive Slave Law and the 1851 Indiana State Constitution combined to cripple the legal status of Indiana's people of color. The Fugitive Slave Laws allowed southern slaveholders, for the first time, to capture blacks on northern soil. This development threatened all persons of color, whether free or fugitive.[8] And Article 13 of Indiana's 1851 State Constitution outlined the following restrictions on the state's "Negros and Mulattoes":

Article XIII

Indiana Constitution of 1851

Section 1. No Negro or Mulatto shall come into or settle in the State, after the adoption of this Constitution.

Section 2. All contracts made with any Negro or Mulatto coming into the state, contrary to the provisions of the foregoing section, shall be void, and any person who shall employ such Negro or Mulatto, or otherwise encourage him to remain in the State, shall be fined in any sum not less than ten dollars, nor more than five hundred dollars.

Article 13 further provided that all fines collected would go into a "colonization" fund designated for Negroes and Mulattoes who wished to "emigrate," that is, to move out of Indiana. Clearly, the article's goal was to keep people of color out of the state and, in the words of a State Supreme Court justice of the day, "to remove those already among us as speedily as possible."[9]

The 1851 Constitution brought together many of the state's earlier anti-black statutes. It codified the 1843 General Assembly law (and earlier constitutional provisions) that prohibited black children from attending public (i.e., white) schools, even though their parents were still required to pay school taxes. It reinforced the 1831 prohibitions against both serving in the militia and testifying in court cases in which a white person was a party. The 1851 Constitution again outlawed interracial marriages. It barred people of color from voting and from holding public office.[10] A harsher and more uniformly enforced document than that of 1831, the 1851 Constitution had very real consequences for the state's black residents. Article 13 of the 1851 Constitution was invalidated by the State Supreme Court in 1866. Still, its passage signified troubled times for the state's African Americans—and an important shift in the state's attitude toward its people of color.[11] As in states both north and south, relations between Indiana's blacks and whites deteriorated as the Civil War grew near. This deterioration did not go unnoticed— indeed, Indiana's African Americans often strenuously and publicly objected to the growing bigotry of the times. In 1860, Samuel Smothers, the black president of Randolph County's integrated Union Literary

Institute, railed against the state's racist laws, saving his greatest indignation for those who denied education to people of color.

> When you support, by your votes and by your influence, the other proscriptive laws of this state, you indeed commit a crime against God and humanity of great magnitude; but when you deprive us of the means of education, you commit an outrage upon the SOUL; *a war upon THE IMMORTAL PART!* [emphasis in original][12]

Yet, once more in the face of grave obstacles, Indiana's people of color settled in, raised families, established churches, and educated themselves. They survived and, in many cases, thrived. Though the 1851 Constitution surely chased more than a few people of color on to states further west and to Canada, many others remained. And despite the ambivalent nature of life in this "free" state, African Americans continued to seek out new lives in Indiana.

African Americans in Muncie

Against this backdrop, Edward and Maria (also Mary) Scott moved to Muncie in 1845, shortly after their 1844 Henry County marriage.[13] Though they were not the first African Americans to live in Muncie, they were probably the first family to move into the city and stay.[14] Maria, born in North Carolina around 1827, was the daughter of Samuel and Marian Bundy, relatively well-to-do pioneers of Henry County's Bundy neighborhood.[15] Edward Scott, born in Virginia around 1810, came from a large and long-free Southern family, many of whom immigrated to Wayne, Henry, and Randolph counties between 1820 and 1850.[16] Both the Scotts and the Bundys had been among the first wave of black settlers to Indiana. First wave families, who often bought and cleared land upon their arrival, had been able to carve out some measure of prosperity within the first generation. That prosperity no doubt helped their children to establish settled lives of their own.[17]

Like many of Muncie's early black professionals, Edward was a barber. His apparently profitable business served his family well—the 1860 census lists the combined value of his real and personal estate at $700.00. Edward was not the only black barber in town—indeed, four of the five adult black men listed in the 1860 census were barbers.[18]

When Edward died in 1861, Maria married Henry Artis, also a barber, who died in 1864. With the death of her husbands came difficult

times for Maria and her children. Although both of her husbands had accumulated some measure of personal wealth during their lives, her own
economic status plunged after their deaths. Maria supported her family
by taking in washing, a service she supplied for the rest of her life. This
economic setback did not hold her back—despite her changed life she
was one of the city's most important early black figures. In 1868 Maria
Artist was one of the primary organizers of the city's first black church,
the African Methodist Episcopal Church of the city of Muncie, Indiana.
Her brother, Jason Bundy, was elected as the church's first leader.

Family, church, and community were important things in 1860s
Muncie. They remained important, and as the city grew, the pattern of
living and worshiping close together became even more pronounced.[19]

In 1870, most of the city's forty-eight black residents claimed either
Indiana or Kentucky as their birthplaces, though a few claimed North
and South Carolina, Virginia, Tennessee, Ohio, and Illinois. Though
there were still four black barbers in town, there were also three day laborers, one farm laborer, a carpenter, a blacksmith, and a teamster.
Most of the women kept house, but two took in wash (Mary Scott Artis and her daughter, Martha Scott Gilmore) and one young woman
worked as a domestic servant.

The city's black population nearly quadrupled during the 1870s,
growing from 48, or 1.6 percent, of the city's population in 1870 to 187,
or 3.6 percent, by 1880.[20] As the numbers of black people in town increased, so too did their institutions. The city's second black church,
Second Baptist was organized in 1872.[21] The city's African American
presence also grew in terms of civic participation—in 1876, a black man
sat, for the first time, on a Delaware County jury.

The Beginnings of Muncie's
African American Community

Muncie's black community established itself, steadily if slowly, between 1840 and 1880. In the 1880s a different era began, marked by the
discovery of natural gas in east central Indiana, which was followed by
the city's first industrial boom. Factories, both large and small, multiplied and new citizens poured into the community looking for work.
Job seekers often came from the upland, piedmont, and deep South, as
the end of Reconstruction and the crash of the southern economy ushered in bleak times for African Americans in those areas. As agriculture

began the radical shift away from the frontier's small-scale subsistence farms toward the large-scale crop farms of the twentieth century, blacks also moved in from the surrounding countryside and from rural areas in nearby Midwestern states.[22]

In 1880, Muncie's African American community was well established. The black neighborhood hinted at in earlier censuses—south of the central business district, centering on East Jackson Street and reaching out toward Adams, Monroe, and Vine streets—solidified. Small businesses took root. Churches grew larger and stronger. Black children attended the city's public schools—when Addie Knight picked up her diploma in 1880, she became the first African American to graduate from Muncie's Central High School. At least one black volunteer firefighter served the city during the latter nineteenth century. And, in the spirit of civic unity, people began to organize around issues that mattered to them. In September 1880, famed abolitionist Frederick Douglass visited Muncie to stump for James Garfield, the Republican candidate for president. His speech, sponsored by the Garfield and Porter Club, the county's black Republican organization, drew thousands.[23]

The Garfield and Porter Club was one of many established in the 1880s. Two other Republican organizations, the Blaine and Logan Club and the Lincoln League, took hold during the decade, as did the city's Colored Masons. Muncie's black citizens organized recreationally, as well as socially and politically. In 1884, a colored semi-professional baseball team was organized, and in late September 1887, the city's black community held a large and very public celebration to commemorate the twenty-fifth anniversary of Lincoln's Preliminary Emancipation Proclamation. Indeed, the city's black population grew so steadily and visibly during the 1880s that, in 1889, the city's *Daily News* reported that "Muncie's colored population was increasing so rapidly it would soon be the largest colored population of any city of Muncie's size in the state."[24]

Muncie's black community was growing quickly, indeed. Between 1880 and 1890, the city's black population grew from 187 to 418. The 1890 decennial U.S. census showed that for the first time, Muncie's black population (3.7 percent), as a proportion of overall population, was significantly larger than the state's black population (2.0 percent). Indiana's African Americans had begun to urbanize, and Muncie had become one of their favored cities.[25]

Muncie's boom expanded in the 1890s. Increasing job opportunities, along with the family and friends already in Muncie, brought in more black residents who continued to cluster on the city's near southeast side, forming the early core of the "Industry neighborhood" that would come to be called "across town" or "Crosstown." Churches and social organizations multiplied and thrived throughout the 1890s, and a series of firsts solidified the black community's presence in town. The first community band was organized in 1895. That year or the year after the city hired its first black firefighter, one of the city's first ten paid firemen. The post office hired its first black employee, Henry T. Burnham, in 1897, and after years of petitions by black residents, the city's police department finally hired its first African American, W. T. Stokes, in 1899. By 1900, Muncie's African American community numbered 739 people, and had grown strong, vibrant, and visible.

The Whitely Neighborhood

> All he wanted was a job, I imagine. Of course, in them days that was all that really mattered. Man with a family, if he had a job, why he could move in the community easily and get along.[26]

John Lucas was born in Ghent, Kentucky, in 1901. In the search for decent work and good wages, John's father first took his young family to Peru, Indiana. When a friend encouraged him to come to Muncie, telling him that good jobs were plentiful there, the family moved. Arriving in 1904, the Lucases took up residence in Whitely, a small and growing town immediately northeast of Muncie.

Whitely was established by William Whiteley, an industrialist who opened an enormous reaper factory just northeast of the city in 1893. He bought all the surrounding land as well, and laid out a small town for which he had a grand vision. Following the model of mega-industrialists like George Pullman and Milton Hershey, Whiteley envisioned his "Whitely" as a model industrial town—well planned, rationally laid out, and self-contained, designed around and for the benefit of his factory. Both the factory and the town got off to a roaring start. Less than a year after the Reaper Works opened, it was completely destroyed by fire. Whiteley, whose model town had no fire station and whose modern factory had no insurance, did not rebuild. His brother, Amos, built the Whiteley Malleable Castings Company on the same spot. Amos continued to promote the town of Whitely, but he never became the town booster his brother had been. The Malleable's foundry changed names and products many times over the years, but it continued to provide African Americans with important jobs until it closed in the mid-1960s.

Despite the initial setback, Whitely took root. It started off as a primarily white town, but African Americans were part of the community from the start. Whitely was annexed by the city of Muncie in 1919, and became the city's most integrated neighborhood during the 1920s and 1930s. Many of that era recall a town that was "fifty–fifty," a place where both white and black families lived together in relative peace.

Muncie's Growing Black Population

When the *Daily News* said in 1889 that the city's "colored population was increasing so rapidly it would soon be the largest colored population of any city of Muncie's size in the state," the paper pointed out something interesting. In *Black Migration to Muncie, 1860–1930*, Jack S. Blocker gives depth to the newspaper's statement:

> Muncie's nearly constant ability to attract black migrants at a faster rate than white migrants over the entire seventy-year period produced a pattern of relative black population growth that resembled the trend found in the state's largest city. Black migration to Muncie created, by 1920, an African American community that was larger as a proportion of overall population than black communities in such major northern cities as Cleveland, Detroit, Chicago, and New York.[27]

The city's boom firmly in place, Muncie had become an industrial mecca. And, clearly, it had also become something of an African American mecca. Even as new migration into the city slowed slightly after the turn of the century, blacks continued to come in at faster rates than whites. Between 1900 and 1910, the city's total number of African Americans grew from 739 to 1,005. Their percentage of the city's total population went from 3.5 percent to 4.2 percent. With new people came new homes, stores, businesses, clubs, and churches. And the city's expanding industrial economy and job market, the driving factor behind all of this expansion, showed no signs of slowing.

Leila B. Davis, born in Germantown, North Carolina, in 1890, came to Muncie with her family in 1910. Like many of those who came during the industrial era, the Davises had moved quite often before they settled in Muncie. From North Carolina, the family first went to Maryland, then New Jersey, then Pennsylvania, before they finally settled in Muncie. The family had contacts in Muncie, and came at the suggestion of Leila's aunt, who had told them "you could get good wages here."[28]

Muncie did hold some measure of economic promise for African Americans, though full equality was never part of that promise. Muncie's blacks did not have the same range of job options and wages as whites. Still, the choices people had in Muncie were better than what they'd had in other places, especially in the south. A woman known only as Mrs. Graham, who was born in 1889 and came to Muncie from Knoxville, Tennessee, in 1913, worked as a domestic in Muncie, work she had also done in Knoxville. Her financial lot improved almost as soon as she arrived:

> Fifteen, I have worked for, I don't think I ever worked for fifteen cents here now, but I have worked in Knoxville for fifteen cents an hour. And then when I first came to Muncie, I was getting about thirty-five cents an hour. And then they raised it to fifty cents. And that's about the most I've ever got, you know, was doing the work I was doing in Muncie, this fifty cents an hour.[29]

Some of Muncie's black women worked in the city's booming factories but, by and large, those who worked outside their own homes worked inside someone else's. All of the city's upper-class white families hired domestics to work in their homes, as did many of the white "business class" families described by the Lynds. In some cases, an entire black family would serve as domestics to a single white family, most often the city's wealthiest whites. These families might live on the white family's estate, each member of the family performing service work for their employers. But this situation was unusual. Most black domestics instead traveled each day to their worksites, where they spent their days cooking, cleaning, or serving, and often caring for their employer's children.

Still, Muncie provided people with opportunities they might not otherwise have had. More than anything else, Muncie in the early twentieth century was a city that promised work.

> And the good part about it was when you could come in and make some good money, when you could make better money than the average place, and you could always get a job. You could always get a job in Muncie when you couldn't get a job any place else.[30]

During the late nineteenth and early twentieth centuries, Muncie's greatest draw was the many jobs its factories offered. James Davis, who arrived in the 1910s remembered that jobs here were much easier to come by in Muncie than in other places. They often paid better than elsewhere, too. But that didn't mean that the job market was completely open. Blacks couldn't get a job just anywhere in Muncie, nor could they get just any job. Black men, outside of the very few medical or business professionals, worked primarily as industrial laborers. Even then, not all factories, nor all positions within factories, were open to blacks. Black men worked primarily at the Whiteley (later Muncie) Malleable plant, also known as the foundry; at Broderick's boiler factory; at the Wire Mill (formerly Kitselman Brothers, currently Indiana Steel and Wire); and at Ball Brothers and Hemingray's glass companies. Some of the city's other factories, like Chevrolet (aka Warner Gear), did hire African Americans—but not often, and then only for janitorial or similarly low-wage, low-skill, and low-status jobs. Henry Sims, who spent his working life in the Ball glass factories of Muncie and of Owens, Illinois, remembered that the glass factory's best paying jobs were open only to whites.[31]

Between 1910 and 1920 Muncie's black population doubled, rising from 1,005 to 2,054. The city's black population reached 5.6 percent of the total, reflected in the now large number of black institutions. New churches sprang up. Schools opened in the city's growing primarily black neighborhoods, and black-owned businesses thrived. By the 1910s, Muncie's African Americans owned barber shops (as always), shoe shops, ice cream parlors, restaurants, saloons, grocery stores, tailor shops, a pool hall and concession stand, a hotel, and a skating rink. Dozens of clubs took root in the century's early decades. In 1919, a black YWCA named after national figure Phyllis Wheatley was organized. A black YMCA opened just a few years later.

At the end of the decade, U.S. forces joined those already fighting the first World War. Over 150 of Delaware County's young black men served during World War I and three of them, Guy Shelton, Leonard Nichols, and Alonzo Terry, made the ultimate sacrifice. African American soldiers of the day saw their participation in the war as a way to demonstrate their patriotism, believing that a valorous display of service might finally earn them full and unrestricted citizenship at home. Many embraced the rhetoric of the day that "an Allied victory would mean an end to oppression of all kinds—at home, as well as abroad."[32] But their hopes were not borne out. Indeed, World War I's black soldiers returned to substandard housing and schools, to lack of access to capital, higher education, and political representation—in short, to separate and unequal lives. In the 1920s, the United States was not yet safe for democracy.

More than 150 of Delaware County's young black men served during World War I. Courtesy Archives and Special Collections, Ball State University.

Muncie's Color Line

"As I say," said James Lyons, reflecting on his arrival in Muncie, "this was a kind of a, it's a northwestern town, but it's somewhat similar to Mississippi and Alabama when I first come here."[33] Lyons's observation and experience mirrored the observations and experiences of many of Muncie's early black residents. Most of Muncie's increasing population, both black and white, had come from the states of the former south. Most southern blacks, like James Lyons, had come to Muncie hoping that northern life would be different. But southern whites brought the Jim Crow south with them, and blacks were dismayed to find in Muncie many of the same kinds of segregationist practices that they had lived under in the deep south. Segregation, always practiced to some extent in the factories, neighborhoods, and social institutions of Muncie, became entrenched during the century's first decades, so much so that even the Lynds noticed, as this passage from *Middletown* points out:

> At a meeting of school principals held at the YMCA to arrange for interschool basketball games, one of the YMCA secretaries said that any school having a Negro in its team could not play in the YMCA building, but would have to play in the high school. In answer to mild protest he said simply, "Well, you know, it's the sentiment here." And so it stood.[34]

Segregation also surprised James Davis, who had lived in Indianapolis before he came to Muncie:

> If you wanted to go to the show you would have to go upstairs and things like that. And if you go to a restaurant, they would hand it to you out the door. During 1924. And I wasn't used to that in Indianapolis. At that time, Indianapolis was better than Muncie.[35]

When Campbell Auditorium opened in Whitely in 1914, both races could use it—but not on the same nights.[36] And the city's parks were segregated as well. Heekin Park, just south of the city's Industry neighborhood, was commonly understood to be off-limits to blacks. Blacks used McCulloch Park, just west of Whitely, instead. But blacks could not use all of McCulloch. One woman interviewed in the 1980s remembered well the dividing line that separated white from black in McCulloch Park. She shared this memory on the condition of anonymity:

> But out here we better not go on the other side, and I know a lot of them [African Americans] ventured over there, like I said, I never did go where I wasn't wanted and I didn't go, but a lot of them went over there and they was run out. And of course a lot of them didn't know they just went on over there and the police made them get out.[37]

Madge Davis remembered McCulloch Park's dividing line, as well. Her memory points out the transparency and fallacy of the "separate but equal" ideological foundation upon which legally sanctioned segregation once rested.

The street down the middle of the park separated us—the colored on this side and the whites were on the back side. They had all the pretty swings and everything. We had a swing and a piece of a tennis court and some sleds and stuff. But anything extra was on their side. Definitely, it was divided.[38]

When the Lynds came to Muncie in 1924, they came to a racially divided city. And they arrived just as the Ku Klux Klan's power peaked in Muncie. In August of 1922, the Klan paraded downtown, with the knowledge and (some said) protection of the chief of police. The Klan marched again in 1924, the same year that the Lynds arrived, this time from the Fairgrounds to downtown, with Mayor John Hampton Sr. and the chief of police leading the parade.[39] Though it is common to attribute Franklin Delano Roosevelt with making African Americans Democrats, in Muncie at least part of the credit goes to the Klan, whose tight hold on the Republican Party during the 1920s gave African American Republicans cause to ponder their party affiliation. In an earlier work on the history of Muncie's African American community, Hurley Goodall and J. Paul Mitchell underscore the difficult nature of African American life in Muncie during the 1920s:

Even today the 1920s remain a bad memory for Negroes who lived in Muncie then. It was a time when racial matters took a backward step, when color became a greater dividing line, when the degree of segregation greatly increased, and when Negroes felt the real fear of physical assault by the Ku Klux Klan.[40]

Despite the difficulties faced in the 1920s, or perhaps because of them, Muncie's African American community strengthened. When the city's first black student, Jessie May Nixon, graduated from Ball State Teachers College in 1925, African Americans took notice. Blacks started up a series of community sports teams in order to counter the lack of blacks on school sports teams and in the city's informal leagues. Churches, choirs, and missionary groups thrived. Muncie had its own black newspaper, *The Shining Star*, during the 1920s and had access to the nation's major black papers as well. Four black medical professionals, three doctors and a dentist, practiced in Muncie during the 1920s. A black orchestra offered itself for hire. Factory and community bands were everywhere and the social scene blossomed. Unwelcome at most of the city's white social events, blacks formed clubs, like the men's

Epicureans (later Bachelor Benedicts) and the women's Ingenues (later Entre Nous). These clubs organized regular charitable and social events and held highly anticipated annual formal dances. No matter what the city's segregationists, Republicans, or Klan desired, Muncie continued to draw African Americans. The city's black community was there to stay.

The 1930s were hard on all of the city's middle- and working-class people, and especially hard on the city's African Americans. During the Great Depression, some of the city's heavy industries managed to keep going. Others, like Ball Brothers Glass Company, whose profits from home canning supplies rose significantly during the Depression, actually thrived. Despite these few bright spots, the city's economy foundered. One quarter of the city's factory workers lost their jobs. And Muncie's African Americans, the city's "most marginal population," according to Robert Lynd in his follow-up study, *Middletown in Transition*, bore the brunt of the layoffs. Blacks had once been virtually assured of the city's "meaner jobs," but the desperation of the Depression meant that whites competed for even the lowest jobs. As the Depression deepened, some work came from New Deal projects, like the city's water treatment plant, or the levees that lined the city through town, or the extensive sewer system laid down in Whitely (which resulted in some of the best-drained land in an occasionally swampy city). But blacks and whites competed for these jobs as well, and there was never enough work to go around. As the city's white business and middle classes began to feel the economic pinch, black domestic workers lost their jobs. And as black factory and domestic workers lost ground, so did the black businesses that served them. Though black migration to Muncie did not end in the 1930s, its pace slowed significantly.

With all of the economic uncertainty of the time, when Muncie's African Americans look back on the 1930s, they fix on something other than tough economic times—something more immediate, more powerful, more threatening. On August 7, 1930, a white mob lynched two young black men in Marion, Indiana, less than forty miles to the north. The young men had been taken from the Grant County Jail, beaten and dragged through the streets of Marion, then hanged from a maple tree on the courthouse square. Thousands witnessed the events. The boys were left hanging all night as Marion's whites rioted downtown and in the city's black neighborhoods.

The 1930 Marion lynching. Reverend Johnson brought the bodies of these two young men to Muncie in order to prepare them for burial. Courtesy Archives and Special Collections, Ball State University.

The next morning a determined black mortician, Muncie's Reverend J. E. Johnson drove to Marion. He intended to bring the bodies back to Muncie so that he could embalm and prepare the bodies, then return them to Marion for burial. As word of his plans swept through Muncie, a white mob began to form. The mob planned to take the bodies from Johnson's Whitely funeral home and drag them through the streets of Muncie. Muncie's Negro community, aided by principled white law enforcement officers, gathered up arms, rallied at nearby Shaffer Chapel Church, and held an all-night vigil at the church, vowing to protect Reverend Johnson and the two bodies. The white mob, no doubt surprised by the strength of black Muncie's reaction (and by the sheriff's support of black Muncie), never fully formed. Johnson finished his work and returned the bodies, under police escort, to Marion the next day.

The community, angered by the Marion lynchings, took pride in the way they had responded. But they also took heed. In 1931, less than a year after the Marion lynchings, a black man was arrested for the robbery and murder of a white woman. A wave of fear swept through Muncie's black neighborhoods and the prisoner was quickly taken to jail in another town.[41]

As they so often do, racial and economic tensions rose together in the 1930s. When Robert Lynd returned to Muncie in 1935, he took note of the city's deepening racial divide, and especially of how difficult economic times were pressuring the black community. Job cuts fell disproportionately on African Americans. Black businesses suffered. And, as the lack of prosecutions in the Marion lynchings so powerfully demonstrated, the marginal status of African Americans continued. Lynd took note of another interesting trend in 1930s Muncie. Black men had begun to experience a disproportionate number of the town's arrests, a trend that escalated throughout the twentieth century.[42]

Despite, or perhaps in response to, these times, Dr. A. Wayne Brooks, the city's only black dentist, ran as a candidate for city council in the 1934 Republican primary. Brooks's run is interesting for many reasons. It points to political complexity in the black community, often seen as united and monolithic. Though many blacks became Democrats during the 1920s and 1930s, others, especially those most prominent and prosperous, remained Republicans. Brooks's run also points to growing confidence in the black community, at the very time when economic and social conditions conspired to push blacks back. Despite the city's ingrained belief in the inferiority of African Americans, Brooks and his supporters were determined to prove otherwise.[43] African Americans began to organize themselves at work. Locked out of the skilled trades of the American Federation of Labor (AFL), African Americans across the country were instrumental in the founding of the Congress of Industrial Organizations (CIO). The leadership training that unions provided for their members and officers would one day be a critical part of Muncie's African American leadership.

Whatever their political differences, in the face of white attitudes that most often ran from indifferent to hostile, Muncie's African Americans took care of their own, as Robert Smiley remembered. Smiley, a member and deacon of Antioch Baptist Church, was one of many who remember either giving to or benefiting from the many charities based in black clubs and churches.

> Out at the church we have what you call a benevolence, and we give money out of that and see what they need and take them to the doctor and different places. . . . We give to people that goes in the hospital or get sick, help them. Raise a collection for those that are in desperate need.[44]

Church and social clubs ran the gamut from Missionary and Choral societies to the Odd Fellows and The Blue Ribbon Club. Much of the town's life occurred in these clubs, from social events to worthwhile causes. African Americans went almost exclusively to black churches throughout their lives, and to black funeral homes at the end of their lives.

World War II marked the start of Muncie's last industrial boom as the city's manufacturers turned to wartime production, the young white men who would otherwise have taken the city's best paying industrial jobs shipped off to Europe and Asia. For African Americans in Muncie, the industrial boom of the 1940s went much further than had the city's previous booms. The acute labor shortage created by millions of men overseas meant that many jobs formerly closed to black men, and to both black and white women, suddenly opened up.[45] Significant numbers of black workers were hired at some of the city's strongest and most stable companies and, importantly, they were not always hired only as janitors. But even in that tight labor market, some industries managed to guard their old racist practices:

> Wire and steel mills, foundries, and glass works employed more Negro workers than ever before, and in some cases even opened their doors to Negro women for the first time. At the same time, progress was very slow in the automotive plants, the major one of which still refused to hire Negro production workers.[46]

This expansion in black hiring sowed the seeds for a future expansion in black leadership as black men became presidents of union locals: James Tinsley, of Ball Brother's Local 93; Frank Nelson and Hurley Goodall of Muncie Malleable's UAW Local 532; Raymond Pittman, Willard Washington, Ezra Cherry, and Ralph Kersey of Indiana Foundry's Local 609; and a host of other African Americans began rising through unions. Finally, the surge in jobs brought another surge in black population. Between 1940 and 1950, Muncie's black population went from 2,985 to 4,400, an increase of 47 percent. By contrast, the city's white population increased by only 8 percent during the same time period.

As African Americans migrated to Muncie, they filled up the traditionally black neighborhoods of Whitely and Industry. Industry, bounded on all sides by white neighborhoods, became an especially powerful site of contention as black families spilled into traditionally white areas. Apparently alarmed by this development, the city-county planning commission, in their 1944 postwar plan for Muncie, included a proposal to address "Colored Housing and Allied Problems." The plan, in addition to promising sewer and street improvements in existing black areas, also proposed something interesting: a long-range voluntary plan that would essentially shift all of the city's black families into Whitely and nearby Austin Heights, and black businesses onto Highland Avenue. The white presenters of the plan were somehow surprised that many African Americans of the day reacted to the plan with shock and disgust. Vocal African Americans scoffed at the idea that the city would actually follow through on promised services and infrastructures in an isolated, all-black neighborhood, and decried the postwar plan as, essentially, an attempt to segregate the city's blacks and institute a planned ghetto. The fury and strength of black reaction led planners to quickly shelve the proposal.

The Fight for Civil Rights

World War II also marked, for the second time in as many generations, the fight by young African American men for freedom and democracy abroad when they had neither at home. At midcentury, Muncie's African Americans looked back on qualified progress and looked ahead to an uncertain future. They were unwilling to surrender the tenuous economic progress made during World War II and just as unwilling to continue living Jim Crow lives. They could not, therefore, heed the counsel of this 1958 editorial writer:

> The eventual answer is that one day Americans of Negro descent will be accepted as private persons not because of their race, nor in spite of it, but rather with no concern for it. Until that happens, no one has any valid solution. Until then, the chief requirements seem to be patience, forbearance, and tolerance, on both sides of the American race question. At least these have borne some fruit thus far.[47]

By the 1950s, Muncie's African Americans had run low on patience, forbearance, and tolerance. They began to question what fruit acquiescence had brought them in the past. And some began pushing the color line. Ray Armstrong's 1952 election to the Muncie City Council from District 6 marked the first time an African American had ever been elected to major public office in Muncie. In 1952, Geraldine Findley became the first African American to teach in the city's schools. In 1956, Robert Foster became principal of West Longfellow School. And in 1958, after years of broken promises to the black community, the city's fire department made its first black hires of the twentieth century, John Blair and Hurley Goodall.

Ray Armstrong was the first African American elected to public office in Muncie. Courtesy Archives and Special Collections, Ball State University.

The most important symbolic change of the 1950s, the desegregation of Tuhey Pool, is one of the stories most often told in the community. Built during the Depression, Tuhey Pool stands as a classic example of Muncie's de facto segregation practice. There was no law or code that prevented blacks from using the pool, but it was understood by all that the pool was off limits to blacks. When the city's integrated pool at Jackson Park was closed down after World War II, young blacks swam in the White River and in many of the deep abandoned quarries next to it. After a series of drowning deaths, the city's black population demanded that the city provide a safe, supervised place for their children to swim. The city did as asked, and a truce seemed to hold for two years.

But Tuhey Pool, still segregated, glistened on the other side of town. The idea of a pool devoted entirely to whites (and supported by all of the city's taxpayers) could not stand. After several unsuccessful behind-the-scenes attempts to desegregate the pool, Levan Scott and Roy Buley took three young black boys to the pool. The boys swam in the pool for about an hour, when about twenty more black children showed up. When a crowd of white youths began to harass the boys, city officials closed the pool. All of the city's pools remained closed while leaders negotiated a solution. On June 12, 1956, a city official made the following statement:

> There has been a misunderstanding on the part of some people that [Tuhey] Pool is for whites only. That is not true. Both pools are paid for with public tax funds and the only way they can be operated under federal rulings is for the pools to be open to everyone in the community.[48]

On June 19, all of the city's pools reopened to all citizens, regardless of color.

As in communities across the country, Muncie's African Americans were heartened by each new victory over Jim Crow and institutionalized racism, whether de facto or de jure. But with all the progress made in the 1950s, Ruth Campbell could still tell this story, about her own experience of being African American and looking for work in 1950s Muncie.

> I had a time. I went downtown because I called, I saw an office job open, and I called. And the girl said, yeah, you come in. And when I got there, she says, "May I help you?" And I said, "Yes." . . . "My name is Ruth Campbell," and I said, "I have an interview at 1:00." She says, "You have an interview?" And I said, "Yes." And she says, "Just a minute." Well, she went in the back, and she came back, and she said, "Well, I'm sorry, but that job's been filled." I said, "You know, if that job's been filled, why did you have me come in for an interview? You just told me over the phone." "Well, I'm sorry that job's been filled, but if you'd like to come in, maybe something else would come up later."[49]

Needless to say, Ruth was never called about another office job, despite her education and advanced secretarial training. Instead, she went to work in the Ball Brothers glass factory's white liner department, alongside many other well-educated and trained African American women.

Employment opportunities and practices became one of the rallying points for Muncie's budding civil rights movement. Many still remember the leaders who emerged during the civil rights era, especially those like Reverend Anthony Jones Oliver, who led the fight for equal access to jobs and opportunity.

> He took men and took them to the jobs and asked the guys if they would hire them. And they said "no," and he wanted to know why. He'd call Washington, D.C., and found out about the contracts they had, government contracts, and threatened them, which [the government] could take away from them. . . . I was with him because he was a leader. That's what I call a leader.[50]

In 1959, Reverend Oliver was appointed Pastor of Shaffer Chapel Church. A year later he organized the People's Economic Progress Group in an effort to expand job opportunities for Muncie's black workers. Reverend Oliver's tactics were controversial, but very effective—he was able to open up jobs and job sites for African Americans that had never been open before.[51] When George Wallace, an avowed segregationist, campaigned at Ball State University in 1964, Reverend Oliver led the protests against him. In that same year, the city formed the Muncie Human Rights Commission, whose primary goal (at the time) was to find peaceful solutions to interracial conflicts. Reverend Oliver's bold and confident tactics, similar to those then practiced by African American leaders across the country, seemed to demonstrate that activism was a better strategy than forbearance—contrary to the city paper's suggestion only a few years before.

As the city's black communities continued to grow at a faster pace than its white communities, a new YMCA opened on South Madison Street, in the midst of growing Industry. A flurry of school construction followed the city's population growth. In 1963, East Longfellow School opened on Whitely's Centennial Avenue. In 1962, Southside High School opened, splitting the community's two black neighborhoods. Black students from Whitely still attended Muncie's Central High School, but students from Industry went to the new school. Symbolizing the contention that would come to define the 1960s, Southside's sport teams were nicknamed the "Rebels." The Confederate flag became the school's symbol.

As in nearly every other American town and city, the 1960s were marked by both progress and conflict. In June 1967, the "Corner" at Willard and Hackley Streets became the focal point of racial tension, as police in full riot gear faced off against teenagers and young adults armed with, essentially, sticks and stones. In October, the simmering disquiet that surrounded the choice of highly charged Confederate emblems as Southside High School's symbols finally erupted into riots. The fights subsided quickly, but nothing was done to address the school's problematic symbols or its institutionalized racism. Three months later, the rioting began anew. This time, several students were seriously injured, and some of the city's prominent black ministers convinced black students and their parents to boycott the city schools. The boycott was firmly supported by African Americans across the city, many of whom kept their children out of all city schools for three days. Black students only came back when school officials agreed to seriously hear and address their grievances.

Another school controversy erupted in 1967. The Muncie Board of Education planned a third high school on the city's northwest side, a plan opposed by a group of Whitely parents for a number of reasons. The Whitely parents pointed out that the new school would draw its students from the city's growing northwest side, whose residents were primarily white members of the middle, professional, and upper-middle classes. This new school would abandon the children of Whitely and the central city's less well-off white children to Central High School, a facility already in a significant state of disrepair. The Whitely parents firmly believed that the city's population projections were overly optimistic and did not warrant three high schools. They proposed instead that the city build one large school on the site of the old Minnetrista Golf Course, a school that would serve the students of Whitely, poorer inner city neighborhoods, and the wealthier northwest suburbs.

The Whitely parents tried to negotiate with the school board for two years, to no avail. In 1969, the parents filed a lawsuit in federal court. The Board of Education began construction on Northwest High School anyway, even as the case was being litigated. Eventually, the Whitely parents lost their case and Northwest High School opened in 1972. Just a few years later a new Central High School was built on the site originally suggested by the Whitely parents. The Whitely parents were vindicated in the end, however. Very soon it became apparent that the city's population projections had, in fact, been overly optimistic. In 1984, Northwest High School was turned into a middle school. No third high school had been warranted after all.

Angered by continued racism and emboldened by new action, in the sixties, Muncie's African Americans made a concerted push to take political matters into their own hands. In 1967, Dan Kelly Jr. was elected to Muncie City Council from District 6. In 1970, Hurley Goodall, one of the above-mentioned Whitely parents, became the first

African American elected to the Muncie Board of Education. In May of 1971, Reverend J. C. Williams ran for mayor in the primary election. The candidate for the Poor People's Party, Williams was the city's first African American to mount a serious bid for this office. And in November of that same year, James Albert Johnson became the first African American ever elected to an at-large seat on the Muncie City Council.

Muncie's black population continued to grow during the 1970s, and African Americans continued to create new institutions.[52] The Roy C. Buley Center, named after the man who had pushed desegregation at Tuhey Pool, opened in 1974. African Americans continued to gather and consolidate power throughout the decade as well. Hurley Goodall's election to the Indiana State Legislature in 1978, the first African American ever elected to that position in Delaware County, signified an arrival of sorts for Muncie's African American community. It would have been impossible just a decade before.

The city's black population continued to grow and to achieve firsts in the last decades of the twentieth century.[53] In 1989, Dr. Sam Abram became the city's first African American superintendent of schools. In 1992, Walter Berry became the first African American ever to serve as deputy mayor of Muncie. In 1995, Ralph McGairk became the city's first African American chief of police. And in 1996, Dr. Charles Sanders was elected president of the Muncie/Delaware County Chamber of Commerce, the city's first African American to hold that position.

In a cemetery about fifteen miles east of Muncie, there is a tombstone that marks the final resting place of Nancy Perry, a woman of color who was among the very first wave of black settlers to arrive in east central Indiana. Nancy died in 1862. Her tombstone is unusual for many reasons, not least of which is the proud, forceful sentiment that she ordered carved on its now fading face:

> I was a slave freed by a lawsuit prosecuted by David White, the Quaker; may God bless his name. My husband's freedom was bought for $675. He made the money on rented land. Who of you that say tauntingly of my race, "They can't take care of themselves," have done better?[54]

Nancy Perry's epitaph is fitting testimony to her own life and the life of her husband, Willis. But it is also an eloquent tribute to the tens of thousands of African Americans who came after her. Throughout history and throughout their lives, Muncie's African Americans have struggled against the economic and social oppression that comes with color. Theirs is, partly, a story about racial struggle and uplift. But it is more a story about daily life, about trying to make a good living and a good home, about raising and educating children in the best way possible, and about finding the faith and community to carry on.

Notes

1. Letter from Hannah Elliott to Mary Parker, September 21, 1829 (FMS 24 f14, JPP, Friends Collection, Earlham College, Richmond, Indiana).

2. For an in-depth analysis of the socioeconomic factors that motivated black pioneers see Stephen A. Vincent, *Southern Seed, Northern Soil: African-American Farm Communities in the Midwest, 1765–1900* (Bloomington: Indiana University Press, 2002). According to Vincent, southern free people of color ". . . migrated [to the new Northwest states] during the 1820s and 1830s in a clear and deliberate attempt to improve their socioeconomic standing" (6). For an analysis that also looks at why African Americans might have chosen the virgin northwest over the established states of the northeast, see Clayton E. Cramer, *Black Demographic Data, 1790–1860: A Sourcebook* (Westport, Conn.: Greenwood Publishing Group, 1997). Exploring their decision to move on to the frontier, Cramer suggests that "[f]ree blacks may have found fewer social barriers to advancement on the frontier than in the more settled East" (37).

3. Prior to the Civil War, people of color, primarily from the southern United States, flocked to the newly formed free states carved from the old Northwest Territories. The number of black settlers in Indiana grew from 1,420 in 1820 to 11,428 by 1860 (Emma Lou Thornbrough, *The Negro in Indiana before 1900: A Study of a Minority* [Bloomington: Indiana University Press, 1993], 31). Although life was better for free blacks in Indiana than it had been in the south, it was by no means trouble-free. Many whites, Quaker and otherwise, strenuously objected to, and often attempted to impede through social and legislative means, the flow of black settlers into the state. Regardless of those obstacles, people of color continued to come to Indiana. Many of those who came to Indiana during this time settled not in the state's cities, but in one of at least twenty-six rural African American settlements that flourished during the middle of the nineteenth century.

4. W. E. B. DuBois, "Long in Darke," *Colored American Magazine*, 17 (November 1909): 353–55.

5. Indiana Constitution, 1851. The amount of bond specified in the 1831 Constitution, $500, is the equivalent of $10,416.67 in 2002 dollars, according to the inflation calculator provided by the Columbia Journalism Review. Counties across the state could certainly use this article to sort black immigrants by class.

6. Thornbrough, *The Negro in Indiana*, 31. Enforcement of the registers varied significantly from county to county. In Orange County, the vast majority of African Americans complied with the act and registered. But in Randolph, home at that time to two (later three) strong, growing, and prosperous black settlements, and a large Quaker population, only 8 of nearly 400 of the county's African Americans complied. According to Thomas Addington, longtime Quaker resident of the county, the Negro Registers were "a plumb failure" ("The Underground Railroad in Randolph County and Vicinity: An Interesting Account of the Antebellum Days," *Winchester Journal Herald* [February 11–August 12, 1903]). With regard to the prohibition on migration established by the 1831 law, the same kind of selective enforcement was practiced.

7. Larry Scott, interview with Elizabeth Campbell, Rachel Mancini, and Deborah Rotman, Winchester, Indiana, October 23, 1997 (on file at Ball State University Archaeological Resources Management Service). James Stafford and Barbara Stafford, interview with Elizabeth Campbell, New Paris, Ohio, July 18, 1997 (on file at Ball State University Archaeological Resources Management Service).

8. For a more in-depth analysis of this trend, see Deborah L. Rotman, Rachel Mancini, Aaron Smith, and Elizabeth Campbell, "African-American and Quaker Farmers in East Central Indiana: Social, Political, and Economic Aspects of Life in Nineteenth-Century Rural Communities, Randolph County" (Report of Investigation 51, Archaeological Resources Management Service, Ball State University, Muncie, Indiana).

9. Hurley Goodall and J. Paul Mitchell, *African Americans in Muncie, 1890–1960* (Muncie, Ind.: Ball State University, 1976), 1 (quoting from an unspecified source).

10. Bruce A. Aldridge, "The Underground Railroad Passed This Way," *Indianapolis Magazine*, 5, no. 9 (1972): 47a; Leon Litweck, *North of Slavery: The Negro in the Free States, 1790–1860* (Coatesville, Ind.: Hathoway Printing, 1961), 70.

11. Randolph County was one of four Indiana counties that refused to ratify Article 13 of the 1851 Constitution, which points toward a different relationship between the county's blacks and whites.

12. Samuel Smothers, Repository of the Union Literary Institute, Indiana Historical Society.

13. The following discussion relies heavily on Goodall and Mitchell, *African Americans in Muncie*.

14. County legal and relief records place at least a half dozen African Americans in the city, some children, most paupers, beginning in 1839. Goodall and Mitchell, *African Americans in Muncie*, 1.

15. Will of Solomon Bundy, December 4, 1858 (Newcastle, Henry County, Indiana, Will Book A-B, 215). Solomon Bundy's will reveals a fairly substantial estate.

16. Edward was probably a member of the Scott clan who came from Virginia in the 1820s and settled first in Cabin Creek. These Scotts later moved to Henry County, but returned to Randolph in about 1880. Larry Scott interview.

17. For an in-depth discussion of the economic advantages that early black settlers were able to gain in Indiana (though not necessarily able to maintain), see Stephen A. Vincent, *Southern Seed, Northern Soil*.

18. Silas Shoecraft also barbered in Muncie during the 1850s, though he left before 1860. When he returned in the 1870s he established a profitable barbering business of his own (Goodall and Mitchell, *African Americans in Muncie*, 2–3). Barbering was an important African American profession in nineteenth-century America and remained so for much of the twentieth century. Though barbers by the 1850s were no longer the all purpose surgeons they had once been even today they remain important members of the community, and their shops are important community centers.

19. In 1860, Edward and Maria lived on East Jackson Street with their five children. Henry Artis(t), also a barber, was counted among their household. Next door to the Scott household lived Madison Bundy, Mary's brother, along with his wife, Elizabeth, and their young son. Another Mulatto family, listed in the census as "Chasuss" (which could have been a variation on Chavois or Chavers, a common name at the time) lived next door.

20. Blocker, "Black Migration to Muncie," 303.

21. Goodall and Mitchell, *African Americans in Muncie*, 4.

22. For a more in-depth analysis of this trend, see Rotman et al., "African-American and Quaker Farmers."

23. Goodall and Mitchell, *African Americans in Muncie*, 5.

24. Ibid., 5.

25. Blocker, "Black Migration to Muncie," 302.

26. Black Middletown Project interview, #L140, John Lucas, 3.

27. Blocker, "Black Migration to Muncie," 304.

28. Leila B. Davis, Black Middletown Project interview, #D143.

29. Mrs. Graham, Black Middletown Project interview, #G159, 6.

30. James Davis, Black Middletown Project interview, #D52, 12.

31. Henry Sims, Black Middletown Project interview, #S62, 3.

32. Goodall and Mitchell, *African Americans in Muncie*, 13.

33. Mr. James Lyons, Black Middletown Project interview, #L112, July 22, 1980.

34. Robert S. Lynd and Helen Merrell Lynd, *Middletown: A Study in Modern American Culture*. (New York: Harcourt Brace & Company, 1929), 480.

35. James Davis interview, 11.

36. Campbell's burned in 1924, but not before it had hosted gatherings of the Ku Klux Klan, an organization that would become a controlling force in Muncie in the 1920s.

37. Anonymous, Black Middletown Project interview, #C146.

38. Madge Margaret Davis, Black Middletown Project interview, #D165, Session 1.

39. Goodall and Mitchell, *African Americans in Muncie*, 17.

40. Ibid., *African Americans in Muncie*, 16.

41. Robert S. Lynd and Helen Merrell Lynd, *Middletown in Transition: A Study of Cultural Conflicts* (New York: Harcourt Brace & Company, 1937), 464.

42. Ibid., 348. Blacks are 5.7 percent of Muncie's population in 1930, but the percentage of black men as total arrests rises from 12.9 percent in 1931 to 15.7 percent in early 1935.

43. Among the core values of Middletown residents (that people should be honest, kind, have community spirit, etc.), the Lynds found that Muncie's residents also deeply believed "that Negroes are inferior." See Lynd and Lynd, *Middletown in Transition*, 402–8.

44. Robert Smiley, Black Middletown Project interview, #S35, Session 2, 14, and 18.

45. Jobs for white women opened up as well. World War II is often seen as the first wave of professional liberation.

46. Goodall and Mitchell, *African Americans in Muncie*, 31.

47. Ibid., quoting newspaper, 43.

48. Ibid., *African Americans in Muncie*, 40.

49. Ruth Campbell, interview by Elizabeth Campbell and Hurley Goodall, February 1, 1999 (Ball Production Employees Oral History Project, Minnetrista Cultural Center, Muncie, Indiana).

50. Robert Smiley interview, 14.

51. See chapter 7, this volume, "Engaging in Religious Practices."

52. In 1970, the city's black population reached 9.6 percent of the city's total.

53. In 1980, the city's black population fell slightly, to 9.5 percent of the city's total, remained near that mark in 1990, then jumped to 11 percent in 2000.

54. Inscription on the tombstone of Nancy Willis, who died in 1862 and is buried in the Old Dunkirk Cemetery, Randolph County, Indiana.

PART II

COLLABORATIVE UNDERSTANDINGS

3

Getting a Living

Michelle Anderson, Anne Kraemer,
and Ashley Moore

It was cold out that day, too cold. It felt like winter had already lasted a year.

As we pulled up in the driveway, the house looked vacant. No lights were on to show that anyone was home. We walked up to the door and rang the bell. We didn't hear the bell echo through the house, so we rang it again. But as soon as the bell rang a second time, a smiling Pastor Renzie Abram opened the door. A wave of heat hit us as we stepped in. It was a nice change from the snow and cold outside.

We followed Renzie into the living room. The colorful couch and the three rocking recliners were adorned with doilies. Several live green plants, family photos, and small religious figurines gave life to the room. As we got comfortable in our seats, our conversation began.

"Now, how can I help you this evening?" started Renzie.

"We're interested in your story, and how you have made a living."

"I have done a whole lot in my life, worked in the factories in Muncie and Dayton, Ohio, received a Ph.D. in ministry and raised eight children," Renzie said.

"It must have been difficult to work, have children, and be going to school."

"Well, I *had* to work, and make a living."[1]

Finding Work in Middletown

In their original 1929 study, *Middletown*, Robert S. Lynd and Helen Merrell Lynd identified two main classes of people in Muncie: the "business class" and the "working class." They wrote:

> Members of the first group, by and large, address their activities in getting their living primarily to *things*, utilizing material tools in the making of things and the performance of services, while the members of the second group address their activities predominantly to *people* in the selling or promotion of things, services, and ideas.[2]

The working class, they determined, included "those who worked with their hands," "those who make things," and "those who use material things"; while the business class included "those who work with their tongues," "those who sell or promote things and ideas," and "those who use various nonmaterial institutional devices."[3]

In the decades before and after the world wars, similar patterns could be found in Middletown's African American community. Like their white counterparts, Muncie's black population was also made up of "those who worked with their hands" and "those who sell or promote things and ideas." But the divisions between the business and working classes—which the Lynds make much of in *Middletown*—were never as pronounced in the black community. And it exists that way to this day: many of our consultants have had their feet in both worlds throughout their lives. Renzie Abram, for example, could be counted among "those who work with their tongues" in his current role as a minister, but he was also among "those who make things" for much of his life.

Renzie Abram was born to sharecroppers in 1942 in Money, Mississippi. His family first migrated to Muncie when he was four years old. During and after high school in the late 1950s and early 1960s, he cut grass, shined shoes, and worked in the kitchen at Ball Memorial Hospital. "Then I heard that they were hiring at a factory, at Warner Gear. And so I left [the hospital] and I began to work at Warner Gear. I was making $3.50 an hour. Now that was good money back then, back in '62. But the unfortunate thing was that they had a lot of layoffs. . . . I worked there for a year and four months. And I got laid off three times. I just didn't see any security. So I left and I went to [the supermarket] Marsh in Yorktown. There's a warehouse there and we made up the cottage cheese in produce. I didn't work there too long, but one of the managers talked to me about . . . becoming a manager and going to school. But I didn't pursue it."

"I left Marsh," continues Renzie, "then I went to Westinghouse. I worked there for about eight months. And then I went to Delco Remy in Anderson, Indiana—that was General Motors—and I found myself a home. I worked there for thirty-three years. I had a chance to retire, but I wasn't ready. So I transferred to Delphi Chassis in Dayton, Ohio. And I worked there for four years. That gave me a total of thirty-seven years and I retired in January of 2002."[4]

During all of this, and in addition to raising a family, Renzie was also going to school. In 1968, he enrolled in Crossroads Bible College. By 1972, he had received a bachelor's degree in theology and by 1975 had received his Ph.D. in religion. A few years later in 1984, he completed his doctorate in ministry. "So at the present time," he says, "I'm retired. But I also minister at a church currently. In other words, I had two jobs: I was a part-time pastor as well as working in a factory."[5]

Like Renzie, Hurley Goodall also got his start in the factories in and around Muncie. "I was going down the railroad track one day," he once told us, "and I said, 'I'm going down there [to the Muncie Malleable Factory] and see if I can get a job! If you could walk, talk, and chew gum at the same time, they [the factory managers] gave you a job!" And they did. He was sixteen years old.[6]

Jobs were easy to find during and after World War II, especially when factory jobs began to open up in Muncie to African Americans. Before the war, very few African Americans worked on the high paying production lines. They were instead relegated to the hot, dirty work of the foundries and steel mills, or to janitorial work in some of the city's other factories. When Hurley first began working at the Muncie Malleable factory, he was hired to pour iron. His uncle helped Hurley gain a position with him in the core room. The core room was better than other jobs in the factory; it was not as hard, hot, or dangerous as pouring iron.[7]

Aside from this, Hurley's factory experience was like many others in Muncie. During his junior and senior years of high school he worked at Malleable from 2 A.M. until 10 A.M. and then attended school from 10:30 A.M. until 3:30 P.M. The need for workers created many jobs for members of the community. But even with the availability of jobs, many times it took perseverance and connections in order to maintain a *good* job. Hurley's mother, for example, was employed at the Ball Brothers Factory. Although she had a college degree, she was unable to get a white collar or administrative job, so she had to get a position in the factory.[8]

Around the same time that better factory jobs were opening up for black men, black women began to find more plentiful opportunities in the local factories as well. Limited to the white liner department at Ball Brothers Glass Company before World War II, women of all races found new opportunities in the city's factories during and after the

Women glass workers pose for a photo holding the glass insulators that they helped to make, circa 1915. Courtesy Archives and Special Collections, Ball State University.

war. (White liners were the milky white circular lids that once fit under glass jar caps.)

Working in the Factory

Mamie Barker is a cutter–grinder for a company now called Muncie Limited, which also has been called New Venture Gear, Detroit Diesel Allison, Chevrolet Muncie, Hydromatic, "and there may have been another name or two," she says. "The company is always changing its name. For example GM buys in and sells out, then we're part of Chrysler or different groups, so the names change several times. We manufacture transmissions—manual transmissions for small trucks."

Mamie, who was a single parent on welfare, recalls that "they [the welfare office] made you look for a job and they gave me an application. I had no clue there was an auto factory in this town; I was twenty-seven and I didn't know. I didn't even know where it was. Once I got there, it was real scary. Real scary. They have racks of gears and stuff floating across your head going from one point to another and then there are big tow motors that are riding up and whizzing up and down the aisles. I mean it's all kinds of stuff that you would never imagine if you had never been in an automobile plant."[9]

After a few years in the plant, Mamie graduated from the Employee-in-Training program, which taught her new skills for her trade job. Many factories are doing away with Employee-in-Training programs now, leading Mamie to believe that the few jobs that remain will be unskilled. African Americans won't have the same kind of opportunities she had because, in order to be a skilled laborer, you must be an apprentice (eight years of on-the-job training) and some small shops will not give African Americans that chance. "I've known several black men that went to small job shops to work and they get harassed out. You can't work under those conditions, you know. Without the Employee-in-Training program, I know I would not have made it."[10]

When asked if she felt lucky to land a factory job, Mamie replied: "I wouldn't say I'm lucky, I'd say I'm very blessed to have worked there for thirty years so I could raise my child and put her through college. I have good benefits and make excellent pay."[11] Many hope for the same chance Mamie had. But as Muncie's industrial economy weakens, those hopes dim. The powerful allure that these jobs once had is weakening, and the unions—once leadership training grounds for African Americans—are in decline as well.

Unions

UAW Local 499's meeting had already begun. As we entered, Mamie's cheerful face welcomed us. She sat behind a table and motioned for us to sit next to her. Extra folding chairs lined the aisle between two sections of chairs. A man read the minutes from the last month's meeting as we took our seats. Of the fourteen people in attendance, five were black. The only two women were black. The group of African Americans sat in the back left corner, except for Mamie who sat at the back table with us. On the right side of the room, two white men sat apart from each other. The four officers—who were all white—sat behind a desk that held a small podium. To the left of the table stood an American flag. To the right stood the flag of the United Auto Workers Union—a field of dark blue in the middle of which was set a gold star, emblazoned with the letters "UAW."

The meeting started with concerned talk about job losses, the theme of the industrial economy for the last ten-plus years. Jobs are leaving, they [the union members] said, because people in other countries will work for so much less. And with lost jobs, of course, comes a decline in the union. Mamie explains that "Union membership has been declining probably for the last ten years with plant closings and companies moving their plants to Mexico where workers are paid like a fourth of the income that we make here."[12] Another member at the meeting put it more bluntly: "Work going out of the country," he said, "is bleeding us to death."

As the UAW meeting continued, we noticed that at this particular meeting, the black members were the most outspoken members in the group. When the shop committeeman in charge of negotiations with management delivered a report to the members, for example, an African American man in the back asked the chairperson how often his committee had met. The committeeman explained that it was just getting started. "Y'all should have started meeting last year!" the man retorted.

The chairperson shifted uncomfortably. "Well," he said, "you've got to be there to understand."

"Which I should be!"

Despite the active participation of many African Americans, however, many other black workers did not and still do not participate in the Union because of discrimination. Mamie Barker, who is a very active UAW member, encourages black members to think otherwise. If they have a problem, she says, they should look it up in their contract books and get help with it. Without question, Mamie is very enthusiastic about her union membership. She chairs the women's committee and is involved in both the recreation and civil rights committee. The civil rights and labor movements, she explains, became intricately linked in the 1960s. For example, Martin Luther King Jr. and Walter Reuther—a key organizer of the United Auto Workers and the Congress of Industrial Organizations (UAW-CIO)—marched together during the Civil Rights Movement. The civil rights leaders and the union both had, and still do, the same goal: "to see that we have equal pay, that we are treated equally and fairly. We want the best for our families."[13]

In Muncie, unions like the UAW played a particularly important role in the African American community. They were the primary training grounds for the city's black leaders—leaders like Hurley Goodall. "I don't really remember what motivated me," he explains, "but I started going to the union meetings and then they elected me as recording secretary right when I got out of the service—so I had to be twenty.

I thought I was hot stuff until one of them told me one time, 'We elected you, Goodall, because you were young, and we didn't like to write, so *you* can keep the minutes.'

"By the time I was twenty-four, I was president of UAW Local 532. I'd say that's when I learned what *responsibility* is all about. Because before that I was one of the young guys that would say, 'Shut the thing down!' whenever there was a problem at the plant. When you get to be president and have that responsibility, you would be like 'Now, *wait* a minute, let's think this thing over.' When you have that responsibility, your thought process has changed, and it makes a big difference how you think and how you react to situations. I learned that lesson the hard way."[14]

While the unions and factories have provided many opportunities for Muncie's African American community, these opportunities are disappearing in the face of cheaper labor elsewhere, leaving many people without jobs. The leaders of corporations are taking the factories to places such as Mexico, South America, and China in order to produce more for less. This has created a huge void in Muncie. Renzie put it to us rather bluntly: "It doesn't look good for anyone who wants to get factory work today. I encourage you to go to Ball State like you're doing and get into another field."[15]

Domestic Work

As we approached the door of the seniors' home in Marion, Indiana, Rosemary Lamb Edwards greeted us eagerly. The interior of the four-story apartment house was softly lit. It smelled clean and felt safe. As Rosemary led us to the cafeteria we passed a quiet living room with a fireplace. Sitting in the fading winter light of the cafeteria, Rosemary's reddish hair shone beautifully. She listened as we explained the purpose of the project and our chapter and why we wanted to include her story.

Rosemary did domestic work, she explained, one of the primary jobs available to black women. It was also one of the very few jobs that straddled the white and black sides of town. Though most black domestics did not live with their employers, Rosemary's family did. When she was a child, both of her parents worked for the Edward B. Ball family, and lived in the Ball's family mansion on Minnetrista Boulevard. There, her father, Fred Lamb, was considered the do-all man. He did everything that was needed around the house, from driver to gardener. Her blind mother, Mary Lamb, was the family's

cook. As a child, she ran and played with the Ball children and vacationed in Michigan with the family. "I was one of them," she says. They
also provided her with piano lessons, education, and supplies for
school. "I had every opportunity in the world I must say."[16]

The Lambs were not Rosemary's birth parents. Rosemary was born
in Evansville, Indiana, in 1929, to a black mother and white father. The
Lambs adopted her at the age of eight. Her life in the Ball home did not
prepare her for the "real world," she says. "It was all Greek to me when
I went out into the world—see, I was raised with the Balls and they
didn't make a difference with me."[17]

Another domestic worker for the Balls, Ruth Robinson, worked to
bring in extra money for her family of fifteen. She did not live with the
Ball family. Indeed, her job was a very small part of her life as wife and
mother—she was married in 1928 at sixteen, and raised fifteen children. Still, she had warm feelings for the Ball family like Rosemary. "I
just felt I was as good as anyone else," she says. "We are all God's crea-
tures."[18]

Ruth Rhinehart Redd did domestic work as well, though her memories are not as fond as Rosemary Lamb's or Ruth Robinson's. Now
seventy-eight, Ruth Redd was born and raised in Connersville, Indiana. In 1944, high school behind her, she decided to attend Muncie's
Ball State Teachers College. She worked her way through college in order to pay her tuition. During her first semester she and another girl

Ruth Redd. Photo by Danny Gawlowski.

worked as domestic workers for a family who lived near campus. Ruth was not allowed to take a bath in the tub in the house or eat at the family's table. The other girl, who was white, had both privileges. Even though this prejudice was blatant, Ruth didn't dispute it. "I didn't argue. I came up here to go to school."[19]

After receiving her teaching degree from Ball State in 1948, Ruth was unable to get a job in Muncie due to the fact that there were no African American teachers in the Muncie school systems. Forced to relocate, Ruth's first job as a teacher was in Kansas City, Kansas. After teaching there for two years, she gained experience and came back to Muncie and was hired as the third African American teacher at Longfellow Elementary School. Longfellow, with its concentration of African American students, employed every African American teacher in the school system at that time.

On Middletown's Black Businesses

John Vargas, "Mexican John" as he was known around town, was a Texan of Mexican parentage, who married, settled in Muncie, and then joined the service. At first, John occupied a transitional space in Muncie's black community. Though he was accepted for the most part, his daughter—Dolores Vargas Rhinehart—recalls that "he was like a man without a country . . . he would cry because there weren't any Mexicans around here who he could relate to, and the blacks, they weren't always crazy about him!"[20] He also felt shunned by his family in Texas because he had married an African American woman. He did not feel that his wife and children would be accepted in Texas. Despite this ambivalence, he became a pivotal member of the black community, and he served them with dedication.

For his first business venture, John Vargas started a restaurant. In 1946, he bought a bus from a local wrecking company, put it in a vacant lot, and invited customers to dine on his Mexican lunch. At first serving sandwiches and soda pop, the family prepared food in their house nearby. A second bus, however, soon joined the first to become the kitchen. A wooden lunch counter connected the two buses and provided seating.

Next, John Vargas built a concrete block building, which started out as mere concrete slab. On weekends it served as a dance floor. "Kids could come dance at the basketball court lighted area," says Vida Burton, the daughter of John Vargas and sister of Dolores Rhinehart.[21]

When the building was completed, one half was the kitchen and eating area, and the other half was the recreation area. The community supported and was loyal to all of Mexican John's businesses. John's wife, Ruth Robinson, now ninety-one—remembers that above all, John was an entrepreneur. John started a mechanic's business with his own money. At the time, for many minority-owned businesses such as his, borrowing money was next to impossible: "Lending institutions refused to let the blacks have the money and take the chance that they take from whites."[22]

Given difficulties such as these, John forged ahead. His humble garage had no doors at first, but over time he saved up enough to put them on. "It was just an empty ground at first," Ruth says. "And we saved enough money to start building a garage. We didn't have it quite completed. We had all of it done except we didn't have any doors on the garage. But later on we saved enough money to put garage doors on—the kind that went up and down, you know."[23]

He and Ruth also had a laundry service that catered to Muncie's white community. "The girls were big enough to work in the laundry," Ruth says. "We bought a Kenmore washer and dryer and that's how we started out." Vida Vargas Burton, Ruth's daughter, adds, "We would run an ad in the paper and then people would call and we would pick up their laundry, bring it here, do it, iron it, and all that; and then we would take it back."[24]

Mexican John died in the late 1950s. Today, his oldest daughter Dolores Vargas Rhinehart carries on Vargas's entrepreneurial spirit in the same neighborhood where Vargas made his mechanic, laundry, and restaurant businesses. "[John] always had an idea for making a dollar. Dolores Rhinehart—that's where she got that from," says Dolores's sister Vida. "If there's a dollar to be made, she can make it. She's a hard worker. And she's been in the beauty business for the last fifty plus years."[25]

Dolores Vargas of Muncie and Carl Rhinehart of Connersville, Indiana, married January 3, 1948. Carl graduated form the Poro Barber and Beauty College of Indianapolis in 1947 and then continued his study in 1953 at American Barber College in Los Angeles, California. Upon moving back to Muncie, John Vargas, Dolores's father, built them a barbershop on the southeast corner of Highland and Penn in Whitely. The Rhinehart's Barber Shop opened in 1954. In 1959, Dolores graduated from the Poro Barber and Beauty College and began to work with Carl in the Rhinehart's Barber Shop. In 1969, the Rhineharts expanded to include a salon and became the sole owners of their business and

Dolores and Carl Rhinehart in their barbershop/salon. Photo by Danny Gawlowski.

purchased the building. Today the barbershop and salon stands proudly in the Whitely community and is operated by their son, Carl Rhinehart Jr.

Like Mexican John, Dolores and Carl had difficulty securing loans for their growing business because of their minority status. But "when we weren't able to get a loan from the bank, we talked to the woman across the street who worked for the president of the bank," and they were finally able to secure a loan. "That was the way that we got that loan."[26]

After fifty-four years in the business, the Rhineharts retired. After a brief time, however, Dolores went back to work. "Oh yes, the reason that I went back, I had a customer that said 'I am losing my hair. Dolores, will you come back in the shop and check it for me?' She was my good customer. She still is. She was the reason for me to go back after retirement." But Dolores also admits that "I'm doing it mostly to get out. It's to keep busy, and getting out and meeting people and talking: what's going on. I like that." Carl agrees: "I go down there and loaf around."[27]

Dolores and Carl say this about the success of their business: "The black community has been very good to us. We have admiration for the people in Muncie because they gave us a chance to make a living and we gave our lives to them."[28] Dolores's customers are loyal to her, just as she is to them. Indeed, this loyalty has enabled their business to exist within the community for years.

But working as a minority business for the minority community can also create problems. "No checks cashed, no loans please, thanks for not asking." This sign hangs above the Rhinehart's barbershop door. Although many customers are friends, neighbors, and relatives who bring in business, customers can often demand too much from the owner. For example, though barbershops and salons no longer provide medical or legal services, many people assume that the barbershop's role historically as a lending institution still holds. Carl and Dolores have gone to great lengths to make sure that no one makes that assumption at their shop. What people don't realize, say the Rhineharts, is that times like these could create trouble for a business, especially if loans became large or in some cases, customers pushed off payment. "In fact, there are some people that still owe Carl money," Dolores says.[29]

Times are not always prosperous when you own your own business. Dolores and Carl made their business their lives. They said it *had* to be, for they always had to be thinking of new ways to bring in more money and to make the business better. No matter what, the Rhineharts say you must always be willing to put money back in the business. Even if no one is coming in, the bills still need to be paid.[30]

It takes unwavering dedication to run a business, they say. But Dolores and Carl don't see that same dedication in today's new business owners. Dolores doesn't think the young work as hard as they did in the past. "We were always open—six days a week, 8 A.M. to 6 P.M. I used to take lunch to Carl so that he could work all day without breaks. Walk-ins were important to us, so he would stay at the shop even if there were no customers. They knew that they could depend on us to be open. People knew we would be there. Now kids will leave if they are not busy. You always have to put the customer first. If we are going to do something, we better do it the best way possible. We bought air conditioning for the shop before we even had it at home."[31]

One cannot overestimate the importance of the Rhinehart's work. Indeed, they are carrying on a time-honored tradition. Barbershops, in particular, have long carried historical significance in Muncie's African American community. Barbershops

> became the place where black citizens not only got their hair cut but also their medical needs taken care of. They also got legal advice and many times money loans from the barbers of the community. They were one of the few businesses that actually employed other black workers.[32]

Barbershops and salons continue to be an important institution where Muncie's black community can come together, talk, and share. But above all, many black people continue to patronize shops like the Rhineharts because most white hair stylists are not educated in the care of African American hair. Barbershops and beauty shops like the Rhineharts were and still are "the only shops they could go to get good service . . . because when you go to school and you learn how to work on white people only, you can't do black hair. So that is one of the reasons why it compelled all blacks to go to their own barbershops and beauty shops."[33]

Mortuaries: Staying Alive as a Black Business

Upon walking into Faulkner's Mortuary on a bitter, snowy day in late January 2003, a wave of maroon carpet and wallpapered walls with a maroon border that stretched around the room waist-high washed over us. Images from "The Other Middletown"—an exhibit of historic photographs of the black community created by Hurley Goodall and other community members—were prominently displayed on every wall. Edgar Faulkner Jr., our second community advisor and

Ed Faulkner chuckles with Sam Williams on the steps of Mt. Zion Church while waiting for a family to arrive for a wake. Photo by Danny Gawlowski.

the mortuary's owner and operator, was doing business on the phone. A friendly middle-aged man named Gary Mason, a lifelong friend and employee of Ed Faulkner's, greeted us and invited us to take a look around. The pictures, with their accompanying life histories and stories, provided great insight into the community. Around the corner six caskets lay open for viewing and selection, a certain reminder that we were in a mortuary. Seated in the front parlor, we could see the chapel through glass French doors. We were a bit anxious about being in a mortuary, but this nervousness dispersed as a warm and cheery Ed Faulkner Jr. came in to talk with us. Dressed in a fine gray suit, his soft smile, friendly handshake, and eagerness to share his story created an atmosphere of lightness and fun. We gathered around in fancy chairs and dove into conversation. We began with embalming fluids and how to make the dead look alive.

Ed explained that, like barbershops and salons, mortuaries have long been a staple business in Muncie's African American community. Early black morticians had a ready market because most white morticians did not want to handle black funerals. Though that has changed somewhat, there is still a strong tradition of sticking with black funeral homes in the black community. Faulkner's mortuary, for example, has been in business for over fifty years.[34]

Ed's parents, Edgar Sr. and Doris Faulkner, opened Faulkner's Mortuary in 1952. "A service with dignity and quality without extravagance," was their motto. They were very dedicated to the principle that the people of this community deserved the best service in every respect. As their business grew, they relocated to a site that was also the home of two other service businesses: Faulkner's Realty and The Indiana Construction Co. Ed Faulkner Jr.'s father worked extremely hard to serve his community in many aspects. Edgar Faulkner Jr. carries on that tradition as the owner and operator of the mortuary today, as well as working as a supervisor at Borg Warner.

Like the Rhineharts, Ed explained that dedication and loyalty were key to a successful business. Ed's employee, Gary, sums it up this way: "The most important thing [Ed] instilled in my head is loyalty. I'm pretty loyal to him. And when you're loyal to your employee, or employer, things work out pretty good for you."[35]

Like the Rhineharts, Ed also explained that being an owner of a mortuary in the black community can be like "having your behind in the sand!"

"What do you mean by 'having your behind in the sand'?" we asked.

"Minority businesses serving the minority community are the hardest thing there is."[36]

Hard because—like barbershops, salons, and a few remaining black-owned BBQ restaurants—there is a constant tension he must negotiate, a tension that goes hand-in-hand with the loyalty that the community has for him. These people are his customers, and if he is not able to bend at some points and provide his customers with choices, then he wouldn't have the business. But if he bends too much, he won't be able to maintain the profitability of his business.[37]

The current situation is especially hard for people like Ed Faulkner and the Rhineharts because the only black-owned businesses that are thriving in Muncie today are mortuaries, barbershops, salons, and BBQ restaurants. Though they survive, black businesses continue to decline. "Black businesses aren't here," says Hurley Goodall. "They were, but with the McDonalds' moving in, the large corporations have pushed out the small grocery stores, restaurants, and other privately owned repair shops and businesses."[38] For example, a small black-owned grocery store and community institution, Parrots, which closed in the early 1980s, could not stay open in the face of corporate superstores— a pattern that our whole nation, not just Muncie's black community, has faced in the past several decades.

The Service and Education: Opportunities for the Next Generation

In Hurley Goodall's house, downstairs in his office, it was very warm. The walls were covered with a myriad of plaques and awards celebrating his long life and many accomplishments.

As we asked our questions we could see gleams of excitement and happiness, and sometimes sorrow, in Hurley's eyes behind his large brown-frame glasses. "Did you graduate from college?" we asked.

"Nope. I graduated from high school in 1945 and I went into the Army. I was one of the first troops that landed in Japan after World War II. At that time the army was still segregated. I was in a black outfit that had all white officers. The outfit that I got into was really interesting. . . . It was all black, a combat engineer battalion, a 1392nd Combat Engineer Battalion that had been fighting in the Philippines. . . .

"Here I'm eighteen years old, ten thousand miles away from home, and didn't know anybody. And somebody came down the hall and saying, 'Where's the cat from Muncie, Indiana? Where's the cat from Muncie, Indiana?' I said, 'Here I am.' It was a staff sergeant. His name was Armstrong. He befriended me and kind of took me under his wing and got me in his squad, or platoon I guess it was at that time. He was from Richmond, Indiana, and he wanted to know how the Bearcats and the Richmond Red Devils had fared in basketball. He hadn't heard anything from home."[39]

Since the era when Hurley joined, many black youths have continued to join the military. People give different reasons for going into the military today. But most suggest that it's because of the opportunities it continues to offer black youths. Renzie Abram's sons joined the military because "jobs were a little hard to find."[40] Mamie Barker's "brother joined the service. There were just no opportunities in Muncie for him."[41] One of Vida Burton's sons "went into the service. Like all young boys, when they leave home and graduate from high school, he was ready to see the world."[42]

Dolores Rhinehart believes that young African Americans seize on the educational opportunities that the service provides. "The blacks are wanting to do more," she says. "They will take the service. I got a nephew that just made some kind of lieutenant before you get to captain. He had a couple of years at Ball State before he got married. He was stationed down in Florida. Through the service, he's got a degree to be a registered nurse."[43]

Like Dolores, many parents believe that knowledge is power, so they encourage their children to get a higher education. Dolores Rhinehart's grandchildren attended Purdue, Florida A&M, and Earlham College. She does not want them to return to Muncie, Dolores says, because they have better options in other areas. "I want them to go someplace where there is more going on for blacks."[44] She told them that a well-rounded education was best, and if the kids wanted to leave Muncie they could—that is, if they had an education.

Mamie Barker told us how important education was to her. She wanted to find a well-paying job when she first got pregnant so that she could save money to send her daughter through college. "You know," she says, recalling her decision, "I'm going to have to find a better job with better benefits, so I can save some money for her college. That was my main goal—to make sure she had enough money to go to college. Without education there's not much of a future."[45] Vida Burton agrees: "I would not care if my kids had stayed in Muncie or not, but Muncie seemed like it did not have that much opportunity."[46] She has one son who now lives in Atlanta, another who resides in Seattle, and her daughter lives in Indianapolis.

"I raised my kids to get the hell out of here," says Ed Faulkner.[47] And get the hell out of Muncie they did. His daughter went to Purdue and then to school in Michigan and is now an engineer for Ford in Detroit. His son played professional football, then turned to a career in coaching.

The Future of Getting a Living in Muncie's Black Community

We headed across town to the Muncie City Building after a long interview with the Rhineharts. We took the elevator up to Phyllis Bartleson's office, the director of the Human Rights Commission, which focuses on maintaining civil rights for all people. Phyllis took us to the conference room. A large table occupied the center of the room. Other than a bulletin board on the wall and a few boxes filled with files scattered here and there, the room was pretty empty. The interview started out slowly, but picked up quickly. It soon had the feeling of a conversation rather than an interview. With previous conversations with our consultants in mind, we asked Phyllis if she agreed that the community was suffering from the lack of black leaders. "Absolutely," Phyllis answered. "It already has. I can see it."

The decline of Muncie's industries has sent ripples throughout the economy. The absence of black doctors and dentists, the rarity of black administrators and other professionals, the loss of black businesses, and the decline of the city's once-powerful labor unions have left black Muncie with a leadership gap. With the lack of blacks in prominent leadership positions and the lack of businesses setting an example for success, many in the community are left wondering about the future for the community if young black leaders do not emerge soon.

"Where are the young people?" Phyllis asks. "Gone. The next generation is gone. They are not mentored, not nurtured; they're gone. Many of the older people here are people with good work ethics that contributed to the building and shaping of the community. They were a stabilizing force. There are few people left, like myself, who are community-oriented, but we're so few. The kids with sense, they're gone and they are not coming back here. The black community of Muncie is left with the two ends of the spectrum: the old ethical people and then the thugs, drug dealers, noncommitted people. They don't care if there is a better life in Muncie, and they won't contribute to the welfare of the neighborhood."[48]

"When I was younger," says Renzie Abram, "Muncie had three black doctors. . . . The people who are in some sense doing well, they end up moving away. . . . The opportunity is a little bit better in another area. You just don't have blacks in the school systems like you used to have. . . . To me it's critical. What has happened is that some have moved away and retired, and they haven't been replaced—black people are leaving."[49]

Hurley and Fredine Goodall's two sons followed this pattern of getting an education and then leaving. "We were able to get them a college education," Hurley explains, "and they both left because they went where the opportunity was."[50] The Goodalls' youngest son attended Ball State University, became a sports writer for the Associated Press, and now lives in Florida. Their son would not have had that same opportunity had he stayed in the community. "He had to leave here to do what he is doing," Hurley says. "Even if he had been hired here, he would probably have been making a tenth of what he is making now."[51]

Like many smaller cities around the country that are losing their industrial base, the professional jobs in Muncie—primarily the hospital and the university—tend to recruit graduates from outside the community, and therefore leave limited opportunities for native Munsonians. Phyllis Bartleson talked about how many of her children's friends would have liked to have come back to Muncie but could not because they couldn't find a job. "They were overqualified, but there is no such thing, according to the law, so they were forced to go elsewhere."[52]

Phyllis's son followed this pattern, too. He moved to Michigan to attend Albion College in search of better opportunities. Those opportunities led to an internship in Korea with the State Department, and he now resides in Atlanta. Phyllis said that he would never have had that chance had he gone to Ball State and stayed in Muncie. And with all he has now in Atlanta, she sees no reason for him to return. "Why would he want to come back to Muncie? To sell dope?"[53]

Selling drugs has become the preferred way to make a living for some young people, according to some of our consultants. Dolores and Carl, for example, discussed how many young African Americans do not want a "real" job because they cannot make that much money. "Young boys say I can make more money in an hour doing this than you make all day," says Carl Rhinehart. "These boys are selling the wrong stuff out there."[54] Mamie Barker agrees: "It's fast money, stupidity, and the lack of education."[55] Drugs seem to be a prevalent reason for the demise of the teenage or young adult work ethic. "That's for the kids who don't have a job, or don't want a job," says Dolores Rhinehart. "And they get hooked onto that."[56]

In the end, community leaders like Hurley Goodall believe that it is possible to maintain jobs for black youths here, but he feels that things will have to change more significantly. One advantage of his being an older African American is that he has seen progress and knows that things have changed already. You can't blame the young people for wanting to leave to obtain a better opportunity, he says; they should do what is best for them. Given the current state of affairs, he says, the best way to earn a living as an African American is to "prepare yourself with as much education as you can."

How We Learned about "Getting a Living"

Dolores and Carl served as the community advisors who provided the most details and conclusions about themes evident in the community. Their experience and respect in the community made many other contacts available to us, such as Dolores's mother, Ruth Robinson; her sister, Vida Burton; and Carl's sister, Ruth Rhinehart Redd, as well as their friend Rosemary Lamb Edwards.

We have a deep respect for the lifelong work and the many sacrifices made by our community advisors to make their livings. They overcame struggles through years of employment and broke through color barriers in order to survive in the community. Sharing homemade dinner and conversation in their homes created friendships, and their struggles and triumphs were highlighted by the memories and photographs that they shared with us. This chapter, shaped by our advisors' stories and experiences, began in the places most important to them, as they welcomed us into their places of work and their individual homes. As they opened their lives to us, we became a part of their story.

"It's not what you make, it's what you do with what you do make," reiterated Dolores Rhinehart after she read an earlier draft of our chapter. For many of our community advisors this thought seemed to sum up the meaning behind getting a living. Anyone can make money, our community advisors explained, but not everyone knows what to do with it. "Knowing what to do with it," we learned, includes things like putting "what you make" back into a business to make it more profitable; but spending wisely "with what you make" extends beyond this—to making a home, training the young, using leisure, engaging in religious practices, and engaging in community activities.

Notes

1. Renzie Abram, conversation with Michelle Anderson and Anne Kraemer, February 7, 2003.

2. Robert S. Lynd and Helen Merrell Lynd, *Middletown: A Study in Modern American Culture* (New York: Harcourt Brace & Company, 1929), 22.

3. Ibid.

4. Renzie Abram conversation, February 7, 2003.

5. Ibid.

6. Hurley and Fredine Goodall, conversation with Michelle Anderson, Anne Kraemer, and Ashley Moore, February 11, 2003.

7. Ibid.

8. Ibid.

9. Mamie Barker, conversation with Michelle Anderson, Anne Kraemer, and Ashley Moore, January 29, 2003.

10. Ibid.

11. Ibid.

12. Ibid.

13. Mamie Barker conversation, January 29, 2003.

14. Hurley and Fredine Goodall conversation, February 11, 2003.

15. Renzie Abram conversation, February 7, 2003.

16. Rosemary Lamb Edwards, conversation with Anne Kraemer and Ashley Moore, February 2, 2003.

17. Ibid.

18. Ruth Robinson and Vida Burton, conversation with Anne Kraemer and Ashley Moore, February 2, 2003.

19. Dolores Rhinehart, Carl Rhinehart, and Ruth Redd, conversation with Michelle Anderson, Anne Kraemer, Ashley Moore, and Dan Gawlowski, February 5, 2003.

20. Dolores and Carl Rhinehart, conversation with Michelle Anderson, Dan Gawlowski, Anne Kraemer, and Ashley Moore, January 16, 2003.

21. Ibid.

22. Hurley and Fredine Goodall conversation, February 11, 2003.

23. Ruth Robinson and Vida Burton conversation, February 2, 2003.

24. Ibid.

25. Ibid.

26. Dolores Rhinehart, Carl Rhinehart, and Ruth Redd conversation, February 5, 2003.

27. Ibid.

28. Dolores and Carl Rhinehart, conversation with Michelle Anderson and Anne Kraemer, February 26, 2003 (not recorded).

29. Ibid.

30. Ibid.

31. Dolores and Carl Rhinehart conversation, January 16, 2003.

32. Hurley Goodall, "The Other Side of Middletown: Making A Living" (personal papers, n.d.), 1.

33. Dolores Rhinehart, Carl Rhinehart, and Ruth Redd conversation, February 5, 2003.

34. Ed Faulkner and Gary Mason, conversation with Michelle Anderson, Dan Gawlowski, Michelle Johnson, Anne Kraemer, and Ashley Moore, January 31, 2003.

35. Ibid.

36. Ibid.

37. Ibid.

38. Hurley and Fredine Goodall conversation, February 11, 2003.

39. Ibid.

40. Renzie Abram conversation, February 7, 2003.

41. Mamie Barker conversation, January 29, 2003.

42. Ruth Robinson and Vida Burton conversation, February 2, 2003.

43. Dolores and Carl Rhinehart conversation, January 16, 2003.

44. Ibid.

45. Mamie Barker conversation, January 29, 2003.

46. Ruth Robinson and Vida Burton conversation, February 2, 2003.

47. Ed Faulkner and Gary Mason conversation, January 31, 2003.

48. Phyllis Bartleson, conversation with Michelle Anderson, Anne Kraemer, and Ashley Moore, February 5, 2003.

49. Renzie Abram conversation, February 7, 2003.

50. Hurley and Fredine Goodall conversation, February 11, 2003.

51. Ibid.

52. Phyllis Bartleson conversation, February 5, 2003.

53. Ibid.

54. Dolores and Carl Rhinehart conversation, January 16, 2003.

55. Mamie Barker conversation, January 29, 2003.

56. Dolores and Carl Rhinehart conversation, January 16, 2003.

4

Making a Home

Abigail Delpha and Cari Peterson

Nestled on a small drive is an unassuming brick house. The door swings open and a woman greets us generously with wide-open arms, beckoning us inside. Phyllis Joanne White's energy fills the room. She greets us with an "Okay, hey there now," and hugs us like children returning from a long journey. We take off our shoes as her voice trails off while she wanders into other rooms and back to where we are standing by the front door.

The front room is warm and enticing. Joanne invites us into her kitchen for what she says is a snack. As we approach the kitchen table, the "snack" turns into a college student's dream buffet. There are chicken wings, various types of drinks, sandwiches with a variety of meats and cheeses, chips, condiments, and a coffee cake. Joanne innocently suggests she did not have the time to make us a real meal and she apologizes for her lack of preparation, but we are still having difficulty picking our jaws up off the floor. We turn to Joanne and tell her if she is sorry for this "snack" then we want to live with her forever, because this is the best-looking meal we have seen while in college. She blushes at the compliment and then immediately smiles and nudges us toward the plates. She pokes at our sides and mentions that we are both too skinny and should have more than one helping.

We wander toward the living room, pausing with Joanne on the way back as she makes sure to point out all the pictures on the walls in the hall and kitchen. One picture by the kitchen is of her grandson holding a basketball, and there are more pictures in her guest bedroom of other grandchildren in basketball team jerseys with basketballs. She has a circle of pictures of her children, four daughters and

Abby Delpha (center) banters with Phyllis White (right) as the Shaffer Chapel's "Golden Girls" prepare dinner for a community-student meeting. Photo by Danny Gawlowski.

one son. Joanne hands us plates heaping with food, and we move back to the living room, where we sit on couches overflowing with coordinating pillows that remind us of a display in a department store. We know we should not jump on them, but cannot help the thought of doing so. The television set is showing a TV movie that Joanne says she was not watching. We enjoy the food and feel the love in Joanne's lively voice. The friendly banter continues and conversation quickly begins to unfold. Her family becomes ours as she relates stories about the people we are told are our new brother and sisters.

Near the end of this first conversation, Joanne receives a call from her youngest daughter, Denise. Soon into her conversation, she calls like a mother would for us to pick up the phone: "I want you to say hello to your new sisters," she says excitedly to Denise. Abigail apprehensively picks up the phone, only to be put at ease by the calming voice on the other end. The phone conversation ends and our spirited discussion resumes. We are comfortable and content. We are at home. In conversing on different topics, that first meeting with our community advisor leads us to discover a much enriched, humble, honest, tactful, loving, and well-spoken woman whose life is led by her family and her faith.[1]

How a Home Is Defined

"When a person walks into your home, your home emits a personality. And they can feel it. They'll know if they're comfortable, they'll know if they will feel welcome in that home, because it emits a personality," says Joanne, who grew up in a crowded house.

Joanne recalls her childhood home and family: "I was the sixth one: three boys and . . . my mom and dad had three sons and eight daughters . . . and we had *one* bathroom." She goes on to describe the amenities, "and see, back then, we really didn't have a bathtub. Taking a shower, no, we didn't even have a shower." She stops to chuckle and continues, "We had an old coal stove and a big tub and we'd pour water into that tub back behind the stove and take baths in the tub." Originally, there was an outhouse and an outdoor water pump, "and then, back in those days, the bathroom was always off the kitchen. . . . Daddy was a carpenter and he finally put a bathroom in for us. We had an outhouse. We had to go out back and use the outhouse, and pump water from the outside. . . . That well water, it was *so* cold." Not only did Joanne's family make use of this commodity, so did the neighborhood families. Joanne recalls, "We used to hear people pumping the water. We hung a water dipper by the well. People would come to the well night and day, pumping water to drink."[2] As the Lynds reported in their 1929 study—though electricity in the home was nearly ubiquitous by the early 1920s—plumbing was slow to come to Muncie, especially for Muncie's poorest families.[3]

"I like my home because it's just mine, being mine; like I said it's a struggle, but I'm relaxed. When I come home I want to feel at home," says Joanne's niece, Daidra Pryor. Daidra is a single mother and a Muncie native. She lives in a Habitat for Humanity house that she worked on for fifty hours to obtain the lot and three hundred hours to help with the home's completion. Daidra's home isn't filled with things that are new, but her possessions are so loved and cared for that they seem new. "These tables came from my grandmother's house; this chair came from my mother. They're not extravagant things, but I work to keep them, or I worked to have them. I try to take pride in what I have and take care of it," she notes.[4]

Joanne led us to her coworker, Mrs. Mallie Ross, who was born and raised in Mississippi, then lived for a time in Dayton, Ohio. She moved to Muncie over thirty years ago with her second husband, George. On the topic of personal possessions, she comments, "The punch bowl that belonged to my mother is the one thing I would want to keep above all else. When my mother passed, I went and got her dishes and pots and pans. I'm still using her bath mat and she passed in 1967."[5]

People's belongings have meaning from the work put into them, and the people they came from. People leave their memories behind in these objects. These gifts help to demonstrate that family helps build a home. When faced with the question of why it is harder to rid themselves of the gifts from family, Mallie says, "You didn't accumulate too many unusual things in my mother's day, and so I guess that is the reason I treasure it so much. However, it's gotten to the point though that I don't know who to give it to, because I don't know if they will value it as much as I do. With the nieces, I don't know if they want that punch bowl."[6]

Daidra Pryor built her house from nothing, and she takes a strong pride in that. "I've done something in here, I've put something in here that no one else could. And I see some flaws, but it's great. It was a great challenge, and it was a great thing to come over here and build something. Hammering nails—it was great," says Daidra.[7] In her case, it is the work that is poured into forming the home that connects the building to a more substantial meaning.

Trenton and Daidra Pryor sit with Cari Peterson and Abby Delpha at the Pryor home. Photo by Danny Gawlowski.

Upon arriving in Muncie from Dayton, Ohio, Mallie Ross and her husband George remodeled their current home. Mallie recounts, "When we first came here, and we tried to make it ready to move into, this room was a kitchen. I had to scrub this floor and try to get the grease off; I almost drove myself nuts! But that is when I decided to put rugs on the floor. And it's the work you put into it that makes it a home for you."[8]

Hurley and Fredine Goodall, who have been married fifty-four years and have lived in Muncie all of that time, attend Shaffer Chapel with Joanne. They both attended high school in Muncie and built the home in which they raised their two boys. "We've always worked well together. We built this entire home ourselves, and people don't believe it," says Hurley.[9] Fredine adds, "Every stitch and nail, I know where it is."[10]

People have to take what they have if they do not build a home and make it suit them. This is an ongoing process. "You have to believe in maintaining that home, and maintaining life in general is a challenge. But a home is what you make it. And me making a home is just gradually doing things that I want to be done, and keep and upkeep," says Daidra.[11] People work with what they have. "It is just what you put into it. My mother taught me, you take what you have and make the best of it, and we are still making this house a home. It is a continuous process. They just put in new insulation. The work isn't done when building a home or making a house a home," says Mallie.[12]

"We didn't realize we were poor because we were happy poor," says Joanne. And although her family's life was hard, she says their hardships were incidental to making a home. Memories first and foremost, she states, make a home. Joanne described, for instance, a scenario that arose because of this living arrangement: "This is really comical. Well, this was when I was in high school, and my ma had gone outside to use the outhouse. And it was cold and windy. You know, one of my friends, this guy [William Faulkner] who I really liked, was coming up the hill on the other side . . . and my mom was sitting up there in the outhouse and the door blew open. And William Faulkner was coming up the hill. And he came to school and said, 'I saw your mother sitting in the outhouse!'"

For Joanne, memories help to explain the relationships that make a home real. Her focus shifts to what they had rather than what they did not have. She has a fond memory of her mother and a strong appreciation for the blessings of family in the home, along with those nearby who shared these experiences.[13]

The Process of Making a Home

A large part of making a house a home, Joanne explains, is doing the things that are needed to make the household operate day-to-day. This responsibility extends from parents to children and children to parents. Joanne experienced these responsibilities from both angles: "With eleven of us in our family . . . my dad worked three jobs. My mom was a cook; she worked at Ball State, and she also used to get on a bus and ride to New Castle, Indiana, to work. And really, we didn't realize back then how dedicated our parents were to us." Because her father worked so much, he would have to come home to sleep during the day. He would sleep through all of the children's whooping and hollering but as soon as one cried, he woke up immediately.[14]

Joanne witnessed the results of her parents' extremely intense work ethic during her adolescent years. "I remember one incident," she recalls, "when I was a teenager . . . I wanted this dress . . . and I can remember this dress. It was a pretty gray dress . . . and my mom said: 'Well, I'll get you that dress.' . . . And she was doing day work, cooking for families in their homes—the week's wages almost were what that dress cost. So they did make sacrifices for us back then. We had all the kids. They weren't making that much money, but they were still trying to make us happy."[15]

Julius and Belinda Anderson have been married for twenty-five years and have four children. Belinda is a longtime resident of Muncie, having been educated at Wilson Middle School and Southside High School. Belinda's father, a fireman, was also from Muncie and her mother was born in Mississippi.[16] Julius moved to Muncie from Arizona in 1969 and attended Southside High School, but was gone for twenty years thereafter to serve in the military. Love is the central part of what makes their marriage and home function so well, say Julius and Belinda. "To make a strong marriage is to make a strong family . . . a strong family makes a strong community," states Julius.[17]

Julius and Belinda say they have a balanced partnership. "You have heard the slogan," Julius begins, "behind every good man there is a good woman. That is wrong. *Beside* every good man there's a good woman. Equally, not behind, but equally." The Andersons have made a commitment to their faith and to each other, and are a tight-knit couple and a strong family, making a strong home. "There is a difference between a house and a home . . . anyone can get a house, but what makes a home is love . . . a home may not be as pretty as a house, but a home is full of love," says Julius.[18]

Single Parent Homes

Strong families do not necessarily consist of two parents and a certain number of children. Joanne and her husband had a fairly large family of five girls and one boy, all of whom have obtained undergraduate degrees and are now grown, married, and live out of town. Joanne and her husband divorced after about twenty years of marriage. Her children proved to be a guiding force for her strength. Joanne raised her children in Muncie in much the same way her parents raised her, she says. Working full time, she relied on her children to return her love and support by taking care of things in the home. "Because they were the older kids," she recalls, "they had to take care of the younger kids." Not only did her children look after each other, they all pitched in economically, all going to work as teenagers. "All of my children worked. That was a blessing."[19] Sharing responsibility and support, she says, strengthened the family: "I love my children so much I would die for them." She explained as she talked about her divorce: "My son and my daughter came to me—they said 'you are the strong one in this household, mama' . . . and that next day I was up and going . . . I love my children, their spouses, and all my grandchildren. I love 'em all, and you know, it's just that I cry with them when they cry, I'm sad with them when they're sad, I'm happy when they're happy—I just want them to be happy all of the time."[20]

Kimberly Williams, a coworker of Joanne's, also discussed the love she had for her children and her desire to make them happy. Kimberly was raised for about thirteen years by her grandparents, alongside her aunt who is five years older. Kimberly has two younger siblings, a brother and a sister, who were raised by her mother.[21] Although she saw her mother throughout her early childhood, she became closest to her grandparents, who prepared countless meals, gave hundreds of smiles and hugs, and supported her personal achievements and losses.

Today, Kimberly does the same for her children. Her two daughters are now in their early twenties. After they were born, she was in a relationship for eight years. Of her family at the time, Kimberly says: "Odd as it is to say, even while he was sometimes abusive, he still took care of my kids . . . even though I and he were going through certain things . . . and my kids always wanted me to do better than him."[22]

After slowly moving out and moving on, Kimberly does not look back. She now tries to help her children avoid the mistakes she made:

"I make sure that I'm taken care of first. And I'm going to make sure that my children are taken care of in their relationships as well. They witnessed certain situations that I had to go through; they don't have to go through that . . . under no circumstance should they ever have to be verbally, mentally, or physically abused. They don't have to tolerate any of it. Get up and go."[23]

Kimberly respected and loved herself and her children enough to recognize that it was time to get out of something that was hurting them all. Now, by guiding her children she reinforces this love: "It's like when your kids tell you something that's going on in their lives, and if it's unhappy, I'm unhappy. I worry because I don't know what's going on, and I don't know where they need help most . . . and when they tell me they're happy, I'm *so* happy. I guess I flow with them."[24]

Love continues to be a large part of making a home for Robert Vance, or Smokey, as most people around town know him. Smokey is a forty-three-year-old single father with three children: a twenty-three-year-old daughter, a fourteen-year-old son, and an eleven-year-old daughter. We were led to him through a coworker of Joanne's, Nicole Watson, whose children attend school with Smokey's. Smokey was

Robert "Smokey" Vance plays with his daughter, Stephanie, and other neighborhood children on the porch of his home. Photo by Danny Gawlowski.

raised in Muncie and has lived there almost his entire life. He was raised by his grandparents, although he saw his mother every single day. He was not close to his father when he was younger, but now sees him more regularly. Although he had his first daughter with a black woman, his younger children are with his current wife, who is white. They have been married for eleven years, but separated for the past five, so he has been raising the two youngest children by himself. There is nothing but heart that goes into these relationships with his children. He feels much like Joanne and Kimberly, and says, "My children are my best friends."[25]

To Smokey, a home is more than love for his children, it is a place to relax and have fun with his children. He describes making a house a home as "having the kids here," because, "without them, it would not be the same. . . . My home is laid back, relaxed, and fun where kids can be kids as long as possible."[26]

Smokey seems to get a natural energy from spending time with his children. What he loves about his children is "being around them, just getting on their nerves," as he goes on to talk about eating lunch with them at school at least once a week, for example. "I keep them thinking," he says with a twinkle in his eye. As we converse, we see this interaction from where we are sitting in resin lawn chairs on his front porch during an unusually sunny, warm Sunday afternoon in March. Smokey watches over his children and his neighbor's children playing in the yard from where he sits on the front porch railing and continues: "Love is a big part of the home, a *big* part. Without love, it would be a boring place to live with a serious attitude. Nobody cares about anybody. Where is the fun?"[27]

The Security and Refuge of Home

Having fun in the home is one concept that most people mentioned when discussing the home; more than that though, it is a place to relax and be yourself, free of the outside world. This perspective was shared by many of our consultants. "Making a home is creating a peaceful atmosphere to come to after a day of whatever. A place where you can relax and be comfortable. A place where you enjoy being," says Belinda.[28]

Hurley also mentions how home should be comfortable: "A home is a place where you can go and just let it hang out. . . . You can do what you want to do, just relax and get all the cobwebs out of your head . . . don't have to please anybody or carry on a conversation if you don't want to . . . there's no pressure to conform to society's norms when you're in your home; you do what you want to do." More than a comfortable place, the home can serve as a retreat of sorts, says Hurley. Fredine agrees, "You can get in here and hide. Hide from everything and everybody."[29]

Because they are so active in the community, the Goodalls are well known by many and rarely go somewhere without getting into a conversation with somebody. Therefore, they find comfort and refuge in their home. Kimberly and Joanne concur. "I do think how a person runs their home is how it makes you feel inside that's person's house. When people come to my house, they are just comfortable," says Kimberly, explaining how she creates comfort.[30]

Mallie Ross is another person to voice this theme. When asked if she feels at home when she is in her house, Mallie quickly responded, "Oh heavens yes! You know you can go away, visit different places, but there is nothing like getting back home where you can just drop stuff here, or put it away, or do whatever you want to do. Just feel at ease."[31]

Discussing the topic of making a home comfortable, many are quick to add that safety and security are also necessary to making a home. "Well, this is the way you make a house a home. First of all, you make your home secure. You make your home safe for your children," says Joanne.[32] Hurley also is concerned about children when considering safety: "The home should be a place where a child can feel safe and feel loved and feel wanted. . . . The home is a safe haven where a family can get together and bond and talk over their differences and concerns."[33] To accomplish this, Joanne says that "sometimes you have to go away from where the problems are too, to make your kids secure."[34] Feeling secure is often about a personal choice to take control and to get away from things that can interfere with the full enjoyment of the home.

For many, this security, although partially reliant on those around them, was mainly based on personal strength. Kimberly, recognizing her need for assistance as a single mom, continues, "But I learned to give myself my own support, because I had to struggle. So I learned that I made a support system for myself that got me through. . . . It was just things that I built up and I made my own rules on certain issues and I supported myself with that . . . I made my own support system and that's how I survived."[35]

Although many of our consultants talk about needing family members, community, and God for support, many still seem to have an inner strength that kicks in to help them pull through. Daidra talks about opening her home to her family members, but having difficulties: "I cannot work and take care of somebody who doesn't even want to take care of herself . . . I'm working day to day . . . and I'm trying to keep what I have."[36] Whether relying on family, friends, faith, or oneself, feeling secure about their homes and lives is a priority for our consultants.

Home encompasses other people besides parents and children. Joanne and her husband were divorced, and she moved back to Muncie from South Bend, Indiana. "I had to come here and live with my one sister, Delores. We all had to live in separate households. Some of my kids lived with my mom, some with my other sister. I lived with Delores until I got the job in the factory, and then we all moved back together," Joanne says.[37]

Many people are reliant on their parents to help raise their children, which brings extended family into their homes. Joanne's niece Daidra Pryor also is close to her family: "My family was my greatest support when I was pregnant and even now. My two cousins are my best friends." Daidra is involved with her son and his school, but still falls back on her family. Her involvement does not require her to venture out into the community to seek for other support or friends. "I have too many family members to worry about friends; if I can't find a friend, then hey, I've got enough family members," she says. Her mother, Delores, takes a big part in raising her son, Trenton. He is in the Latchkey Program at school from which Delores picks him up. When Daidra gets off work at 6 P.M., she picks him up from her mother's house. "My mother feeds Trenton no matter what, and that helps because then I only have to worry about his homework getting done when we get home," says Daidra.[38]

This involvement may be due to the involvement of this generation's grandparents or to the example that their parents set by involvement with their children. Gwynne and Ron Orcutt, two white Muncie natives with an interracial grandchild, are heavily involved with their granddaughter, Dominique. "I've just seen too many grandparents that aren't involved. My parents—and Ron's too—were always involved; so we just kind of grew up that way. Your whole family was always together," says Gwynne.[39]

Smokey's grandparents raised him, as well as two brothers and five sisters. His mother lived across the street and saw him everyday, but it was his grandparents who instilled his main morals and his family values. "My grandfather taught all of us about responsibility and work ethic. He would have all of us do chores, we would work on the lawn, shovel the snow, whatever. He showed us that you have to work for what you want. I have my kids do chores too; they have to keep their room clean," says Smokey. "And my father was never there for me, so I don't ever want my kids to wonder if I love them, so I am very involved with them like my grandparents were with me," Smokey reiterates.[40]

Being raised by her grandparents helped instill the family values Kimberly possesses. "The love that I have for my grandmother is different from the love I have for my mother, because I wasn't raised by my mother. The love that I have for my father—well, I don't have any love for my father, because he wasn't in my life—period. But my grandfather was, so therefore, I poured all my love into him and he poured all his love into me," she says.[41]

Kimberly and her youngest daughter, Keisha, are both single mothers. Kimberly is helping Keisha raise her son, who is three years old. "I have a different love for my grandchild, and I just cannot explain it," says Kimberly. "I love my children, and my grandbaby is a different love than my children. It's like there are certain things that I wouldn't let my children do, but I let my grandbaby do—nothing bad of course, but it is because I love him so much," she admits.[42]

There seems to be a different type of involvement that grandparents have with their grandchildren. Whether it is the relationship itself or that grandparents have more time to be involved with the youth—either way, they play a part. "When you are grandparents, you have free time and you are on your own. So when you pick them up, they can be the center of your world, but when you have your own kids, you have no time at all. You are either at work or raising your kids. Now I can relax and do my own thing, and say okay, 'Now I'm done with me, now I can concentrate on you,'" says Gwynne.[43]

This assessment of time is a key that grandparents have more time than parents do for their children. "People are so busy now," laments Fredine.[44] "Parents don't have enough time for their kids, and that is my job, to do stuff with my kids, to be here for them," says Smokey.[45]

Generosity, Memory, and Family Relationships

The family is the center of the home, so the times when family gathers are often the most memorable. These gatherings and celebrations vary in scale, but they always share at least one thing in common: generosity. Generosity is a constant in this community. Almost unquestioningly, it is expressed through a welcoming smile and an enveloping hug. Daidra made a pure example of this. As we students were leaving her home after a conversation, she easily could have dismissed us, but she did not. After she offered us delicious lemonade, fascinating conversation, a tour of the house, and time to hang out with her son, we prepared to depart, commenting on the wonderful aroma in her home. Daidra stopped us in our tracks, turned to us and put her pointer finger in the air. With a child-like gleam in her eye, she said, "Hold on," and rushed out of the room, continuing to talk as her voice trailed down the hall. Moments later she emerged: "I have a surprise for you—close your eyes," she said. As we waited together with our eyes closed, we were anxious to see what would happen. "Okay, you can open them," she said. "Your choice." What she had presented to us was a way to remember and savor her home. Inside a nondescript cardboard box was a selection of fragrant candles, each emitting their own distinct, rich scent. The baked apple pie scent turned out to be a favorite for one of us, later evoking the memory of the warmth and kind reception received in Daidra's home, along with the unfaltering generosity.[46]

Most people discussed extending their homes to those who are family members and some who are not. The Goodalls took in Hurley's mother for quite a period of time. They had lived with her when they first got married and she lived with them "until the last four years of her life." The Goodalls also recalled memories of hosting others in their home. The comfort they experienced was extended to others. Their children would have friends over to enjoy ping-pong or pool games in the basement. They still host parties and social events based around a popular entertaining space in the home: "I've always enjoyed the garage in the summertime, because we put screens up," says Fredine. "It just makes another room in the house, and we can sit out there with our friends, have a cookout in the backyard . . . usually on Memorial Day we will have some kids over and cook hotdogs and barbeque chicken and ribs or something . . . that kind of thing," says Hurley as he fondly recalls the additional uses of this space.[47]

Space

Because of the enjoyment people got out of these specific spaces and people, they were able to feel more relaxed in their homes. Space in the home has been important to some of our consultants, like the Goodalls' fondness for their screened-in garage. There are boundaries of the home for many of our consultants, we find, as they talk about relations with neighbors and friends and the purposes of certain spaces, and how these areas are used in support of the generosity they show to others. When talking about his home, Smokey says, "People feel at home, because what most people can't do in their homes they can do at this one." He continues talking about his personal guidelines, "If I do not trust them, they are not coming in, because I've got to know them, and they have to know me. Don't take from me, I won't take from you." During the summertime, Smokey describes people from all over the neighborhood coming to his porch. However, he does not let just anyone into his house. There are boundaries for who is allowed where in Smokey's household—depending on how well he knows the person and what the season is.[48]

Kimberly also talks about gatherings in the home when she was younger. To her, the space was very open, reflecting her personality: "It was like my apartment, one time," she begins, "And I didn't have *anything*—I didn't have any furniture. I didn't have anything but lawn chairs, a stereo and a TV in my house, beds for my kids. And everybody was always at my apartment—even with no furniture. I didn't even have a kitchen table. This space was all we had." She may not have had much, but people would come over, she says, "Because I made it comfortable. It was comfortable in my home. It was safe in my home."[49]

Both Joanne and Smokey seem to have had comparable experiences with welcoming people into their homes. Joanne continues talking about how to make a home: "and then, what I always did was let my children know . . . their friends could come in and meet me, and come into the home and just . . . they would come in and cook. They would spend the night; they would do everything. They loved to come. And my kids loved it. We couldn't wait to get home. I wasn't just free with them, let them do anything they wanted to do, but they felt comfortable enough and felt that I had made a home for them. Even when we were in a two bedroom house, it was still a home because the kids loved to come there . . . and I see them today, you know, those kids are grown today, some of the white kids, they remember me and I say 'you know, I don't remember you.' And they say 'Miss White, you know you were so sweet to us. We could *always* come to your house.' I didn't remember them, but it's just something that kids keep. The happy memories stay with them."[50]

Making others feel welcome and wanted is a large part of making a home for many in the black community in Muncie. The size, location, or amenities of the space are not as important as the memories and people that fill the space.

Food

Bringing people together to make memories is not usually altogether difficult for this community. One significant way the space is filled is with food. "Food is a way of tearing down walls,"[51] said Julius when talking about bringing people of different backgrounds together. Family get-togethers often revolve around food. When talking about her family get-togethers, Daidra explained that her aunts would *all* pitch in: "Each of them brings a four-course meal."[52] Hurley and Fredine talked about cooking meals for Hurley and the crew when he worked at the fire station, "Even on the holidays, Fredine would bring the kids to the fire station and then sometimes, you know, we would prepare a meal in there for anywhere from three to seven guys . . . and they would bring their families and we'd all sit down like a big family."[53]

Food had its hand in bringing together families and people of different ages, interests, and races. Uniting people in the home helped people to feel at home; at the same time, it allowed them to extend their generosity to others. It permitted them to be a part of welcoming people by letting the personality of the home play an active role in welcoming guests. Outside of the structure of home, the home was shared with others by extending the generosity and support the family had for each other and their community.

Children

"I always told my kids that family is all you have, and when it comes down to the bottom line, they'll be there for you," says Ron Orcutt as he discusses the challenges of being part of a biracial family.[54] The importance of family has been embraced by all our consultants. To some, family is neighbors, brothers and sisters, or fellow church members. Regardless of family designation, discussion of children was central in the thoughts and recollections of most of our consultants when talking about home. The topic of children emerged repeatedly in conversations with people of different ages and backgrounds. We discovered that many show their support by getting together with their children often. Two things that seem to affect the relationship between parents and children is whether or not they live in the same town, and, from the older generation, the process of children moving out of the house. For others, their relationships with their children depend largely on the struggles they have had together.

Joanne and Kimberly, single mothers, became more like good friends with their children, since they depended on each other for strength and survival. Kimberly can attest to this: "My kids became so much stronger, together, more like sisters. My kids call me by my first name. They don't call me Mama. After all of that was said and done, we became friends. But then they became teenagers, and they rebelled . . . but now, they seem like they've changed a bit. And we still go through certain stuff that, as a mother trying to tell her two children—and they're grown—they are slowly understanding. But you just have to stay focused." Joanne also agrees that she has a special relationship with her children: "My daughter Denise called me one night . . . and she was writing poems. She read those poems to me and I cried . . . and we cried together and she said: 'Mom, this made me feel good. You know mom, you're my best friend . . . I can talk to you and you'll tell me if I'm right, and tell me if I'm wrong.' That made me feel wonderful."[55] As a single parent Smokey also says that his children are the center of his life: "They're my best friends."[56]

For both the Goodalls and the Andersons, their relationship as a married couple seems to be of great importance in relation to how children were viewed. They concentrated on making their relationship strong and then using this strength to positively guide their children. "Freddie and I were really—we were a team—and that was my strength, I think," Hurley says fondly. Fredine talks about her and Hurley's approach with their children, "We just couldn't take a lot of foolishness. They could have a say in things, but we were their bosses." Even though there was a negotiation of power, "We definitely involved the kids in everything we did," says Fredine. "And we always put them first," adds Hurley.[57] Despite their different family structures, our consultants were focused on their relationships with their children, and able to build strong homes by building strong families.

Children's Future

Although our consultants have strong ties to their children, many do see an increasing problem with the way children are developing today. They are deeply concerned because children are no longer the center of the home and community. Joanne comments, "If there's no restraint with the younger generation, things will get worse." The situation will get worse if individuals do not change their behavior, agrees Kimberly: "Some people just go out and do what they want to do—they don't care about their kids."[58] Ron also agrees by explaining how families have changed: "I guess then again, it is just the way we grew up, and when we did, families were always together. They were playing cards, they were just always together. And now families aren't like that, kids are just put in front of TVs with their technology things."[59] Fredine notes that some parents do not take time to take care of children's basic needs. "When the weather's good and we're walking outside we meet these little ones going to elementary school. I just look at them and I say, 'Oh, they just need somebody to take care of them.' They just really do. Some of them, they're not dressed right. They don't have on what they're supposed to have on. I just don't know what to think. I don't know."[60] People are not giving the time that children need. The problem partially stems from single parents struggling to make a living and raise children at the same time, and partially from a general societal apathy toward the training of a child. When asked if single parenting is a growing concern in Muncie, Joanne and Kimberly quickly responded: "Of course it is." Not only are single mothers prevalent, but so are single fathers, according to Kimberly: "What we're seeing now is male parents raising the children as well. So it's just changing. It's just doubling on both sides a little bit."[61]

One significant problem that is occurring is an increase in dangerous activities. "Like I said, they were doing that drinking and stuff like that back then, people were still making homes for their children, it just seems like it's harder-type drugs now. People fought with their fists; now they're using guns," comments Joanne. Many discuss young drug dealers and prostitutes. As these children are left more on their own, they struggle to find a place to be accepted by somebody. Children in the community today, our consultants say, are growing up too fast. The problems are more visible. "The parents act like they're scared of the kids," says Kimberly.[62] This problem of parents not being as actively involved in molding their children leaves much responsibility on others, like the schools, to try to take care of children. Hurley talks about a group of educators venting about the things expected from the schools—bathing, clothing, and feeding children. "Those things are the responsibility of their parents," said Hurley.[63]

Slowly, the traditional tasks of home and family are being dispersed outside of the home, leading to a conflict of who exactly is responsible for the welfare of the young. To relieve some of the growing problems of single-parent homes, drugs, and lack of control over children, our consultants offer many solutions. Changing this generation of children, Kimberly says, "starts in your home. That's where it starts; it's how you educate your kids."[64] With a solid home and supportive family as a base, children can be positively active in the community.

One other significant way children are grounded, say our consultants, is through the instilling of morals and values, which is also a key way for many in the community to bring the center back to family and home. Morals and values have played an intimate part in Joanne's life and in the lives of her children. She admits that her parents always made her go to church. It did not matter what she had planned the night before; she was expected to wake up and go, no matter what. Hence, faith became one of the principal sources of the morals and values that helped her build her home. Faith instilled in her a deep sense of right and wrong, and she expected the same of her children. When her marriage broke up, she moved back to Muncie and lived with her sister. In doing this, Joanne says that she wanted to take her children back to her roots—to Shaffer Chapel, the church where she grew up, and the one on which her children would learn to rely.

When first on her own, Joanne relied heavily on this place of familiarity. Indeed, she came to depend on it for balance. "Sometimes you lose your softness because you have to become the man and the woman," she says. "So, you know, that's why many black women stay prayed up and that's why we talk about religion all the time. Because we have to have God in our lives to continue, you know, to do what we're doing—to hang on to."[65]

Joanne depended, and still depends, on this tried-and-true system to help her raise her children right, in the context of Shaffer Chapel and in the context of a larger community. With her home as her backdrop, she has faith that her children's own faith will help them with their decisions. "I believe that . . . if I've done my job as a parent, kids are going to go out and they're going to do things like all kids do. But if it's instilled in them, and you teach them—you take them to church, and you go to church, that is instilled in them—that'll sustain."[66]

Faith continues to cycle through her family. "Like I tell my daughter Denise when she has problems," Joanne says, "Every day, like I used to do with you guys, when you get up in the morning, say, now we're going to take this time and stand around the table, stop eating, hold hands, and say a prayer and go out to face the day.'"[67] The actions taken in the home to shape her children's values, and to strengthen her in turn, have thus been essential to maintaining the health and unity of the family.

Defining Neighborhoods

There are varying levels of comfort for African Americans residing in Muncie. Kimberly and Joanne see this as something that is throughout

A summer afternoon in the Whitely neighborhood. Photo by Danny Gawlowski.

Muncie, while Smokey and Daidra seem to feel more comfortable in their own neighborhoods, as they define them. Smokey says, "My neighborhood is really this apartment complex. I feel safe here." Daidra, who also sees her neighborhood as small, says, "I might go out to dinner with the people I work with, and I might not. I might deal with them, and I might not. I don't really deal with the people in this neighborhood. I go home, me and my mother, and that is who I communicate with. I know my family is going to have my back, and certain other people have my back. So I go where I feel safe, and I feel safe here."[68] When they feel safe in their neighborhoods, they feel safe in their homes. At Smokey and Daidra's homes, we witnessed kids playing outside and interaction in these areas. In contrast, Kimberly defines her neighborhood very broadly, "This is Industry, and the boundaries would be Macedonia, Madison even back of it, 12th Street, and Main Street." Joanne used to live in Whitely and comments, "When I was young, Whitely was a mix of black and white, and it is still like that now."[69]

Joanne's definition of her neighborhood is similar to Smokey's. She defines her neighborhood as, "My street, and my neighbors across the street really look out for me."[70] People do rely, then, on certain individuals in the neighborhood to secure some level of safety. These neighborhood definitions are very precise and demonstrate the different perceptions people have about the neighborhoods in which they reside.

Race

Even in 2003, Muncie residents still encounter racism. Joanne has endured racial discrimination even when she lived in Whitely. "We all lived in the same neighborhood and went to high school together. We used to have race riots when we were in Muncie Central, too. It was so ironic because the white friends that we were friends with during the day in school, laughing and talking, would come out in Whitely and drive through calling us all kinds of names. They would come out and call us 'niggers' during the night,"[71] says Joanne.

Past and present, blacks and whites face different forms of racial tension. Ron, a white man, recalls a more recent incident he had when working at General Motors in Anderson. "There was this one black guy, and at work he was as friendly as could be. One night his car broke down, and I offered to take this guy home. We both lived in Muncie and worked in Anderson. We got within two blocks of the guy's house, and he asked me to drop him off. So I asked, 'Don't you live on down there?' and the guy said, 'Yeah, but I don't want anyone to see me with you.'"[72]

Smokey does not bring up specific incidents, but describes how he deals with discrimination. "I know that I have to make an effort, so when I go walking around the neighborhood I say 'hi' to white and black people I don't know. This makes people see that I am just a nice person, regardless of my color." In these interactions with others, many find that people are becoming more accepting of one another. Kimberly says, "This area is mostly black, but you know white people are moving in and you know, I'm okay with it." Smokey tells of a neighbor that openly admitted, "Smokey, I haven't really had interaction with black people, let alone had a black friend, but I've really gotten to know you. And this has opened my eyes; I am much more accepting of black people now, because you make me feel at ease about the issue."[73]

Safety

Communities are often the neighborhoods in which we live. Neighborhoods fall apart and become unsafe when faced with certain challenges that make the process of creating a home feel very isolated or difficult. There are many examples of isolated incidents that continue to chip away at the structure of the neighborhood. During one conversation at Kimberly's house, when a group of Joanne's coworkers are asked if it is harder to raise children in those neighborhoods and how, they speak of the problems: "It's harder, because now there are crack houses out there in Whitely," says Joanne. Kimberly speaks of one problem facing the community, "Prostitution is a problem. Right down on Madison and Kirby is a big place for prostitutes who are white and black; and Willard and Jefferson. With that place, one side is predominately white, and the other is predominately black." Joanne continues, "Where my sister lived, the prostitutes used to walk up and down on Elm Street, and the residents pushed them out." The way to prepare the next generation to face challenges in raising a family in an unsafe neighborhood is "train your children to stand up for what is right, respect others, to pray to keep it safe," Joanne resolves. With this break in the community there are fewer safe places to go and people are pushed into their homes. Speaking of local neighborhoods, Kimberly mentions, "I know of a cross burning right down the street from Miss Phyllis (Joanne), right in her neighborhood." Joanne adds to this by stating, "They made it so bad for people that they moved out, burning their crosses there, and people were afraid for their children."[74] It is later mentioned by Kimberly that this happened as recently as 1983 or 1984.

Kimberly also explains how she feels in her neighborhood, "There was another household, next door, and they were drug dealers. I don't bother anybody, and I don't want to be bothered. I don't want to say I don't socialize with anyone else, but I don't, because it's better that way. I stay to myself, and when you stay to yourself, people don't really bother you." However, Joanne says, "You are still accountable to somebody. You have people coming by; somebody has to look out for you. And it could be your daughters that come over, your mother comes over, and they check on you," says Joanne. When asked if it is possible to make a home under these conditions, Joanne replied, "You can still make a home despite that, you just need to know what's going on." Kimberly followed with, "You can make a home anywhere, because you have to, because it ends up being all you have."[75] Making a home in the community can be accomplished, despite these problems. But this trend of isolation may be pushed further. If a home is all one has, then one loses out on the community, neighbors, support, and safety outside the walls of the structure.

Kimberly and Joanne do depend on certain neighbors to secure trust and safety. "The neighbors who are close by, we are the only people that look out for each other. If I have to go out of town for two weeks, they keep an eye on my house. If they had to go, I always kept an eye on their house as well," says Kimberly. The people that do not rely on the neighborhood being safe or watching out for them, then rely on family, which Kimberly and Daidra both seem to do. This situation becomes a breakdown of the community in raising a child. With reference to building a home, Joanne sums this all up the best: "A home is a place where love abounds, where you feel safe and secure with the people who dwell within that home."[76]

But at the same time, these women are also concerned about how parent and children interaction affects overall safety in their neighborhoods. "*Oh* it is in your face," says Joanne, "right there for everyone and anyone to see. In the front yards, kids talk back to their parents; and it is just everywhere you turn. And you can't punish someone else's child because you don't know what they will do. People are crazy these days; they will shoot you or say 'Why is my child your business?' So it is better to just stay away,"[77] describes Kimberly.

Smokey explains that in his childhood, "if we did something wrong, our neighbors would punish us just as if we were their own. My grandfather taught us respect and I try to teach that to my children and the kids in the neighborhood. If a child is doing something wrong, I let them know I don't approve. Of course I don't spank them or anything, but if they talk back to their mother in the front lawn, and then come over here. . . . I expect people to punish my kids as if they were their own, or let me know about it, so I do that for them."[78]

In the end, this change in the open forum of problems creates another breakdown in the home, because without the community to hold these children responsible, [children] think they can have free reign. Without communication, people are not telling other people about these open displays of deviance or disrespect that children demonstrate, and this leads to a breakdown in the parent–child structure of the home and neighborhood. A neighborhood depends on the community. "It takes a village to raise a child,"[79] Julius states.

The only other option to fleeing this insecurity is to move, but is the problem really just in Muncie—and if it is, why don't these people move now? "People say they have no way to get out; oh yes you do! You can get up and leave—just work hard enough and move on. You have a choice to be here and you make that decision," says Kimberly. "Sometimes, you have to go away from where the problem is, too, to make your kids secure," states Joanne. But if this is true, and there are problems facing these people in the community, why have they resided in Muncie for so long? "I love the way Muncie used to be. I'm just biding my time until I decide to leave," she says. Her children are really scattered throughout the country and that plays another role in her decision. "This one says 'come live with me,' and this one says 'no, with me'; if I pick one they are going to say I love them more. I don't want to choose so I don't," Joanne says. "But one day, I will have to make a choice," Kimberly says.

Interracial Relationships

Today, more than ever, interaction between the races seems to result in more interracial couplings. Joanne also admits that it has always been there but now it is more open. "Now there are so many more, and it's out in the open; the world is going to be full of those biracial children," she says. Kimberly's nephew is an interracial child. She comments, "When the nephew came, that was what it took to bond the two sides of the family. When my brother married his wife, who is white, I was like, '*oh, they are not going to accept this*,' but then we got to sit down and meet them. They were just so crazy about my brother. And then when my brother's son came along, they were just like '*aww*.'. . ."[80]

Joanne also has interracial couples in her family. Joanne's interracial relations include her daughter being married to a mixed Japanese and black man, and three of her nephews being married to white women. By having these relationships, people become more accepting of each other. Joanne says, "Both sides of the family get to know each other and see we aren't that different. We all believe in family reunions, and having get-togethers, and you love your kids just like I love mine."[81]

Gwynne and Ron Orcutt both had insight to this aspect of interracial couples as well. "I guess when you get so self-centered, or self-thinking that you don't realize that their community is thinking too," Gwynne continues, "it's just so weird when it's in your life, you start to realize that people hurt other people's feelings so badly over something that you have no control over." Ron, who was in the first full graduating class of Southside High School, grew up with ideals and morals that do not allow for interracial coupling to occur. However, "You just deal with it. Because it's family,"[82] says Ron. It is this new generation that binds the community and starts the interaction of once-separated parts coming together to raise the children.

The main reason why biracial coupling continues to be an issue is because parents are worried about their children and the future of a new baby. They don't want them to face prejudice or hurtful actions. Joanne told us, "When my kids were in high school, I told them to stick with someone of their own race; I did not believe in interracial marriages at that time because the children would have problems coping with society. That is what I told them then, because the children will have such a rough time, because back then they did have a rough time."[83] Parental concern seems to be universal. Helping biracial children deal with prejudice from classmates and community members can make it difficult to concentrate on other aspects of home life. Ron says that "when Kim, our daughter, came to us about it, I was very upset, because it isn't something I believe in. I grew up in a different time; it's hard to make it out here the way it is. And it's just tough, and I didn't want my daughters to go through those things, but having said that, I love my granddaughter, and if anybody messes with her, they are going to have to deal with me." Gwynne also adds to this by saying, "I told Kim, what bothers me more than anything about this is that you always would get up in the morning for middle school and say, 'Do I look okay, do I look too fat in this outfit?' But you aren't considering that your little girl can't just change her clothes, and that is what you were concerned about when you were young. What about them laughing at her for her not being able to change her color? And it bothered you so much that people would make fun of you for what you had on, but she can't change."[84] This parental concern and drive to protect is among the reasons there is still resistance to biracial relations.

To make biracial relations today even more complex, the generation actually engaging in these new and open relationships does not always see the potential problems. Smokey has two children with a white woman and admits, "It was never an issue of us being together. People realize that one race is not as bad as the other as long as you get to know them."[85]

This attitude seems to prevail among the younger generation, and because it does, the older generation seems to be moving toward greater acceptance of these relationships. Ron says, "You've got two different cultures here. They are different from the way they dress to the way they speak. I realize that things will be hard, but I want her to have both, not just from one side. You can learn a lot of things that way, and if you are going to be in this situation; then you might as well do it. That is my main concern, just for Dominique to get both equally."[86] Joanne also mentions her new outlook on the scenario. "People are people. God made people. If you fall in love with someone of a different race, if you love that person and God's in it, then I bless them. Because we're all God's people anyway. . . ."[87] Gwynne concurs: "Yeah, I agree that our generation is more accepting of it, because we have seen the changes and realized there isn't anything we can do about it. And that generation before us is very narrow-minded."[88]

With the current grandparent generation moving toward accepting these changes, and the current parent generation not seeing the problems in it, the children's generation seems even more accepting of the issue. "I'm not black, I'm both and I'm glad that I'm both. I'm white and black, and I'm proud," says Jasmine Taylor, a Wilson Middle School student.[89]

Students like Jasmine see both sides of the story and want equality for all types of people. On the topic of Black History Month, Jasmine comments, "I think it is good to have Black History Month; but if I was completely white I would feel, 'Where's our month?' But I think that Mexicans should have a month, everybody should have a month. Because it is just leaving one group out if we don't." Younger students like Jasmine do endure racism, but they have learned and grown from these experiences. They found that they respect others more from dealing with more from this point of view. "When I was little," says Jasmine, "people used to call me 'white girl', or they would talk about me because I'm mixed and they aren't used to it. They would call me a half-dubbed biscuit, but I didn't care because I realized who I am and I'm proud to be who I am." This being the case, some of her friends say she "tries to act black" though. "I don't try to act," Jasmine says, responding to this sentiment. "This is who I am. I don't try to act white [either]. . . . There is not one 'perfect color,' no one is 100 percent black or white."[90]

As Jasmine's comments suggest, efforts to make people aware of racial equality seem more apparent in this upcoming generation. Perhaps neighborhoods will become more unified and more secure, because stronger communication will be more prevalent. "You can't isolate yourself from the world," says Hurley. "You have to expose children to other things, other people, and hope that you can expose them to the right kind of people who will be the right kind of role models for them . . . people can't gain social skills in a vacuum."[91]

Building for the Future

To make a home in the place that Muncie has become, people are willing to face hard questions. Hurley says, "I'm very discouraged because no one knows what the answer is. I mean, we've got all these social workers, and different organizations, and things just continue to deteriorate and get worse." Finding the cause of the breakdown in today's home may be the first solution to fixing it. The next question is, "Can we look for answers outside of Muncie or are we going to have to cure the problem ourselves? I think that's where the majority of the community has blinders on. Almost every social problem that develops in this country develops in the black community first, because it's the most vulnerable. But it's just a mirror of what's going to happen in the white community later on." Additionally, says Hurley, "Muncie is a microcosm, and Muncie is Middletown. Everything that happens here is happening all over this country."[92]

The problem of deteriorating communities is real not just in Muncie, but across the United States. In Muncie at least, "there's a pocket full of us that's not willing to give up, to give in, or to give out. We're willing to fight with every fiber of our body and being, to hold onto that which we know is right . . . and what's right is a strong family," says Julius Anderson, who has started a married couples group.[93] The couples are from all different parts of town, all different nationalities, but the one thing they have in common is their faith in God. They come together once a month and talk about problems facing married couples. "What we need to continue to do is to be a help," says Julius. "Education is the key."[94] Like Julius, Daidra would like to educate the future generation as well. "I would eventually like to open my own day care center," she says, "that would help young girls in the same situations that I was in. My Aunt Betty wants to do it with me."[95]

There are lots of others like Julius and Daidra who are working to make a difference in their communities. With all of these active community members pushing forward and working progressively, there may be a chance for Muncie to build stronger homes, stronger neighborhoods, and a stronger, better community. Some are pessimistic. "The community has always had these problems and people try, but who knows if it will get better. I want to say that there is hope, but you just don't know," says Kimberly.[96] But others are more optimistic. "There is always hope. You can never give up on hope," says Joanne.[97]

Notes

1. Phyllis Joanne White, conversation with Abigail Delpha and Cari Peterson, January 21, 2003.
2. Ibid.
3. Robert S. Lynd and Helen Merrell Lynd, *Middletown: A Study in Modern American Culture* (New York: Harcourt Brace & Company, 1929), 97–98.

4. Daidra Pryor, conversation with Abigail Delpha, Danny Gawlowski, and Cari Peterson, February 11, 2003.

5. Mallie Ross, conversation with Abigail Delpha and Cari Peterson, February 26, 2003.

6. Ibid.

7. Daidra Pryor conversation, February 11, 2003.

8. Mallie Ross conversation, February 26, 2003.

9. Hurley and Fredine Goodall, conversation with Abigail Delpha and Cari Peterson, March 23, 2003.

10. Ibid.

11. Daidra Pryor conversation, February 11, 2003.

12. Mallie Ross conversation, February 26, 2003.

13. Ibid.

14. Phyllis Joanne White conversation, January 21, 2003.

15. Ibid.

16. Julius, Belinda, and Brenton Anderson, conversation with Carla Burke and Carrie Kissel, March 23, 2003.

17. Julius Anderson, conversation with Abigail Delpha and Cari Peterson, February 26, 2003.

18. Ibid.

19. Phyllis Joanne White conversation, January 21, 2003.

20. Kelli Daugherty, Phyllis Joanne White, and Kimberly Williams, conversation with Abigail Delpha and Cari Peterson, March 18, 2003.

21. Kelli Daugherty, Phyllis Joanne White, and Kimberly Williams, conversation with Abigail Delpha and Cari Peterson, February 10, 2003.

22. Ibid.

23. Ibid.

24. Kelli Daugherty, Phyllis Joanne White, and Kimberly Williams conversation, March 18, 2003.

25. Robert "Smokey" Vance, conversation with Abigail Delpha and Cari Peterson, March 23, 2003.

26. Ibid.

27. Ibid.

28. Belinda Anderson, writings to Abigail Delpha and Cari Peterson, March 24, 2003.

29. Hurley and Fredine Goodall conversation, March 23, 2003.

30. Kelli Daugherty, Phyllis Joanne White, and Kimberly Williams conversation, March 18, 2003.

31. Mallie Ross conversation, February 26, 2003.

32. Kelli Daugherty, Phyllis Joanne White, and Kimberly Williams conversation, March 18, 2003.

33. Hurley and Fredine Goodall conversation, March 23, 2003.

34. Kelli Daugherty, Phyllis Joanne White, and Kimberly Williams conversation, March 18, 2003.

35. Kelli Daugherty, Phyllis Joanne White, and Kimberly Williams conversa-

tion, February 10, 2003.

36. Daidra Pryor conversation, February 11, 2003.

37. Kelli Daugherty, Phyllis Joanne White, and Kimberly Williams conversation, February 10, 2003.

38. Daidra Pryor conversation, February 11, 2003.

39. Gwynne and Ron Orcutt, conversation with Carrie Kissel and Cari Peterson, February 26, 2003.

40. Robert "Smokey" Vance conversation, March 23, 2003.

41. Kelli Daugherty, Phyllis Joanne White, and Kimberly Williams conversation, March 18, 2003.

42. Ibid.

43. Gwynne and Ron Orcutt conversation, February 26, 2003.

44. Hurley and Fredine Goodall conversation, March 23, 2003.

45. Robert "Smokey" Vance conversation, March 23, 2003.

46. Ibid.

47. Hurley and Fredine Goodall conversation, March 23, 2003.

48. Robert "Smokey" Vance conversation, March 23, 2003.

49. Ibid.

50. Kelli Daugherty, Phyllis Joanne White, and Kimberly Williams conversation, March 18, 2003.

51. Julius Anderson conversation, February 26, 2003.

52. Daidra Pryor conversation, February 11, 2003.

53. Hurley and Fredine Goodall conversation, March 23, 2003.

54. Gwynne and Ron Orcutt conversation, March 26, 2003.

55. Kelli Daugherty, Phyllis Joanne White, and Kimberly Williams conversation, March 18, 2003.

56. Robert "Smokey" Vance conversation, March 23, 2003.

57. Ibid.

58. Kelli Daugherty, Phyllis Joanne White, and Kimberly Williams conversation, March 18, 2003.

59. Gwynne and Ron Orcutt conversation, February 26, 2003.

60. Hurley and Fredine Goodall conversation, March 23, 2003.

61. Kelli Daugherty, Phyllis Joanne White, and Kimberly Williams conversation, March 18, 2003.

62. Ibid.

63. Hurley and Fredine Goodall conversation, March 23, 2003.

64. Kelli Daugherty, Phyllis Joanne White, and Kimberly Williams conversation, March 18, 2003.

65. Phyllis Joanne White conversation, January 21, 2003.

66. Kelli Daugherty, Phyllis Joanne White, and Kimberly Williams conversation, February 10, 2003.

67. Phyllis Joanne White conversation, January 21, 2003.

68. Daidra Pryor conversation, February 11, 2003.

69. Kelli Daugherty, Kimberly Wiliams, and Phyllis Joanne White conversa-

tion, March 18, 2003.

70. Kelli Daugherty, Mallie Ross, Nicole Watson, Phyllis Joanne White, and Kimberly Williams, conversation with Abigail Delpha and Cari Peterson, January 24, 2003.

71. Phyllis Joanne White conversation, January 21, 2003.

72. Gwynne and Ron Orcutt conversation, February 25, 2003.

73. Robert "Smokey" Vance conversation, March 23, 2003.

74. Kelli Daugherty, Phyllis Joanne White, and Kimberly Williams conversation, March 18, 2003.

75. Ibid.

76. Ibid.

77. Ibid.

78. Robert "Smokey" Vance conversation, March 23, 2003.

79. Julius Anderson conversation, February 26, 2003.

80. Kelli Daugherty, Kimberly Williams, and Phyllis White conversation, March 18, 2003.

81. Ibid.

82. Ibid.

83. Ibid.

84. Gwynne and Ron Orcutt conversation, February 25, 2003.

85. Robert "Smokey" Vance conversation, March 23, 2003.

86. Ibid.

87. Phyllis Joanne White conversation, February 21, 2003.

88. Gwynne and Ron Orcutt conversation, February 25, 2003.

89. Delores Pryor, Jayné Carey, Carrie Deja Gauldin, Jessica McNeary, Catrice Marks, and Jasmine Taylor, conversation with Carrie Kissel and Carla Burke, February 26, 2003.

90. Ibid.

91. Robert "Smokey" Vance conversation, March 23, 2003.

92. Hurley and Fredine Goodall conversation, March 23, 2003.

93. Julius Anderson conversation, February 26, 2003.

94. Ibid.

95. Daidra Pryor conversation, February 11, 2003.

96. Kelli Daugherty, Phyllis Joanne White, and Kimberly Williams conversation, March 18, 2003.

97. Ibid.

5

Training the Young

Carla Burke and Carrie Kissel

(Carla) "I once was lost, but now am found; was blind, but now I see." These simple words taken from the inspirational song "Amazing Grace," clearly describe the feelings I had before and after entering Family Night at Garfield Elementary on the fourth of February 2003. That night Carrie Kissel, Ashley Moore, and I all arrived a few minutes late to the event, because Ashley and I got lost while trying to pick up Carrie. Once we arrived at Garfield I followed Carrie and Ashley like a chick following its mother, because I didn't know what to expect. This was the first time I had done fieldwork. I found myself trying to work up questions in my mind that I wanted to ask and even points that I wanted to hit that I thought would be helpful in writing this chapter. I started to have a flashback of my first stage play; my palms were sweating, my temperature was rising, and I felt nervous, lost, and blinded to what I was about to experience. Well, we found an open door and—show time!

(Carrie) A strong February wind bit our ears and fingertips as Carla, Ashley, and I, searched for an unlocked entrance to the low brick building of Garfield Elementary School. I reviewed my strategy as we passed dumpsters and more locked doors, completing a half lap around the school, finally entering the cafeteria. Garfield's Family Night program began only an hour after class, an hour that I spent eating dinner and talking on the phone with my mom. Since none of us had been to Garfield before, we spent the ride navigating. As a result, I didn't think about how I wanted to take part in the event until I was walking into the building.

I had attended a basketball game at Muncie Central's Fieldhouse the week before, but I didn't feel like I had really engaged in the participant-observation strategy described in my Anthropology 101 lectures: Take an active part in the occasion while observing the details of what occurs. At the game, I took notes of some of the items I noticed about the students, fans, cheerleaders, and teams. Being a native Hoosier, I had a genuine interest in basketball. But since my loyalties didn't lie with either team, I didn't really participate as a fan. An older man, watching me scribble a line in my notebook, asked if I was a scout—I think it was a joke. But I knew at that point that I didn't fit in.

I realized that in attending Garfield's Family Night as a college student, too old to be an elementary student and too alone to be a parent, I would stick out here too. But I decided to ditch the notebook in an attempt to look less conspicuous. Maybe I would be easier to talk to that way. I wanted to find out what was important to the community about training their young.

With these thoughts running through our minds, we followed a mixed family of five to the cafeteria door. The father of the family, a stocky black man wearing blue sweat pants, a black leather jacket, and a baseball cap held the door not only for his wife and children, but for us as well. This simple act of kindness melted the hesitation each of us felt.

Low, octagonal, purple-topped tables surrounded by small chairs filled the cafeteria. Bulletin boards covered the back wall. Each class had its own bulletin board, although the boards were not in any particular order. A large object stood in the middle of each class's board— a frog took up the center of the third-grade board—and a few smaller stars, frogs, or other shapes surrounded each large picture. Long rectangular tables set up across the cafeteria from the entrance held bingo prizes—household products like bleach, dishwashing soap, colanders, and bubble bath—as well as a podium. At the podium stood two teachers who took turns at the microphone reading the words for vowel bingo as we took our seats.

(Carla) Carrie and I decided to split up. I sat at a table with a family of three—a mother, her daughter, and son—who were very excited about playing bingo. Before I even got a chance to get comfortable, a teacher had put a board and chips down in front of me. I have never been very fond of bingo, so I didn't pay too much attention to the game. I was too busy observing the family in front of me. The mother encouraged her family. "Pay attention so you can win," she would say. The sister would help her brother, too, by putting chips on the words he missed. This was very refreshing to my eyes. There are many children that have no parental support, so to see this was delightful. As I looked around the cafeteria, I noticed many families having the same interactions. One young child caught my attention. She seemed to be playing bingo, but on closer inspection I saw that she was pretending to sweep, using the board as a broom and the chips as her dust. Watching her brought a smile to my face.

As the night wore on, games were won and prizes were given out. Interestingly, the prizes were useful household products, a great idea because the children were not really concerned with what they won; they were just happy that they did. And the parents seemed pleased to get something useful.

Our Consultants on Training the Young

We are not the first to explore the importance of education in the city of Muncie. Robert and Helen Lynd, authors of *Middletown*, defined the themes of training the young as the students, the teachers, the subjects learned, and school social life.[1] These divisions helped us to identify topics that we might discuss with our consultants when preparing for interviews.

At the beginning of this project, we were assigned two advisors from the community who volunteered to help guide us on our road to discovering how education is important to Muncie's African American community. Julius J. Anderson grew up in Phoenix, Arizona, but moved to Muncie with his family at the age of fourteen. He attended Franklin Middle School and graduated from Southside High School. After graduation, Julius enlisted in the U.S. Navy and retired after serving for twenty years. He returned to Muncie and currently works for Ball State University. Julius and his wife, Belinda, have three children. Brenton, the youngest, is a junior at Central High School and is the only child living at home. As one of many community activities, Julius serves as the only black member of the Muncie School Board.

Delores Pryor was born in Muncie and grew up in the Whitely neighborhood. She is a member of Shaffer Chapel. Both Delores and her sister Phyllis Joanne White, advisor to the Making a Home group, volunteered their time to help this project. Because Delores grew up in the community and has been working at Wilson Middle School for twenty-seven years, she provided us with many contacts in the community. While Delores sent us into the community to talk to families about training the young, she also provided us with examples of informal and formal education in one of Muncie's African American families as we observed her interaction with both her adult daughter, Daidra Pryor, and her granddaughter, Jayné Carey, who lives with her.

In our first meetings with our community advisors, we weren't quite sure of where we wanted our chapter to go. We used the Lynds's chapter topics to develop questions. Julius and Delores added to our list of ideas with points they felt needed to be discussed. Themes they felt to be important to the community were: what values are held and how they are taught to children; the role that African American educators and administrators play in the schools and in students' lives; and if there is a presence of African American history and culture in the curriculum.

Both Julius and Delores had intentions of introducing us to positive leaders in the Muncie community. Julius's agenda was to examine the structured family, beginning by talking to older couples, such as Frank and Evelyn Wilson and Q. L. and Willa Mae Stevens. By talking to couples with strong foundations, Julius wanted us to see the outcome a structured family has on their children's successes in education and in life. Julius also planned for us to talk to educators and middle-aged and young families, but we ran out of time to talk to everyone. Delores introduced us to educators like Shelia Williams, as well as students like her granddaughter Jayné, along with Jasmine Taylor, Catrice Marks, Deja Gauldin, and Jessica McNeary, also students at Wilson.

Both Julius and Delores gave us ideas of events to attend to become more familiar with training the young in Muncie. We attended programs like Garfield Elementary's Family Night, Washington-Carver Family Literacy Night, Black History Month programs at Wilson and Garfield, and the Sisters of Promise Girls' Night Out at Union Missionary Baptist Church. Through our attendance at these events, we became a part of the Muncie community by getting to know families. By observing the programs and talking to the individuals involved, we discovered the importance of family to the successful education of their children.

"Family is *very* important to education," says Shelia Williams, who has taught physical education and health at Wilson Middle School for twenty-six years. "If you took a survey of the statistics it would probably show over 70 to 80 percent of the students who are from homes where the parents are encouraging, or the parents are helping them with their homework, parents are coming to their games—these kids probably have the best self-esteem, they learn better, they're the ones who will go on and succeed in life."[2]

Training the young, our community advisors insisted, begins with family. In the way they are brought up, children learn the values important to their culture, including the significance of formal education, respect, and effective communication. Educators like Shelia Williams point out that parents must take an active role in teaching children basic information before they begin to attend school. After students are enrolled, our community advisors stressed that parents should help with homework, be present at school events, and build working relationships with the teachers at school. The standards of these relationships and values are then communicated to the young through discipline and rewards granted at school and at home. Through this process of training the young, children learn the appropriate ways to act within society.

The Importance of Formal Education

"There's lots of things I couldn't have done," said Howard Grimes. "If I hadn't had the education I had, I wouldn't have got the job."[3] We found this quote in the transcriptions of the Black Middletown Project tapes, archived in our university's library. We immediately thought of the treatment the Lynds gave education in *Middletown*. Describing the value of education within Muncie in 1925, the Lynds wrote: "It is no exaggeration to say that it evokes the fervor of a religion, a means of salvation, among a large section of the working class."[4]

As it is for many Americans today, formal education is important to our community consultants, but more as a necessity for success than as a course of salvation. Phyllis Bartleson, director of the Muncie Human Rights Commission, makes this observation: "As time goes on and our use of technology increases, we're going to have to have more education. And the ones that don't have it are just going to be left behind."[5] Children will need the skills they acquire at school to function not just as employees, but also as citizens of the world. "They're going to have to get a global understanding," says Dr. Sam Abram, Executive Director of the Community Alliance to Promote Education (CAPE) of Delaware County, retired superintendent of schools, and cousin of Renzie Abram. "I didn't have to worry about that when I was a student, but today they must know. They're going to be too close to too many situations not to understand the different cultures. They're going to have to be aware of what's going on. When our granddaughter stays with us, she is ready to watch news from five to seven o'clock. We talk about all these things that are happening, and that's something else that must happen with kids. Our kids today are more exposed to horrendous kinds of happenings, and they need people to help them know how that fits. It's deeper than just knowing and repeating things, it's getting in and understanding what's happening in these areas. The young people have to learn . . . what it means to live in this country, compared to another country, because it's going to be different for them. [This] needs to be in the learning process in the homes and in the schools so they can just learn how to live."[6]

By teaching the value of education at home, parents will be preparing their children to attend school. Dr. Sam Abram says, "I think that the home, school, church, relatives, and siblings should all come together to help young people at an early age to become students. There are things that I think that adults should do at their own expense and sacrifice just to teach the children in their lives that something is important. An example would be, I think that adults should model reading. Reading is the most important skill that students must learn."[7] Phyllis agrees: "I believe that education should be introduced at home," she says, "as early as possible. In the womb, if necessary. There's nothing wrong with a mother-to-be reading to her baby. . . . It should be a lifelong road that we travel."[8]

Education in Muncie's African American Community in the Past

When African Americans first began to move to Muncie, they had little opportunity to take part in formal education. The first school opened in Muncie in 1829, and the first free public school in 1855.[9] However, in 1831 and 1852, the state legislature added exclusion laws to the constitution to make it illegal for blacks to settle in Indiana, and they were prevented from attending public schools.[10] Records mention a few black families living in Delaware County.[11] But with these exclusion laws in place, there were probably no blacks in the newly-established schools until the laws were repealed in the 1860s.

In 1881, Delaware County historian Thomas Helms reported that thirty to forty African American children attended public school, four of whom were in high school. Mrs. Addie Knight, the first black to graduate from Muncie High School, gave a speech at the 1880 commencement that was "received by a sympathizing assembly with great applause."[12]

The first African American graduated from Muncie High School (pictured here, circa 1900) in 1880. Courtesy Archives and Special Collections, Ball State University.

Even though Knight's audience supported her speech, the Lynds reported that by the 1920s, "Negroes are allowed under protest in the schools."[13] The general feeling in Muncie was that the black children should not attend school. By this time, the city had opened fourteen elementary schools, Wilson Junior High, and Central High School. The black students attended schools according to their residence since schools in Muncie were never officially segregated, even though many venues for leisure prevented blacks from entering or provided separate spaces for blacks and whites.[14] While there was no official segregation in the schools, Frank and Evelyn Wilson shared a story with us about racial separation that their son experienced in school in about 1949 to 1950. The third graders were assigned names of other students for a Christmas gift exchange. "I asked my son, how did the teacher divide the names, and he said, 'She called us up to the desk,' so I don't know if she had a pile of white and a pile of black, or if it was just a coincidence . . . I got to talking to some of the other mothers, and I found out that this black had this name, and that black had that name, and there was white in there too, but I got concerned. I talked to another mother, and we went up to the school to check it out. At first we went to the principal and talked to him, and he called [the teacher] into the room. Of course she was really upset. We didn't raise any fuss. We said, 'We know that we've been in a segregated place.' We just didn't want our kids to face it so soon."[15]

Many black families had been sharecroppers, and child labor, especially during planting and harvest, was necessary for the families' survival. In industrial families as well as farming families, children during this time rarely had the opportunity to learn in a classroom setting.[16] There was no point to education for many people of color, even after they came to Muncie, as there was no opportunity here. "At that time," says one woman interviewed for the Black Middletown project, "colored people didn't educate their children to anything, [they] thought that was all they had, housework and washing."[17]

One woman, who described her education in the Muncie Community Schools to the interviewers of the Black Middletown Project, attended Jackson Elementary and Wilson Middle School before graduating from Central High School in 1936. She was frequently the only black student in her high school classes—the many students who dropped out did so mostly because they didn't want to go. But others quit school because of work and money.[18] Another participant in the Black Middletown Project, Dorothy Armstrong, regretted not finishing high school. She completed eleventh grade before quitting school to get married, while her brothers dropped out because they wanted to join the workforce.[19] The reasons mentioned in the Black Middletown tapes closely parallel the explanations the Lynds list for dropping out of school. They found that lack of interest was the chief reason cited by students and their families, but that lack of opportunity and financial problems were often underlying causes.[20]

For many older individuals, finishing high school was a great accomplishment. Oftentimes, boys received their first suits upon graduating, and girls their first fancy dress clothes.[21] "Getting a high school diploma meant to us what finishing college means to kids today," Hurley Goodall told us.[22]

The Significance of Higher Education

On Martin Luther King Jr. Day, January 20, 2003, the community held forums and informational sessions at Muncie Central High School. One was called "Careers: Planning the Future." Students sat in chairs lined up along the stepped terraces of the band room and listened to a local elementary principal give tips on identifying interests, goals, and sources of information about job and educational opportunities. "How many of you plan to go to college? Do any of you want to go into the military? The G.I. Bill is a good way to get money for college." All of the students present planned to attend higher education, and only one was going into the military to get it. "College isn't for everybody," the speaker reminded the students, but still this group of high schoolers planned to go.

For black Muncie students today, college is an important goal. But even before higher education was as common as it is today, some African Americans in the Muncie community were able to attend college.

"Even though my mother was a college graduate, none of my brothers or I got a chance to go to college," says Hurley Goodall. "We hope we've got our family to the point where their education is not complete until they at least have gotten their bachelor's degree. If they have that door opened, then they can determine for themselves what kind of life they want."[23]

Many were not able to go to college immediately after high school. But because higher education was so important in the community, some of our consultants attended college as nontraditional students. Delores Pryor introduced us to her husband's aunt, Fronia Stigler. Fronia worked at Head Start for nine years after taking various factory jobs as she raised her own three daughters and two nephews. She says, "My goal when I got out of high school was to go to college. . . . I always wanted to be a schoolteacher, since I was a child. But then my father . . . lost his sight the year that I finished school, so that made it impossible for me to go to college. At the time that I finished school in 1959, blacks couldn't get school loans to go to school, and my father wasn't able to work, and nobody was working but my mother, so I came out of school, got married, and got a job. I did two semesters at Ball State during the 1970s . . . but I didn't get to finish."[24]

Phyllis Bartleson went back to college as well. Her minister at Trinity United Methodist, Reverend J. C. Williams, was a prominent black leader in Muncie in the 1970s. "He was an outstanding proponent of education," she says. "We even had older people going to Ball State, a number of kids—black, white—their parents. We were encouraged, even if we weren't actively pursuing a specific degree—take a class!"[25]

Vivian Conley, a well-respected woman in the community for whom a branch of the Muncie Public Library is named, was also inspired by Reverend Williams to attend college. Phyllis and Vivian attended the same church. "Miss Vivian was . . . very instrumental in the

Nontraditional Students Association on campus," Phyllis remembers. "She was not only very active on the campus, she was also very active within our church."

Conley attended Ball State at the same time as her daughter and three of her grandsons. "She encouraged many of our church membership," Phyllis says, "as well as her other children and grandchildren who went to other churches to pursue higher education."[26]

The importance of higher education to the community continues. Shelia Williams, whose three children are currently attending college, business college, and graduate school, always stressed the value of formal education with her children. "We would always tell our kids, 'We know that you're going to go to school and do everything you're supposed to because you're going to be a teacher one day, and you're going to go to college.' And they just automatically believed that's what they were going to do. My oldest daughter was a Rhodes Scholar, so that tells you something!"

Most of the middle school and high school students to whom we talked want to go to college. In addition, many of these young adults are interested in careers that require advanced degrees. Many of them aim high—becoming lawyers and doctors are among their most popular oc-

Wilson Middle School students gather around Jayné Carey to spend the final hours of the school year flipping through her yearbook. Photo by Danny Gawlowski.

cupational goals. In our interview with five middle school students at Delores's house, her granddaughter Jayné Carey said, "I really want to be a doctor. My mom used to dress me up as a different [kind of] doctor every Halloween. My mom taught me if you really want to do it, just go for it."[27]

Migrating from Muncie

While our consultants generally felt encouraged that so many young people in the community want to attend college, they were also frustrated by the trend of youth moving away from Muncie permanently after they finish college. "It's a challenge everywhere," Dr. Sam Abram says. "Those jobs [factory and foundry] are not there anymore. If students aren't going to be flexible enough to fit into that, it's going to be difficult, not just to stay here, but to stay anywhere. It's not going to go away soon because communities don't have a way to really jumpstart new opportunities so that there will be jobs."[28]

As discussed in earlier chapters, this stress on education forces a paradox: education offers salvation and success, but it also compels many to move on to find professional jobs that require a new kind of mobility. "That's one of the most frustrating things—you work hard to educate your kids, and someone else gets the benefit from it," says Hurley, who is now suggesting new methods for Muncie. "Maybe our community can begin to open up and encourage our kids to stay here. I just recently talked to the superintendent of schools to see if we could consider a 'grow our own' program for the schools, where we identify students who, if they take the proper classes, we will see that they get a scholarship to Ball State. Then if you get the grades, there will be a job waiting for you after graduation."[29]

Although many black youths do indeed leave Muncie, many want to stay, college education or not. Jayné Carey, for example, says she wants to fulfill her dreams of becoming a doctor by opening a practice in Muncie. "It's probably the only place I *would* become a doctor," she says. "The reason why everybody wants to move out is because nobody's here. If you keep on moving, there's not *going* to be anybody here!"[30]

African American Staff in the
Muncie Community School System

Black teachers were not hired in Muncie schools until the 1950s. In 1954, with the opening of Longfellow Elementary in the Whitely neighborhood, Geraldine Evans Findley was the first black to be hired. Two years later, Robert Foster was the first black principal to be hired at West Longfellow Elementary, also in Whitely.[31]

Dr. Sam Abram, who moved to Muncie just before he started school as a child, majored in secondary education in social studies at Ball State because of a love of history learned from his high school teacher, Mr. Hiatt. He had wanted to teach at Central High School. But his future brother-in-law, also a teacher in the Muncie system, advised him to teach elementary school instead: "He said, 'You're not going to get a job here—you need to change your major. They don't hire colored . . . teachers in high school in Muncie.'" Dr. Sam Abram was hired at Longfellow just two weeks before school started in 1960, when another teacher transferred out of the school. He became a principal in 1966.

From 1970 to 1973, Dr. Sam Abram held the position of administrative assistant to the superintendent. At that time, Dr. Robert Freeman was the superintendent and had a strong influence on Dr. Abram's career. Dr. Abram says, "I attribute a lot of my success to his strong insistence that if you work for me, you will become the best, or you don't work for me. He had very high expectations of everyone around him. In fact, I hadn't been on the job very long before he came to me and he said, 'What are you going to be doing three years from now?' And I said, 'I don't know.' He said, 'Well, you need to find out. I can tell you right now [that] three years from now you won't be my administrative assistant. I've never kept an administrative assistant longer than three years. They're always doing something better, so you need to decide what you're going to do.'"

Dr. Freeman sent Dr. Sam Abram to Indiana University to apply to a doctoral program, but for family reasons, he decided not to attend. Instead, he was accepted in Ball State's program, and finished his Doctorate of Education in 1974. Dr. Abram says of his educational opportunities, "The Lord blessed me, and I was able to go. I've always found that when you're trying to do the right thing, there are good people who will come along and who will help you." With the support of Dr. Freeman, Dr. Abram's wife Millie, their three children Sherri, Judith, and Michael, several professors at the university, and many others, Dr. Abram became the first black superintendent of the Muncie Community School System in 1989.[32]

In 1972, Muncie Community Schools opened the first building to be named in honor of an African American, Washington Carver Elementary. By this time, there were a few more black teachers in the school system, but the black school board members didn't feel that there were enough. In 1974, the school board drew up a "Plan for Progress," giving hiring suggestions to make the schools more diverse. While 12 percent of the

17,230 students were nonwhite, only 4.5 percent of the 857 teachers were nonwhite at that time. The board recommended that by 1975, the system should have increased the number of nonwhite teaching staff to reflect the ratios of the student body. These individuals felt it was important to place nonwhite teachers in the schools "where a high percentage of non-whites attend, to meet the needs of identification, discipline, and educational benefits such teachers could provide for these students."[33]

Hurley, the city's first African American to be elected to the School Board, says that during his tenure on the board from 1970 to 1978, there was a "dramatic increase in the number of black teachers hired in the system. At one time, we had over forty in the Muncie school system. I don't think we're close to that now; I'd guess it's less than twenty."

"It still seems to be a problem, however, with teachers of color, and retaining those teachers," says Phyllis about Muncie's schools. "They've made some strides, but I don't think they're quite there yet. I think that within the last few years, they've become more receptive to inclusiveness than they have been in the past, which is encouraging for not only members of the black community, but also for the community at large."

Julius Anderson explained the significance of having African American teachers in our schools. "Kids need to have role models in

Southside High School Associate Principal Mike Gorin answers the phone in his office as a student waits. Gorin, on the edge of retirement, is currently the only black male on the high school staff. Photo by Danny Gawlowski.

their life and that's why it's important to have Afro-American teachers in our schools."[34]

"We Have a Very Rich Heritage"

"Now who is Langston Hughes? Tell Daddy about him," a man said to his daughter as they walked out of the Boys and Girls Club one evening. Information regarding black history and culture was not always covered adequately by the mainstream education and media.

"It's important to know who you are and where you've been, as a race, as a heritage," says Rhonda Ward, a native of Muncie who is currently the site director of the CAPE Learning Center at Garfield Elementary. "It's important to be able to know that we have done so many wonderful things, and people have worked so hard to get us to where we are. Because I truly believe that if it hadn't been for some of those people, I don't know where our race would be. It gives you a sense of pride, too—you feel good knowing that our people have done all these wonderful things."[35]

For some of our consultants, black history and culture were not taught in the schools at all. Julius introduced us to Frank and Evelyn Wilson, who operate a local business selling flags. Frank and Evelyn Wilson have been married for sixty-two years. Evelyn began school at Blaine Elementary in 1925. "One thing we didn't get was any black history," she says. "I didn't know too much about black people until I went to Central—I started reading, I went to the library and got books on black people. . . . Even though I didn't have it in school, I sought it out. I just read anything black I could read."[36]

Some of our consultants found that students in the South learned more about black history and culture than children in Muncie did. When Fredine moved to Muncie from Montgomery, Alabama, she taught Hurley many aspects of black culture. "I didn't know anything about Emancipation Day, or about the Black National Anthem, I was never taught anything like that. But she was, when she went to school in Montgomery," Hurley said.[37]

During her school years, Fronia Stigler moved back and forth between Muncie and Mississippi a few times, graduating from high school in Mississippi in 1959. "In the South, we had Black History Month, and it's really [more] highly emphasized in the South than in the North," she says. "Now at the time that I went to school, schools were not integrated. I went to an all-black school and had all black teachers. We were taught black history all the time, and we had a week, a whole week, when we had important people come in, and we had programs . . . and a lot of speeches. I don't remember them ever having anything when I was going to school in the '50s here."[38]

Phyllis Bartleson shared a similar experience with us. "George Washington Carver, Booker T. Washington, and there was one more— I can't even remember the third one. But I thought, as a child growing up and going through the school system, that these were the only two African Americans who had done something in the history of this country." Phyllis felt that the classes and lectures organized by Reverend Williams at Trinity during the 1970s were the basis of her knowledge about black history and culture. "I learned more about my history as an African American than I had ever learned in all those years in a classroom—about the outstanding African Americans in science and medicine, and inventors, and other kinds of achievers."[39]

Fronia says that the curriculum was a little altered by the time her daughters were in school, however. "I'll tell you when Muncie began to change. It was after Martin Luther King Jr. . . . and the Civil Rights Movement. Things are much better here than they used to be."[40]

Even though the curriculum had changed, some families still felt their children didn't receive education about black history and culture in school. The Stiglers and many other parents took pains to supplement their children's education. "I bought black history books that they could read about the people of the past," says Fronia, "and I've always had black papers delivered so they could know what the black people were doing because very seldom was anything in the regular paper."[41] Hurley recalls a similar situation: "We always took magazines like *Ebony* and *Jet*, and we bought a nice set of encyclopedias put out by *Ebony*."[42]

African American History in the Schools

That training the young includes information regarding black history and culture has proved to be an important theme with our community advisors, whether the children are taught it at school or at home. "As African Americans . . . we have a responsibility to teach our history," Phyllis says. "We have ancestors, and we come from a very *rich* heritage, and we can trace that heritage all the way back to the beginning of time."[43]

With this in mind, schools today seem to make more of an effort to pay special attention to the contributions of black individuals to general history and culture. The schools and community plan special events to celebrate Black History Month. We attended one of these at Wilson Middle School on February 20, 2003. This event included performances of several spirituals, one original step routine, and an original poem, as well as a fashion show and an awards show featuring prominent African American figures such as Harriet Tubman, Billie Holiday, Wilma Rudolph, Jesse Owens, Martin Luther King Jr., and Maya Angelou, among others. We watched the performance with the seventh graders, but all of the students were required to attend the program to raise their awareness of black history and culture.

Other efforts are made by administrators and teachers to get more diversity into the classroom. We asked Shelia Williams if she was able to incorporate information about black culture into her classes. Since she teaches health and physical education, we imagined that diversity education might be more difficult than in an English or history class. But Shelia disagreed, saying, "I bring in videos about the dances of different cultures all the time. I had a drill team come in once and do a step routine for the class. I make sure the students realize how important the different cultures are to all of us."[44]

As the director of the Muncie Human Rights Commission, Phyllis worked on a committee that reviewed new textbooks for the Muncie Community School Corporation. "We were trying to . . . incorporate people of color into the classrooms via the textbook. It may have been a math book, for example—if there are pictures, are there children of color depicted? Are there examples that depict people of color in the written text?"[45]

"My math book is inclusive of different cultures," says Jasmine Taylor, a Wilson Middle School student introduced to us by Delores. "It has a box on every page with a picture, and it may mention the first black woman to do a certain thing. But the teachers don't talk about it; we have to find it out for ourselves. I have an English teacher who says she incorporates stories by blacks into what we learn, but I haven't seen it. I remember one story last week, but that's during Black History Month. She never mentions it any other time."

"We always watch that same slavery movie every year," says Catrice Marks, another Wilson student and a friend of Jasmine's, "but [the teachers] never talk about [black history] in class."

"Yeah, and we watch that sharecropper movie," Jasmine adds.[46]

In our conversations with community members, we found that people feel that the schools limit the teaching of African American history to the month of February, separating it from mainstream history. Along with African American history, Jasmine and Jayné feel that

Jasmine Taylor performs with SWEAT (Steppers with Energy, Attitude, and Talent) during a Talent Show at Wilson Middle School. Photo by Danny Gawlowski.

Latino American and Native American history is also missing from the curriculum and should be taught.[47]

"We make history all the time, but we only hear about it during Black History Month, and in the school [Wilson Middle School], we only get a week!" says Shelia Williams, a teacher at Wilson, discussing the segregation of history in the curriculum.[48]

Belinda Anderson, Julius's wife, discussed why black history needs to be taught more in schools. "We live like this every day, so it should be an everyday thing that is taught," she says. "I mean I know that teachers will not be able to hit every culture every day, but take out some time and touch on everybody. Because everyone has done something, not just the white race. That's history." Julius added, "If you don't know where you come from, you'll never know where you are going!"[49]

Values Instilled:
"Respect Is Something That You Have to Earn"

As our consultants spoke about the education their children received, they also talked about important values that the young should learn.

Values such as self-respect, respect for others, manners and politeness, effective communication, and work ethic were themes around which many conversations and events revolved.

"I have respect for myself, and for other people," says Kellie Woods, senior at Southside High School and Belinda Anderson's niece. "[My self-esteem] probably has gone up higher [as I've grown up]. I've learned from my mistakes, and I've seen other people slip away, and it makes you want to strive to be better."[50]

"One thing I always insisted on—and I still do—is respect," says Fredine Goodall. "If they don't have any respect for themselves or for anyone else, I just can't take that!"[51] Shelia Williams agrees: "I think one of the basic things that we've been getting away from—because we've been so conscious of making them learn what they should learn out of the books—and that's respect. You tell the kids respect is something that you have to earn—you don't really *learn* it."[52]

"I teach a lot of manners," Shelia continues, "because kids can be running down the hall and knock somebody's books off, and they just bust out laughing and walk off. They think it's funny. I cover that a lot in my health class, especially when we're covering self-esteem. It doesn't take anything from you to say thank you or to say 'I'm sorry, excuse me.'"[53]

Fronia agrees that these are critical points for parents to teach their children: "Teach them to love themselves, and to always try to see some good in everyone, not to be critical." When Fronia worked with the young children in Head Start and at Huffer Nursery in Muncie, she taught them "how to sit, and how to get along with each other . . . and good English, teach them words—most of the things you're teaching are manners, and how to communicate with each other, how to follow rules."[54]

Respect is closely tied to the ability to communicate effectively, as well as politely. "There are certain skills every child should have," says Dr. Sam Abram. "One of the courses we told to each of our children that they had to take was speech. . . . It's important that you learn how to present information, how to debate, and how to defend yourself verbally, not physically."[55]

The middle school students who we talked to shared the opinion that learning how to interact with others was an important part of being raised. "If somebody hits you, hit them back," says Catrice. "But if it's just a name, ignore it."[56] Fronia echoes these sentiments. "You treat people right, and you do what's right. I didn't allow my girls to fight unless somebody hit them. . . . A name doesn't hurt you, as long as you know you're not what you [were] called. Now if somebody hits you, that's a different story. The only thing that hurts is a lick. If anybody calls me a dog, I know I'm not a dog, so it doesn't bother me."[57]

By learning values like respect, manners, and communication, parents and teachers train children for their futures. In order to be successful, children must know appropriate ways to act and interact with other people. Without these lessons being taught, individuals would have no way of communicating to potential employers in an interview, to coworkers, or to society in general.

Many of our consultants believe that these values are ultimately important to developing responsibility and a solid work ethic. Julius introduced us to Q. L. and Willa Mae Stevens, who have been married for fifty-three years. Q. L. is from Paducah, Kentucky, and Willa Mae was born in Richmond, Indiana. They decided to move to Muncie for the job opportunities, and raised their family here. Q. L. told us a story about his children's involvement in the family business, Q. L.'s Barbecue, that reveals something important about the value of work to this community. "When they were little, nine and ten, they loved working there! But when they got to be teenagers, my son said, 'Dad, this is too much work, I don't want no part of it, don't be trying to fix it up for

B. J. Crumes, grandson of Q. L. Stevens, returned to Muncie to become the cook for his grandfather's barbeque business. Photo by Danny Gawlowski.

me.' He was honest, and I loved him for that. When he got old enough where . . . he could get other jobs, I didn't try to stop him because my parents didn't do us that way, they didn't try to stop us as long as we were trying to help ourselves."[58] For Q. L., it mattered more that his son was working than that his son was working for him.

With values such as respect, manners, communication, and the work ethic once being taught in the homes, children grew up with a good foundation. Schools used to reinforce values that were taught at home. But as the way to bring up families has changed over time, these values are not as prevalent. Hurley feels that this puts the schools in a bad situation. People are frustrated with the learning environment that must focus on discipline instead of on education because the children don't have stability at home. "If the parent was more structured, that child will be a structured person," Delores Pryor says.[59] "Respect, love, and many other values, gave them a strong foundation at home," Julius Anderson says. "But kids nowadays never respect their parents, and when they have kids, they expect the teachers to teach their children these values. We've got to meet the teacher half way." Belinda adds, "It's not just the school's responsibility, it's ours."[60]

If children are not trained to uphold these values in their home life, they need to learn them at school. "A lot of times," Shelia Williams says, "if you don't really stop them and bring it to their attention, and they don't get it at home, they won't learn it. They'll think it's okay to bump into you and not say I'm sorry, or not say thank you, or just blurt in on somebody's conversation without saying excuse me."[61]

"I think it's critical," says Phyllis Bartleson. "There needs to be a separate class that focuses just on being a good worker and being a productive member of society . . . being to work on time, how you conduct yourself, and how you approach people, how you interact with co-workers."[62] If children are not taught to value a good work ethic, they will not be successful in life. They must know how to work in order to develop careers.

Rhonda Ward incorporates values such as the work ethic, self-respect and respect for others, manners, and effective communication into her Seven Daily Goals, which her Community Learning Center students recite each day. We will try our very best; we will believe in ourselves; we will be responsible; we will respect differences in others; we will work together; we will help each other; we will be proud of our Garfield Community Learning Center. These values were strong in Rhonda's own upbringing. While growing up, Rhonda's parents kept her and her siblings on a strict schedule. After school and sports practices, they ate dinner, did their homework, and then completed their chores before going to bed. "We came up in a strict environment, but my parents gave us freedom to do things," Rhonda says. "I look at the way kids are these days, and I think, 'We could not do that.'"[63] Nowadays lessons may no longer be learned at home, she feels that it is important to teach children to follow these goals.

"As times are changing, kids just aren't respecting their adults anymore. Parents, they don't care! Those family values aren't there anymore" says Brenton, son of Julius and Belinda Anderson. Kellie Woods agrees, "From my perspective, having positive role models in people's lives has changed. Children are raising children, so there's another generation coming in."[64] Even though values in Muncie's community are changing, they remain important to training a child. "They help mold and shape you," Belinda says. "You become a better person when you do have values; without them you have no direction."[65]

Teachers, Parents, and Children

"Parents, family, schools, churches, relatives, and community should all work together," says Dr. Sam Abram, "to help young people at an early age become students." Dr. Abram's comments articulate what many in the black community said when we asked "what does it take to 'train the young'?" Education, discipline, respect, love, and overall positive attitudes were principles that came up repeatedly. Having a positive attitude helps develop effective communication lines between the parents, teachers, and, most importantly, students. Fronia Stigler states, "It is very important that schools offer programs for parents and kids. It helps the child to be aware that their parents are interested, and children will not get into trouble when they find out that the parents know the teacher. It just makes it better for communicating."[66] Having a positive relationship between the parent and the teacher is healthy for the student.

When interviewing our older consultants about raising their own children, many spoke of positive parent–teacher relationships, especially between black students and white teachers. This surprised us because it was at the time when racism, discrimination, and prejudice were at their peak. Q. L. Stevens, for example, who is a father of three, remembered that when he and Willa Mae were raising their children, "the communication between the principal, teacher, students, and parents was great. Everyone got along."[67]

Q. L. and Willa Mae Stevens. Photo by Danny Gawlowski.

Q. L. also shared with us that "on many occasions where a child had a problem with the teacher, he or she would go home and tell their parents, and without any conference with that teacher, the parent would go to the school and confront the teacher, in front of the class, just off of their child's words." Q. L. found this approach suspect: "I feel that parents who jump on their child's teacher are teaching the students the wrong lesson. Parents are showing the student that 'anytime you do anything right or wrong I am going to come up to your school and cuss your teacher out in front of you.' This shows the child how to be a bully."[68] Parents and teachers, Q. L. suggested, must come to an understanding with one another. Not everyone will agree how to handle each particular problem, but if both parties come together with positive attitudes and on their best behaviors, then something should be accomplished, and that is the main goal.

After much discussion about what it takes to have a positive relationship with parents and teachers, we began to explore what makes a good relationship between students and teachers. In addition to values (respect, for example), it also takes open ears and minds to have a positive relationship with students and teachers.

Shelia Williams offered examples from her own experience: "to make a difference, [you] have to know the kids' backgrounds. The kids of one-parent homes may be the parent for younger brothers and sisters [and they] are angry when they arrive at school [because of home problems.]"[69] As Shelia says, you have to be able to listen and try to understand what is sometimes going on at home, and maybe be willing to lend a helping hand. That is what it takes to have a positive relationship.

"[You] can't take things personally," Shelia continues, "[you] have to respect people who were raised differently from how you raised your own kids. Set standards high from the beginning—ask what they expect from themselves, from the class, what their goals are. Kids may think you're mean, but [you are only] preparing them for the real world."[70]

We saw this sentiment in action one afternoon when Shelia Williams took us on a tour of her school. A child stood alone in the hallway, clearly for some disciplinary reason. She stopped and approached him. In a calm, caring voice she asked, "Why are you in the hallway?" He had been talking in class, he said. Shelia went on to say, "You know that what you were doing was wrong."

"Yes," he answered.

"So what have you learned from this experience?"

"Not to let it happen again."

We were impressed with her kindness, and the gentle way she treated the boy. As we walked away Shelia told us that "children have to know what they did wrong without it being yelled to them."[71]

Teachers do make powerful impressions on students. Dr. Sam Abram remembers one of his teachers. "I had a teacher that turned me on to thinking that learning was fun and important; his name was Mr. Roland J. Dygert," he says. "I learned so many things from him. My first goal of what I wanted to be came from Mr. Dygert."[72] Dr. Abram feels that getting to know one another is the key to positive relationships between teachers and students. "Another important thing," he says, "about students, learning, and training the students, is for them to have adults around that they can get to know, and [when] the adults get to know them, they will become comfortable with the learning environment."[73]

Yet teachers can create both positive and negative environments. Some teachers in the past apparently felt that they did not need to educate the black students, because they were just too dumb to learn. Fronia Stigler, for example, shared an experience she had in school. "My seventh grade science teacher," she remembers, "really didn't like black people, [he] would give me Fs no matter what I did."[74] But this experience didn't discourage Fronia: "Blacks have to prepare their children to look for prejudice without teaching hate. Hate only hurts you, not the person you hate."[75]

Frank Wilson remembers a similar story. His son's guidance counselor "told him that he would not be able to make it in college like Purdue," Evelyn adds, "She told him that his parents couldn't afford it. . . . But the funny thing was, he was in the top ten of his class. He was in the National Honor Society. It just made us more determined." In spite of the counselor's advice, Wilson's son went on to Purdue and graduated in the top of his class with an Aeronautical Engineering degree, and went on to higher education in the medical field. "Ever since he was a kid, he was interested in airplanes," Frank says. "When he got ready to go [to college], he asked me, and we had scrimped so much to get him there, 'What can I take to earn the most money?' . . . I said, 'Well, aeronautical engineering would pay you the most.' He said, 'That's what I'm going for.'"[76]

Here They Feel Youth Are Important

On Thursday, February 27, 2003, we returned to Garfield Elementary. In just three weeks, the amount of sunlight at 6 P.M. had changed so much that we felt like we were in a different place. Or maybe we had changed. We felt comfortable now, showing up at events as outsiders and talking to strangers, trying to find out the stories that belonged to these people and places.

Once again, the first door we tried was locked, but without too much difficulty, we made our way inside and to the cafeteria. For the Black History Celebration of the Garfield Community Learning Center (part of the Community Alliance to Promote Education of Delaware County), the tan accordion-style partitions divided the room, but stood open in the center. We saw a few women in long dresses, visible on the other side of the panel, pouring fruit punch and setting out cookies for the reception after the program. Parents, grandparents, and other family members sat at the low, purple tables, waiting for the program to begin. At the front of the cafeteria, where the bingo prize tables had been a few weeks ago, two rows of chairs stood.

We shared a table at the back of the room with the assistant principal and a third-grade teacher, sitting near a bulletin board featuring a giant hot air balloon. These women recognized us from Family Night, remembered a little about *The Other Side of Middletown* project, and were very interested in how everything was going. Dr. Sam Abram spotted us from across the room and came over to thank us for coming.

After a few minutes, the program got underway. Fourteen children filed into the room and took the seats at the front. Rhonda Ward, the site director for the Garfield Community Learning Center, welcomed the audience and introduced each item on the evening's agenda. After reciting a poem in unison about Carter G. Woodson founding Black History Month, the children took turns presenting brief biographical speeches about some prominent figures in black history like Martin Luther King Jr., Sojourner Truth, and Frederick Douglass. Finally, the children sang a song. "Remember, the girls sing the first phrase, and the boys go second," Rhonda told the students just before they began.

> Sing about Martin
> (Sing about Martin)
> Sing about caring
> (Sing about caring)
> Sing about peace, all around the world.

While singing, the children used sign language symbols for some of the lyrics. This song seemed to us to represent the connection between community and training the young. Throughout our interviews and events, we noticed the importance of family to education—this was evident here as well: "Let's give our parents a hand for all their support," Rhonda said in her closing remarks for the Black History Celebration, just after Dr. Abram stressed the importance of the parents and the community becoming involved in the time students invest in school and in CAPE.

All of the themes we had identified from our conversations with consultants were apparent in this event sponsored by the Garfield Community Learning Center. Simply by being involved in CAPE, these students and their families demonstrated that formal education was important to them. The Black History Celebration represented the interest in increasing children's knowledge of their African American cultural heritage. Throughout the program, the children behaved well, followed directions, and were respectful as the others gave their speeches. Rhonda told the parents that the students were working on thank you notes to send to a guest speaker, showing us how the community concerns itself with training the young to have proper manners.

"You're not doing anyone a favor by not educating them," Vivian Conley warned the community of the burden they would have to face by only preparing a nucleus of individuals to join the workforce. "The mainstream will have to pay for those who are left behind."[77]

Training the young remains a key issue in Muncie's African American community.

Still, things have changed significantly since Muncie hired its first black teacher in the 1950s. Some of our younger consultants, for example, feel quite encouraged about their education and the future of Muncie. Indeed, throughout our experiences in this project, we noticed that Muncie has numerous programs that encourage education, promote self-respect, and support family ties. "When it comes to education," Phyllis Bartleson says, "it basically has to be a community encouragement that begins in the home and extends to the neighborhood and our extended families, like church families . . . to encourage our young people to do well in school, to be prepared."[78]

Jasmine Taylor, a student, praised Muncie's support of its youth: "I'm glad we have a community that likes us. Here they feel youth are important. They're willing to help us do what we want to do as long as it's good."[79]

Notes

1. Robert S. Lynd and Helen Merrell Lynd, *Middletown: A Study in Contemporary Culture* (New York: Harcourt Brace & Company, 1929), ix.

2. Shelia Williams, conversation with Carla Burke and Carrie Kissel, February 14, 2003.

3. Dennis M. Rutledge and Vivian M. Gordon, interview with G46. (Archives and Special Collections, Ball State University Libraries [Hereinafter cited BSU: ASC], Black Middletown Surveys, 1979–1982, Mss. 345, Box 2, Folder 10), 4.

4. Lynd and Lynd, *Middletown*, 187.

5. Phyllis Bartleson, conversation with Carla Burke and Carrie Kissel, February 21, 2003.

6. Sam Abram, conversation with Carla Burke and Carrie Kissel, February 21, 2003.

7. Ibid.

8. Phyllis Bartleson, conversation with Carla Burke and Carrie Kissel, February 27, 2003.

9. *Muncie Morning Star*, "Early Schools Held in Cabins," September 16, 1938 (BSU: ASC, Stoeckel Archives, Local History Subject Files, Box 21).

10. Hurley Goodall and J. Paul Mitchell, *African Americans in Muncie, 1890–1960* (Muncie, Ind.: Ball State University, 1976), 1.

11. Goodall and Mitchell, *African Americans in Muncie*, 1–2.

12. Thomas B. Helms, *History of Delaware County* (1881), in Goodall and Mitchell, *African Americans in Muncie*, 3–4.

13. Lynd and Lynd, *Middletown*, 480.

14. Goodall and Mitchell, "History of Public Education in Muncie, Indiana, 1850 to 1990," Table 1.6, 10–12.

15. Frank and Evelyn Wilson, conversation with Carla Burke, February 7, 2003.

16. Hurley Goodall, personal documents.

17. Rutledge and Gordon, Interview with D143, Side 1, 1st Session, Starks.

18. Ibid., interview with A165, 2–3.

19. Ibid., interview with C146, 1–2.

20. Lynd and Lynd, *Middletown*, 184–86.

21. Hurley Goodall, personal documents.

22. Hurley Goodall, class discussion, January 13, 2003.

23. Hurley Goodall, conversation with Carla Burke and Carrie Kissel, February 19, 2003.

24. Fronia Stigler, conversation with Carrie Kissel, February 12, 2003.

25. Ibid.

26. Phyllis Bartleson conversation, February 27, 2003.

27. Jayné Carey, conversation with Carla Burke and Carrie Kissel, February 26, 2003.

28. Sam Abram conversation, February 21, 2003.

29. Hurley Goodall, conversation with Carla Burke and Carrie Kissel, February 19, 2003.

30. Jayné Carey, conversation with Carla Burke and Carrie Kissel, February 26, 2003.

31. Hurley Goodall, personal documents.

32. Sam Abram conversation, February 21, 2003; Sam Abram, conversation with Anne Kraemer, Michelle Anderson, and Ashley Moore, February 12, 2003.

33. "A Plan for Progress," (BSU: ASC, Stoeckel Archives, Hurley Goodall Papers, Mss. 90, Box 2, Folder 15), 2–4.

34. Julius Anderson, conversation with Carla Burke and Carrie Kissel, March 23, 2003.

35. Rhonda Ward, conversation with Carla Burke and Carrie Kissel, March 6, 2003.

36. Evelyn Wilson, conversation with Carla Burke, February 7, 2003.

37. Hurley Goodall conversation, February 19, 2003.

38. Fronia Stigler, conversation with Carrie Kissel, February 12, 2003.

39. Phyllis Bartleson conversation, February 27, 2003.

40. Fronia Stigler conversation, February 12, 2003.

41. Ibid.

42. Hurley Goodall conversation, February 19, 2003.

43. Phyllis Bartleson conversation, February 27, 2003.

44. Shelia Williams, conversation with Carla Burke and Carrie Kissel, February 14, 2003.

45. Phyllis Bartleson conversation, February 27, 2003.

46. Jasmine Taylor and Catrice Marks, conversation with Carla Burke and Carrie Kissel, February 26, 2003.

47. Jasmine Taylor and Jayné Carey, conversation with Carla Burke and Carrie Kissel, February 26, 2003.

48. Shelia Williams conversation, February 14, 2003.

49. Julius and Belinda Anderson, conversation with Carla Burke and Carrie Kissel, March 23, 2003.

50. Kellie Woods, conversation with Carla Burke and Carrie Kissel, March 26, 2003.

51. Fredine Goodall, conversation with Carla Burke and Carrie Kissel, February 19, 2003.

52. Shelia Williams conversation, February 14, 2003.

53. Ibid.

54. Fronia Stigler conversation, February 12, 2003.

55. Sam Abram conversation, February 21, 2003.

56. Catrice Marks, conversation with Carla Burke and Carrie Kissel, February 26, 2003.

57. Fronia Stigler conversation, February 12, 2003.

58. Q. L. Stevens, conversation with Carla Burke and Carrie Kissel, February 10, 2003.

59. Delores Pryor, conversation with Carla Burke and Carrie Kissel, January 22, 2003.

60. Julius and Belinda Anderson conversation, March 23, 2003.

61. Shelia Williams conversation, February 14, 2003.

62. Phyllis Bartleson conversation, February 27, 2003.

63. Rhonda Ward conversation, March 6, 2003.

64. Brenton Anderson and Kellie Woods, conversation with Carla Burke and Carrie Kissel, March 26, 2003.

65. Belinda Anderson, conversation with Carla Burke and Carrie Kissel, March 23, 2003.

66. Ibid.

67. Q. L. Stevens conversation, February 10, 2003.

68. Ibid.

69. Shelia Williams conversation, February 14, 2003.

70. Ibid.

71. Ibid.

72. Sam Abram conversation, February 21, 2003.

73. Ibid.

74. Fronia Stigler conversation, February 12, 2003.

75. Ibid.

76. Frank and Evelyn Wilson, conversation with Carla Burke, February 7, 2003.

77. *Conversation with Vivian Conley, Spoken from the Heart*, 1994 (V22), BSU: ASC.

78. Phyllis Bartleson conversation, February 27, 2003.

79. Jasmine Taylor, conversation with Carla Burke and Carrie Kissel, February 26, 2003.

6

Using Leisure

Sarah Bricker and Mia Fields

"Honey, we had our own little way of life!"[1]

Geraldine Burns, a retired government employee, is talking about the Whitely community where she was raised. "Back then, if one of us got to acting up, and didn't do right, we were liable to get a whipping from anyone [of the adults]." She chuckles heartily as she recalls walking home from Longfellow School: "They kept you straight, I tell you! If anyone was fighting or doing something they didn't have any business doing, your momma would sure find out about it, and you're liable to get another one [whipping] when you get home!"[2]

Geraldine, a gracious host, welcomes us into her home. Her hospitality comes from years of experience. She gives us glasses of her delicious lemonade—it has since become a class favorite. Sitting around the dining table, draped with the kind of mint green lace cloth you might expect for Sunday dinner, we chat while munching on banana bread and fruit cocktail. She tells how much she enjoys it when we come over to socialize with her and Fredine Goodall.[3]

Geraldine valued the close-knit community she had "coming up," she says with sparkling eyes, reminiscent of an innocent child. She looks behind her for something; it is as if she is looking back for something in her memory, something in her past. Finally, she locates a simple picture on the wall. She hops up with enthusiasm, and goes to it and stares at it for a while before bringing it back to the table; she smiles with pride as she shows it to us. It's a picture of four simply-sketched houses and a floating phrase that reads "A small town is like a big family."[4]

"My house was just like Grand Central Station," says Geraldine. "Grown men, they always say, 'Ms. Geraldine do you remember me?'

and I say 'Who's your mother? Who's your father?' you know, so I can go back and relate." She leans forward, pulling us in, imitating the men, "'Oh, I used to come on your porch and sit all the time.' Everybody came and sat on my porch, my house was just like Grand Central Station really." She turns toward the window, "That porch right there."[5]

Heading toward the kitchen to refill our lemonades, she continues: "My mother said that I wore out two living room suits and two record players or phonographs. . . ."[6] Geraldine is proud of this. She models her hospitality on her mother's. When she was "coming up," her parents welcomed her childhood friends to the house on summer nights.

Summer brings extended hours of freedom for schoolkids and Geraldine remembers hot Midwest summer nights, asking neighborhood girlfriends to, "C'mon over and sleep on my porch tonight!" After dinner, two or three girls would gather on her porch, ready to giggle and gossip. As the sun went down, the scarce street lamps that marked every other corner created spooky shadows. "I remember Mary Belle Johnson would tell the best ghost stories! She was good. Anything would scare us. . . . We would get our pallets all made up on the porch—they were like sleeping bags, but not with all the zippers and stuff. It was a neighborhood thing on the 1800 block of Hines."[7]

Mary Belle Johnson's son, Eric Johnson, explains to us that his mother and Geraldine are the "best of friends."[8] Eric has lived in Muncie over the past year to help care for his mother. Though he grew up in Muncie, he worked his way through Highland Park Community College in Detroit, then Michigan State University. His education settled him in Indianapolis for over twenty-five years. He presently works for the Marion County Division of Family and Children Services, but commutes back and forth from Muncie every day.

Eric's childhood memories of his grandfather telling "haint stories" on the porch suggest that his mother may have picked up this skill from her father. "We would sit on the porch for hours," he says.[9] "My grandfather would tell ghost stories. All the kids would come around and sit on the porch and he'd tell ghost stories. All the younger kids would get really scared, and my grandfather would just laugh. Sometimes my grandmother would get on him about scaring us so bad with his ghost stories about how he grew up in Kentucky. And he would tell us story after story about ghosts and 'haints.' People from the South . . . called them 'haint stories'." We ask him what "haint" means. "It's derived from the word 'haunted.' If you ever hear someone speak of a 'haint' you know he's probably from the South. . . . I can remember that my grandfather said that as a boy coming across the field, he went to the well to get some water or something, and he was going back up to his house, and he said this 'haint' was standing in the doorway like this (Eric spans out his arms), and he ran back out, dropped all of his water, and then he got a whipping when he got home because he lost all of his water! He said he didn't care because he was running from this ghost or 'haint'!"[10]

We began to inquire more about the ghost stories and haint stories. When they told these stories with such nostalgia, we could almost see ourselves as kids, anticipating and hoping to be frightened.

Renzie Abram was thrilled to tell us about a man he knew named Elder Hosea Barnes who told the story of "Black Annie" one day during a church service. Elder Barnes also spoke of "Bloody Bones" and "Blue Eyes." Renzie couldn't remember most of them, but "Black Annie" stood out in his mind. As Renzie dug into his memory, he recalled Elder Barnes telling the congregation about the trees that hung low on Willard Street. They would summon "Black Annie" to come and get you if you didn't run fast enough.[11]

Our classmates and professors got a kick out of the story when we told them about it the next day. We were all taken back to our childhood

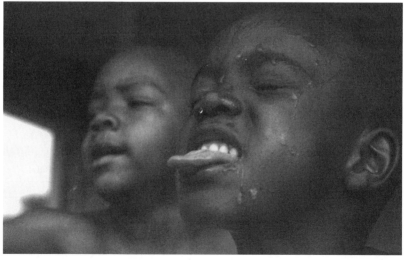

Playing on the porch of their home, Tuvanne Burtley reaches out to feel the drops of rainwater falling from his gutter as Javaris Dett tries to catch a few droplets on his tongue. Photo by Danny Gawlowski.

days wondering, "What *is* the full story of 'Black Annie'? What did she do?" As conversation stirred in the classroom about "Black Annie," we seemed to be like kids again, drawn in, saying "ooh, what happens next!?" The next time we had a chance to talk to Renzie, we asked him if he could get in contact with Elder Barnes to help jog his memory about "Black Annie." We were hungry for the meat of the story.

At a dinner meeting with the community advisors one evening, the spooky story of "Black Annie" crept into conversation once again. Renzie started out telling the group that he had spoken with Elder Barnes recently, and got the "Black Annie" tale straight. The mention of "Black Annie" caused a frenzy in the room. Everyone blurted out his or her own unique recollection of "Black Annie." One person said that it was a story told by parents to encourage kids to come in before dark. Renzie told of how Elder Barnes remembered him and the neighborhood kids walking from Kirby Street. Then to First Street. Next, to Second Street. Finally, to Willard . . . where it all happened. The trees would hover over the street, closing in on the children who had yet to make curfew. They would take their time walking through the other streets, the fear of Willard growing as they got closer. Renzie reported "then they would *really* run when they hit Willard." The story goes that once you've hit Willard, if you're not already running "you're going too slow and Black Annie will come out of the trees and get you!" Even as the group's attention was fixed on Renzie telling the story, many couldn't help but murmur their own rendition to the person next to them. Someone called out "What did you imagine this Black Annie to look like?" Everyone seemed to be baffled by this question. Commotion began to die down, except for one woman who candidly stated "Oooh, I don't think *anybody* ever seen her," rousing laughter again.

Learning about Leisure

By midsemester of the project, as we trudged through tedious nights of writing, Eric Johnson had secured a place in the community for us so we wouldn't lose contact with our consultants. He drew us into people's lives, and ensured that our interpretation of their stories would not venture far from the people we had met. Cleverly, he had invented a Sunday afternoon social hour—or *hours*, as conversations tend to carry on. After worship at Shaffer Chapel, he invited people to stay and socialize. Our responsibility to Eric deepened through these dialogues.

We found ourselves seated in the red-cushioned church pews of Shaffer talking with Eric, the Jones family, Viola Boyd, and Ralph

Vaughn, all members of Shaffer Chapel. Eric and his brother Ralph, lounging in front of us, leaned into the back of their pew. As though in the passenger's seat of a car, they tried to get in on the backseat conversation, taking the lead at times, and other times listening. Robert and Denise Jones had ushered the service that Sunday, and sat in the pew behind us with their son, Robbie. Viola took a seat two pews back and came in and out of the conversation. The pews did not separate us, but rather each person's story led into the next—voices filling the sanctuary to replace the songs of praise from the previous hour.

"Freestyle barbecues," as Ralph puts it, "that's the backyard barbecue . . . it's whatever happens, happens." Robert says, "You'd be surprised. You set a grill up and a cooler and the next thing you know you got a crowd. And if it's the right people, it can turn into, 'man what's going on, there's a party out there,' and the next thing you know. . . ." Conversation about backyard cookouts led to stories about basketball in the parks, movies, shopping downtown. Convinced of the importance of cookouts, we ask Robert to recall one, the time and place. He responds, "Where I live now. . . . I got a nice backyard, and if I set out a grill and put some music out, eventually, somebody will come by. They'll see me out there, and I know a lot of people and they'll stop." Ralph laughs, nodding, "It works every time."[12]

"And somebody will see *their* car," Denise says before Robert continues, "and they'll stop. And if I stay out there from say, the middle of the afternoon until evening—by the time the sun starts to set I'll have a crowd. And I might not be grilling anything but hot dogs. But it's just the *idea* of people getting together and, you know, just having a good time."[13]

We ask about the time frame, about how much time you need for a barbecue. It depends on what you want to cook, they say. Hot dogs aren't a big deal, but with "all these excellent chefs around here," Robert says, "if you want to do the ribs right, you have to start early. Actually you have to start the night before." It's going on three o'clock. We started talking at 1:30 after church, and now we are all getting hungry.

"Yeah, because sometimes you have to—what do you call it?" Robert asks.

Mia answers, with a little laugh, "Marinate."

Robert nods his head and assures us. "And if someone knows you have some barbecued ribs, I guarantee you'll have a crowd."

Eric jumps in. Not heard the first time, he tries again: "The aroma . . . it kind of pulls you in. See, everybody knows each other. It's no problem about barging in on anybody. You've known this person all your life. It's no big deal about just stopping by."[14]

As we listen, we're reminded that the winter months hang over Muncie. We will probably miss these cookouts. But if we're still here when they start, Robert will welcome us to his backyard cookouts.

Our regrets about possibly missing these cookouts are quickly redirected when Robert's voice lures us back into conversation. Backyard barbecues remind him of Q. L.'s Barbecue Drive Thru, a well-known black-owned restaurant. Ralph's voice gets louder. He .was mad one night, anticipating Q .L.'s ribs and finding the Drive Thru closed for the night. The anticipation of the barbecue's taste and more importantly, the reality of missing out, spark laughter amongst us.[15]

Ralph's story gives us the idea that a sense of community is still around, though not as common. However, some people we have talked to, without a doubt, see much of this informal sense of community as a thing of the past, and they miss it.

One reason Hurley Goodall feels the sense of community is lost is because it used to be important that the black community maintain and support black businesses and restaurants like Q. L.'s in Muncie. He mentions that a lot of times these restaurants were places for people to get together leisurely and discuss issues. He says it is unfortunate that these businesses aren't as prevalent as they used to be. As he sat down and talked with us in the student lounge, Hurley pulled out a two-page listing that he found in the archives detailing all the black-owned restaurants and taverns that were once running strong.

As we looked over this list we noticed a shocking pattern. When the first documented restaurants came into existence in the 1920s, there were only a few; the number gradually growing as years progressed. We were very interested because Hurley, being as knowledgeable as he is of Muncie history, was shocked himself. He pointed out the 1960s section where the numbers grew to nearly twenty businesses. Today, the number has dwindled down to a few, similar to how it started out. He suggested that it might be due to the franchises that are taking customers away, causing the black-owned restaurants to go out of business. It seems that society is more concerned with food than fellowship. We were reminded of our visit to Q. L.'s Barbecue, one of the few remaining restaurants. It seems that Q. L.'s success came not only from its popular barbecue, but from serving drive-through customers, catering to a society that has grown accustomed to "grab-and-go" service.

Hurley feels the lack of fellowship is a sad reminder of the change in this community. He went on to express his disappointment that instead of going to these restaurants and socializing with one another, families go home after work and shut the doors, locking themselves inside. "We're forgetting how to talk and interact, I think." He poses the question: "What has the community lost by losing small neighborhood restaurants?"[16]

Making Our Own Fun

Escaping the scrutinizing eyes of grown-ups, whether they were teachers or parents, gave children a sense of complete sovereignty. Maybe the excitement of being released after school was too much for some, but for others a fun-filled evening of street games and innocent mischief lay ahead. Older and younger women remember teasing each other after school just for fun. They recall laughter resonating and echoing throughout the block as kids "played the dozens," a witty and improvisational game of jokes. We laugh, reflecting on petty pastimes as Erica Long, a student in her early twenties, animatedly tells us what a typical session of "the dozens" would sound like in the streets of Whitely where she grew up.[17]

"Your momma's behind hangs *soo* low that everybody calls her the street sweeper!"

"Unt, uh, your momma's *soo* fat that when she bends over, her head is in Muncie and her butt is in Anderson!!"

"Shut-up, that's why your momma's *soo* skinny she can hula-hoop with a Cheerio!"

We compare "joning sessions," humorous taunting associated with "playing the dozens," which usually involves mocking each other's mothers. Sometimes it could get too personal (when it comes to mothers) and ended in hurt feelings or even a minor scuffle. But that didn't happen often. "It's all in fun, we *know* that they're just jokes."[18]

Eric Johnson remembers that from the 1930s (when his parents were growing up) through the 1950s (when he was growing up), few children had television, and computer games didn't exist yet.[19] Many activities were done outside. We couldn't fathom not having the luxury of instant electronic entertainment, but at the same time, we could relate to Eric's stories of playing gleefully outside. We remember how we used to change out of our school clothes with so much excitement that we couldn't tie our gym shoes up fast enough. We'd run out of the house, swinging the door wide open, and greet the friends who so eagerly waited for us to join them in doing exactly what we had done the day before. Games of hopscotch, double-dutch jump roping, box ball, bicycle riding, or even playing sports as close to "by the rules" as we could—or wanted.

"When riding bikes," Eric Johnson recollects, "we weren't allowed to go very far: around the block, down the street, and in the
neighborhood . . . me and my brother and my uncles—all we did . . .
just played in the streets." He points at himself in black and white
pictures running down dirt roads. "They were more like big brothers,
my uncles. As you see here, we'd run down the street playing football."[20] Many boys who played high school football when Eric was
younger went off to play college football, and some even went on to
play professional football. Eric said that these young men were es-
teemed in the community as role models for younger kids. "When I
was a young child, I had always wanted to attend a Big Ten school
and play football."[21]

Play extended beyond the block to the surrounding fields, woods,
and parks. Night fell. The crickets chirped in the thick summer air.
The full moon and bright stars peeked through a blanket of deep blue
sky. The patter of children's footsteps on the prowl whispered
through the grass. "A lot of times," Eric continued, "when I was
younger we would catch fireflies and put them in jars. Yeah, that was
the big community thing. All the kids would get their jars and run
around trying to catch as many fireflies as we possibly could . . . we
would try to make lanterns—when they'd light up, you know," he
chuckles, "we thought we could go in the park and see in the dark. It
was fun!"[22]

Bridging Learning and Fun

Some of the elders in the community organized public places
where kids could learn and play while hanging out with other kids.
Growing up in the early 1900s, childhood memories were shaped by
and depended upon the efforts of black leaders. Black citizens, kept out
of the white "Y" movement, networked in the 1920s to initiate new
branches of the YWCA and the YMCA, recreational facilities for black
youth.[23] Renzie Abram remembers,

> But as far as leisure. . . .
> We would watch the whites.
> They would swim downtown.
> But we couldn't swim, play ping-pong, pool—anything.
> But we *could* go (he says almost bubbling over with laughter).
> You know, they didn't keep us out.
> But we knew that we had our branch to go to.[24]

Recreation, kept separate, taught kids what it meant to be black in the Muncie community. Every person who brought this to our attention experienced it differently, and talked about it in distinct ways.

At Shaffer Chapel we sat in the midst of people who passionately conveyed their memories to us, our eyes darting from one to another, listening as though we sat in what seemed to be verbal combat. Some voices carried so much that the other voices blurting out their tidbits of information were drowned. We loved how they let us into their worlds, allowing us to view the past through their eyes. See things they once saw. Feel things they once felt.

Viola Boyd jumps into the verbal fray. She remembers that when they wanted to go swimming they would have to go to a place called Phillips Lake, also known as the stone quarry. Blacks were not allowed to swim in Tuhey Pool along with the white kids. Phillips Lake was located off of

Blacks were not allowed to swim in Muncie's Tuhey Pool along with the white kids. They instead swam in lakes, rivers, or quarries. Courtesy Archives and Special Collections, Ball State University.

Jackson Street along the White River. A wall full of graffiti hides the inconspicuous lake today.[25]

They revealed the many mythical stories and legends about this quarry such as its depth. There were rumors that it was bottomless, they recall, and that some had succumbed to its mystical waters, lost forever. A railroad bridge ran across the quarry and it is said that many years ago, a train jumped the track and crashed into the quarry, never to be found again.

We looked at each other, thinking the same thing: "We've got to go check this place out!" We knew it was a pretty hip spot when Eric commented "you had to *know* how to get in there."[26]

There are still aspects of recreation and sport that show separation between Muncie's black and white communities, but change continues to come. John Young-El, a Water Pollution Control Facility Operator, settles in at the head of the conference table in the Human Rights Personnel Office at City Hall. We sit to either side of him. John was one of our advisors during the project—the first person we interviewed—and his powerful presence fills the room. Our first conversations led to phone calls, which led to further visits. John's persistence, his complete availability to us, is connected to his passion for history. The archives that we're building together, the chapter we're shaping, they are becoming part of his identity. "If I had political power, I would use it to make a racial change in this country. I would try to figure out a way to eradicate racism. I would try to figure out a way to get all of the history in the history books. . . . Once you get started you're going to have to compile information. Do exactly what you guys are doing, gather information and then document it."[27]

Director of the Muncie Commission on the Social Status of Black Males, John has helped organize a Youth Golf Program in Muncie. "It's an opportunity for the kids to learn that there is a sport out there that they're not being told about."[28] We ask him what it is like for the kids to play golf. "Black kids," he says and stops for a brief pause, "a lot of them came in not knowing what to expect. . . . For whatever reason, the school systems don't particularly promote blacks in golf."[29]

John frames his involvement with the Youth Golf Program by referencing his brother, a professional golfer. Because of their commitment to one another, his brother helps him advance opportunities for black youth in Muncie. "There's a closeness between my little brother and myself . . . well, what can I say?" He talks as if his brother is in the room with us. "God had different plans for us, look where we are today, here *you are, you're* a professional golfer, *you have* a golf program for the youth in the city of Indianapolis. . . .'" John anticipates his brother's visits: "My brother is very, very busy. But he always makes time for me . . . he still finds time to come down here one day out of the week during the summer months and run *our* golf program for us."[30]

Like John, there are several adults in the community who dedicate their time to youth. He invited us to attend the Commission on the Social Status of Black Males meetings. Each month the commissioners meet in the gymnasium of the South Madison Street Community Multiservice Center, or "Multi."

Navigating the housing projects—some of which have been recently demolished, and others that are being rebuilt—I [Sarah] worried about my tardiness to the commission meeting. I plunged through the doors ten minutes late, and was greeted by the smell of bacon and eggs and the sound of carefree chatting. Uncomfortable for a moment, I relaxed after spotting Lonnie Jordan, a familiar face, straight ahead, seated at a table in the gym. He joked about seeing me everywhere and I kidded back that I've actually been following him around town. He invited Mia and me to venture with him and Bessie to the Crispus Attucks Museum in February. Simultaneously, he took off his hat, shook it a bit, and joked that we should chip in for gas. Lonnie suggested that I meet Dee Harris, the director of the Multi. I introduced myself after the meeting and asked if some of the people in our class could start volunteering. Dee was excited, enthusiastic—and he radiated a deep passion for kids. I wanted to come back.

Kids can drop in at the Multi every weekday after school for snacks, recreation, and tutoring. The intentional connection between learning and play is reflected in the Multi's seasonal and daily patterns. During winter weekdays after school, the gymnasium resonates with thumping basketballs. Elementary school children race from the gym to the main room, begging for more snacks. Everyone visits the storage cubby—at least a couple of times—to swap their basketball for a new favorite. The little boys enjoy shooting hoops with the male volunteers. Danny Gawlowski, a fellow classmate and this project's photographer, teases a young boy with a dodge ball. We catch the little boy smiling playfully, laughing, and rolling around on the floor hugging the ball tight to his chest so Danny can't steal it away. He later shows off his ability to spin the basketball on his fingertip, making eye contact with us proudly. Three older girls toss a plastic ball around the other side of the court, while a younger girl takes Carrie Kissel's hand firmly. She steers Carrie, a classmate of ours, around the gym in what appears an aimless adventure. Kids run around, sometimes two to a hoop, sometimes up to seven.

Basketballs pound off the backboard or sift through the net as volunteers sing out "Good shot."

The gym's jubilant mood hangs on at the start of the tutoring sessions. Some grumble, but others race for their tutors, clinging to them. Some can't let go of their play, the occasional boy sneaks to the cubby to energetically toss a football at his buddy . . . until asked to return to tutoring.

The Multi is one of the few, though important, community centers that mark the landscape of the city. Another is the Muncie Boys' and Girls' Club, once just the Boys' Club. "I was a hell-raiser there," smirks John Young-El.[31] He worked for the Boys' Club when he was in high school. "I never really got to go to camp when I was a kid . . . but I got a job working [at the Boys' Club] after school." John pulls both hands up behind his head, and leans back in his chair across from us, "We did some things that we shouldn't have done there . . . we had some booze parties there . . . bought a bunch of liquor . . . and lo and behold we got busted. . . . I got fired and then got my job back and they made me paint the entire basement of that building."[32] Though John had his bouts with adventure, he was a role model at the Boys' Club. "And by the grace of God in the past three years I've had two people tell me I made a positive impact on their lives when they were teenagers. Simply by being at the Muncie Boys' Club."[33]

The Roy C. Buley Center is a grayish-brown, stone, medium-sized community center that sits on the corner of Broadway and Highland Avenue in Whitely. I [Mia] had volunteered a couple of times at the Buley Center, which is a popular community center located where West Longfellow School used to be. I remembered that a lot of the kids from the neighborhood would come in and play basketball or recreational games. I played ping-pong with the kids or helped them with computer games in a designated area off to the side of the gym. Ping-pong was *the* thing for the younger group. The kids loved to play so much that they would, at the drop of a dime, challenge *anyone* to a match—especially, but not exclusively, those who had learned how to play a short while ago and had since tightened their game. One young boy, who lived near the center, challenged a volunteer to a match and became so passionate about it that he began to make up his own rules. He insisted that she was cheating every time she scored against him.

According to Donald Stone, an employee, the Buley Center is about more than just fun and games.[34] The kids that come to the center range in age from first grade to high school. The elementary school kids have time designated for them from 3 to 6 P.M. Designated time for

To the rhythms of a nearby parked car throbbing music out from its trunk, the boys of the Buley Center gather around for an impromptu "Dance-a-thon." Photo by Danny Gawlowski.

the junior high and high school kids is from 6 to 8 P.M. During these times the employees and volunteers will help the kids with homework. When their homework is finished, then they are free to play any of the games for that day. On Tuesdays and Thursdays, Motivate Our Minds (or MOMs), a tutoring program, provides tutoring from 4 to 6 P.M. On Wednesdays, the Buley Center takes kids to the Muncie Center for the Arts for various programs. Donald goes on to say that in addition to those activities planned throughout the week, there is a program for young girls called "Buley's Elements," which is a rhythmic stepping troupe. Also, on Mondays and Wednesdays the Buley Center hosts karate classes, where the basic fundamentals of martial arts are taught to both children and adults.[35]

Sitting in the beautifully decorated lounge of Ed Faulkner's mortuary, Ed tells us that unlike many of the children, he did not attend the community centers much because he was heavily involved in football at school, which took up most of the after-school time when centers usually operate.[36] Ed stressed that it was very important to him and his wife, Ermaline, that their son and daughter be busy and involved as they were growing up. Ed crossed his legs as he settled into the plush chair. His brow raised, changing the expression of his face from relaxed to serious as if to say, "listen to me closely, now." Their children took piano and dance lessons. Ed and Ermaline encouraged their children to engage in extracurricular activities at school such as cheerleading and sports. Activities are good for kids, Ed said emphatically. When their time is taken up throughout the day, there is no room for trouble to tiptoe in.[37]

"The First Time I Realized I Was Black"

We were to meet at the Conley Library on this particularly cold Sunday afternoon to talk with Eric Johnson. The sky was remarkably clear and the sun dazzled so, that I [Mia] thought of the coat-free beginnings of spring. It was late January, and Muncie had a fresh blanket of snow. I had arrived early, and to my surprise the library was closed. I assumed that it would be open at this time, but it had not opened at all that day. A change of plans—I called Eric to ask him to meet us at Kennedy Library. Sarah pulled in, I told her the new arrangements, and we started out. Eric got to Kennedy a little after us. We waved our hands as he scanned the room. He was dressed well, as though he had just come from the regular Sunday morning services at Shaffer Chapel. As it turned out, he had. His bright smile told us that he was very pleased to talk to us and share more of his memories.

He begins to talk, in his deep, velvety, and gentle voice, about basketball, the beloved sport of Hoosiers.[38] Young black men were not as prevalent on basketball teams in the 1950s and 1960s as they are today, he says, even if they displayed more talent than some of the white team players. As a result, he and some of his black schoolmates formed intramural teams and competed in city tournaments. "I think the first time I really felt the sting of racism and discrimination it revolved around basketball. . . . When I was in the fifth grade, about ten years old, we won the championship that year, and we had our pictures in the paper, and it felt really good . . . that was a big deal back in the '50s . . . and in sixth grade, my last year in elementary school, we were in the city championship [game] and we had the lead. The score was 17 to 16 and I distinctly remember that because I shot at the wrong basket and hit." He pauses to laugh. "But anyway, we got the lead back and were winning . . . and with about ten seconds to go [the scorekeepers] just switched the score around . . . and a coach knew. So we lost and we were furious and just crying." He says they protested, "they cheated on us, they just did it because we're black!" Eric's coach showed little sympathy. He told them it was just a basketball game. They needed to grow up. To take it as a lesson in life, that things are not necessarily fair. That was his first encounter with racism, and it deeply affected him. "I think I was upset about that for two or three years."[39]

Trusting Others

"It's still difficult for me to trust people," a woman from the community confides. We've been talking on the telephone for about ten minutes. Her voice is strong and direct, and hits me in the gut. This must be rare, I thought, this kind of honest and open conversation about race. Not many white students will have this kind of experience, I (Sarah) think to myself. I appreciate her honesty. She doesn't avoid this experience, but rather shares it, as a mentor would. Phone to my ear, notebook in hand, I remember last week, when we sat together, talking. She had told me a story then . . . a story of her girlhood:

> Women have a hard time being *com*fortable with one another.
> I don't care what color you *are*.
> And that's because we were never—in a situation like the *guys* were—
> the *guys* know how to really have *fun*—and talk with each other
> and-maybe-stay-three-or-four-hours-together-just-having-*fun*—
> because they always had activities that the guys, *could do.* . . .
>
> And then *black* girls *truly* were set aside—
> and when we were trying to blend in,
> you were always talked about,
> never-appreciated-for-who-*you*-were. . . .
>
> It was *frust*rating and it was *mostly frust*rating
> because I grew *up* with *white kids,*
> My best friend . . .
> she-would-come-to-my-house—I-slept-at-her-house.
>
> We ate each other's *food,*
> Licked off the *same* ice-cream cone
> And all that.
> But she left and changed schools during junior high
> And I saw her walking with her little *blonde* friends—
> She didn't even *know me* (smirking). . . .
> And that's the first time that I realized I was *black* . . . (laughing).
> *That's* when I realized there was a dif*fer*ence.[40]

Other community members talked to us about friendships, too. We began to ask about their childhood memories—how friends come and go in people's lives. Relationships shifted when kids changed schools. In 1962, Muncie opened Southside High School, diverting students who'd thought they'd be attending Muncie Central. Our small group of consultants at Shaffer Chapel on Sunday afternoon remembered the tension they experienced at that time. "When they brought Southside into the mix, that split us," Robert says about the black community.

"Right in half," Eric Johnson breaks in.

"The railroad tracks were a dividing point," Ralph Vaughn points out. "All of those south of the railroad tracks went to Southside and north of the railroad tracks went to Central." Robert adds, "then you have all those kids who knew each other and used to play together. Now they're going to different schools. It's kind of polarizing. The community as we knew it started to change."[41]

Activity at the Parks

In the Kennedy Library we sit at a table in the midst of quiet chatter. Bessie Jordan, a social worker, looks at her husband, Lonnie, somewhat distant across the table, who's allowing her to be the center of attention. Lonnie, a retired steel mill worker, grew up in Arkansas, and he feels Bessie has more to contribute because she has always lived in Muncie. Shuffling his newspaper, he chimes in every now and then adding his two cents. She teases him, saying that he is more involved in the conversation than he pretends to be. She tells us that currently, she and Lonnie enjoy researching their genealogy and taking trips to places that provide the resources necessary to dig deep into their ancestry. The Jordans are also great collectors; it is one of their most passionate leisure pursuits. Lonnie collects original postcards and stamps of African Americans. Bessie, who admits that she was influenced by her husband, collects Aunt Jemima figurines. "I used to think they didn't look so good," she says as she explains how black culture was once depicted so negatively, "but those people worked and got a lot of their children in college . . . by just being the chefs, the cooks. . . . I learned to appreciate them over a period of time."[42]

Bessie remembers that, when she was growing up in the 1950s and 1960s, almost everything in Whitely was centered around McCulloch Park. The park used to have a large shelter house, torn down in the

1970s, where many families would have get-togethers or small parties. She remembers the small park zoo, now gone, that was once so popular. There was a bear, monkeys that jumped from tree to tree, and concession stands scattered here and there where you could buy popcorn and Popsicles. On Fridays and Saturdays, McCulloch Park had a venue set up so that people could show off their talent, such as group singing. There were areas for basketball tournaments, and baseball diamonds for those who signed up early enough.[43]

Historically parks have been gathering places for blacks not only in Muncie, but all across the United States. John Young-El tells us that years ago, McCulloch was segregated and blacks were restricted to the east side of the park. "Even today," he says, "to a degree the parks are still a gathering place for blacks during the summer." He says that Heekin Park, on the south side of town near the neighborhood known as Industry, does not see as much action as McCulloch does on any given day, except in the summertime when Muncie Black Expo has its Summer Soul Fest. One memory of the park that stuck out was when he was a kid on the Fourth of July. The city used to have a fireworks show at McCulloch Park on the river, and crowds of people would line up across the bridge to watch it. John felt that he was blessed because he lived in downtown Muncie at the time so he could go up on the roof of a building and observe the fireworks from there.[44]

"When I was a child, it seemed like everybody in Muncie was there," recalls Renzie Abram, as he explained how he remembered the Fourth of July at McCulloch. He laughs unashamedly of his adolescent immaturity when he admits to going to the park and doing "things we didn't have no business doing," like smoking cigarettes in Heekin Park behind Garfield Elementary School. He also remembers Heekin Park with caged bears, a big huge goldfish in a pondlike area, and even a fox! Growing up, Renzie's family lived in Industry, also known as Crosstown, so they would walk over to Whitely on the northern end to go to McCulloch Park.[45]

That same Sunday afternoon that Eric Johnson arranged for us to talk to the Joneses, we got further information that expounded on things about the parks we had only heard in passing. He was excited to set up the meeting for us. Eric had become so involved in helping us with the research that he often forgot that he, too, was part of it. Denise Jones, along with her husband Robert and son Robbie, seemed to be a bit confused about our reason for wanting to talk with them, so we explained briefly as we set up the tape recorder. They initiated conversation and not long after, others joined us.

Denise used to participate in softball for girls at Carver, Heekin, and Westside Parks. Robert remembers having a lot of fun when he was growing up. He grew up in Midtown, which is a small community between Whitely Bridge and Willard Street. He said there used to be a train in McCulloch Park that the kids could ride all through the park. He told us, "the Cincinnati Reds had a farm team that played baseball there, and I can remember when I was eight or nine years old that they would give us a dime if they hit a foul ball—and we could catch it before it went in the river." Furthermore, he said a movie screen would be set up in McCulloch, and they would show "The Three Stooges" and cowboy films. Family reunions often took place in the parks, and continue to take place there today. Heekin Park, as it has more cabins and shelters, is better suited to large social gatherings.[46]

Our consultants enjoyed reminiscing about the adventures they experienced in the parks as kids and young adults. Even though the parks are not as lively today—it wasn't until later in the semester that we realized this—activities still *just happen* in the parks.

Memory, Story, and Relationship

Group conversation enables memories to flow from person to person. One person's experience leads to another's—weaving the webs of memory and relationship. During our conversations at Shaffer, the spark of memory drew people together. It wasn't just about us learning from these people and their experiences. It was also about each of them layering story upon story, guiding each other through story and memory. As a group, we had not sat together like this before. It was a new dynamic, a new conversation.

"But you know," Denise begins, "even now, this past summer on Sundays, while we're on our way to church, the park will be packed."[47]

"Packed," Ralph adds. "And there isn't anything going on. No bands playing."

"What started that," Robert says, "was the older guys my age wanted to play basketball without having the true athletes of their time—" he chuckled—"playing against them. It's like fathers playing against sons. They didn't want to do that. The fathers wanted to play against the fathers. So Sunday mornings, you didn't have to worry about the court."

"So that's how *that* started?" Ralph jumps in, baffled. "I was wondering what was happening."

"But it got popular," says Robert, explaining the difference between those first basketball games and the games you see today. "And now the younger guys are starting the 'Oh that's where the old guys are around during the summer. . . .'"

The conversation bubbles on. "Yeah," Robert points out, "it used to be nice and quiet, and you played a couple games. That's all you could play anyway. And you sit down and get your beer . . . but then the younger guys found out. They started coming. And with the younger guys came the younger girls. *Then* you got *prob*lems. . . ."

Laughter consumes us as Robert's voice trails: "*Then* you got *prob*lems. *My* goodness." An artful storyteller, Robert continues, "it was like we would hide from the kids. We can't keep up with them anymore. I mean, we still have our memories but we can't keep up with them.

"Then it got to the point where the crowd started getting bigger. And a couple of enterprising young men brought some ribs out there. Then they set up and they started cooking. And then the next thing you know you had your own carnival out there." Robert's voice trails off, disappointed about the change.

"There were cars parked all over the place everywhere," Ralph says. "And then the boomers were going in the cars."[48]

At its most memorable, leisure takes its own course—lacks plans, time frames, and structure. With open-ended sayings, people casually explain gatherings, "The next thing you know . . ." and "It's whatever happens, happens." Memories span from informal "get togethers" of the past, on porches, in the yard, and at the park, to "freestyle" barbecues and basketball today—activities still in the yard and still at the park.

"Freestyle." The word resonates because it captures how leisure happens; it takes form through spontaneity. Our conversations with community advisors and consultants were freestyle at times as well. That Sunday when Eric Johnson invited members of the Shaffer congregation to stay after church and chat, it was never specified who would stay, nor for how long. A group did assemble after church and we began to talk, but even then the group remained freeflowing—it wasn't long before others sat down to join us. There is a rhythm to the way that leisure happens here, but that rhythm is difficult to discern. It has been even more difficult to represent leisure, especially the currents of talk and interaction that weave through leisure. The structure of organized paragraphs, sentences, somehow weakens the power of engaged and free-flowing dialogue. We have struggled to write in a way that doesn't lose the meaning.

This flow of informality, the way the time passes quickly while engaged in talk, extends into nearly all conversations. During some interviews, consultants made phone calls to add additional voices into the mix. The urge to call a friend who knew "more" about the topic of conversation might spring up in the middle of dialogue. Someone would jump up, almost the moment the thought came to her, to dial the phone while the rest of us continued the conversation. Phone calls didn't interrupt the flow of ideas. Nobody waited for a phone call to end, nor for the one who made the call to rejoin the conversation. Instead, the calls wove into the conversation with ease.

Our leisurely talks with consultants developed into relationships. We talked around kitchen tables, in living rooms, church pews, the library, at City Hall, on the telephone. We talked in places where people talk everyday. We learned about the meeting of past and present—talk, activity, and memory—interconnected layers of leisure uncovered. Our consultants' stories reminded us that free time is especially enjoyed when spent with friends and family. "We just made our own fun," was commonly repeated.

Many mourn a kind of leisure lost. They miss days upon days spent outdoors as children—and regret that their own children and grandchildren spend their precious days watching television and playing video games. Some feel that young adults don't have the same opportunities in Muncie anymore. The informal parties and dances at the Old Armory are in the past. They miss the near constant get-togethers at each other's houses, playing cards, dancing, all the babies sleeping in the bedroom on one big bed.

Our conversations continued to unearth aspects of leisure that people miss. The activities that brought people together—the relationships. Family and friends.

Our shared afternoons and evenings with our consultants have a leisurely spirit—full of talk and laughter. Leisure brings *us* together in conversation and fellowship. The things people do may not be the same, but they still do things the same way. Spontaneously. Freestyle.

Let's Get Ready to Rumble: On Structured Leisure

That night, the men's high school basketball game was not just any game, but the Muncie Central Bearcats against the Muncie Southside Rebels. The front page of the Muncie *Star Press* read, "old rivalries are set to renew battle: the Rebels and the Bearcats meet for the sixty-sixth time tonight for 'bragging rights.'"[49]

A Muncie Central basketball player works on his free throw during the varsity practice. Muncie Central has won more state championships than any other team in Indiana, was depicted in the movie Hoosiers, *and was determined to be a major unifying force in the community in* Middletown. *Photo by Danny Gawlowski.*

When the Southside players jogged onto the floor, the gymnasium raged with noise. The Central players began the starting lineup and Southside students abruptly hid their faces behind newspapers. This rivalry runs deep.

The game was really close, with Southside ahead by only a few points. Tension consumed the crowd, frustrated coaches, sparked adrenaline. Southside won. Cheering flooded the gym and a frenzied Southside fan unfolded a Confederate flag, shook it out, and unfurled it across the bleachers. We were shocked, tense. Once the symbol of Southside High School, the rebel flag has a very particular history in this community. The rebel flag still is powerful.

"I call it the fist fight of the century," Ralph Vaughn says.[50] A football player for Muncie Central in the early 1960s, he explains the rivalry between Southside and Muncie Central. When the student population split after Southside was built, tension mounted in Muncie. "In '61 we were all on the same team. In '62 we were split. . . . I played that first (football) game . . . that was a 'grudge match' . . . what contributed to it was that when Southside came on line, the rebel flag was their flag. It went for years. . . . That's why they were so upset and made sure they didn't lose that first game," Ralph explains.[51]

"[High school basketball] is nothing now compared to what it was in the '50s and the '60s," says Eric Johnson. "You couldn't even get into a high school game if you didn't have a season ticket when I was coming up. . . . High school basketball was huge. If you were a boy growing up in Indiana, especially Muncie, [it was all about] basketball. There were basketball courts and [hoops] everywhere. Everybody seemed to have a basketball [hoop] in their backyard."[52]

Eric reveals that during that time, in the 1950s and 1960s, Muncie Central only had three or four blacks on their basketball team, and many talented black boys did not try out because they dreaded the potential rejection. But in his sophomore year, Eric decided to be one of the brave ones and tried to make the eminent Muncie Central basketball team. Several boys didn't make it, but Eric made it quite far. In fact, he made it up to the final round, but later discovered that he was cut also. The coach told him it was not because he did not possess the ability, but because he missed a practice. A practice that was rescheduled. A practice that Eric knew nothing about. "There were a lot of ways [for coaches] to eliminate those they did not want on the team," Eric concludes.[53]

Things changed when Southside High School came into existence. Eric says with the new high school, blacks were not necessarily welcomed with open arms on their basketball team, but it provided more opportunity. During Eric's senior year, Muncie Central's coach wanted to be more competitive and began to realize that he had to put the best players on the team in order to win. This meant taking more blacks. But the pressure from the opposing community was harsh. That coach left, and a new coach replaced him, eliminating blacks again. Consequently, Eric carries on saying that "I was a football player! I played football and ran track when I was in high school." He recalls that there really were not any sports available for the girls to participate in except cheerleading. Even so, black girls were not allowed to cheer with the white cheerleaders. Instead, many participated in the "cheerblocks." Eric calls to mind fondly that the girls would put on their special outfits and stand in a particular spot, the cheerblocks, and "just yell."[54]

We learned more about these cheerblocks when we talked with the group of consultants at Shaffer. Viola Boyd remembers that the cheerblock at Muncie Central included mixed races, but she never saw a black cheerleader during her high school years. She recalls that she and other girls wore complementing purple and white shirts, Muncie Central's school colors, in the cheering blocks shouting:

"BASket! BASket! BASket BOYS!
YOU make the BASket *WE'LL* make the NOISE!!"[55]

Two cheerleaders exchange secrets and gossip on the sidelines of a Muncie Central basketball game. Photo by Danny Gawlowski.

I [Mia] identified with bittersweet memories of my high school days of how it was considered a blessing to see a black face cheering in uniform on the sidelines. Viola continued to tell us the cheerblock would help fire the crowd up with their chants and build excitement, starting the rumbling, stomping sounds in which the entire crowd would join. She said at one game, the year after Muncie Central won the state championship, the cheering block was so proud of their school that they decided to rub in their title, trying to intimidate the other school's fans. They would holler across the gym, reminding the opposing school that Muncie Central was the state champions. Abruptly, and quite candidly, the other school's fans then responded "THAT-WAS-LAST-YEAR!!" Viola remembers being so embarrassed, and they didn't say it again for the remainder of the game.[56]

The Night Life

Geraldine's home has been *the* place to socialize for years. The company may vary, but she remains the host. Not surprisingly, it has become common for two of the groups working on this project to meet at her house.

She recalls the past, when friends and family played cards from late evening into early morning. "We entertained at home. My kids slept in every bed in Whitely because we couldn't afford babysitters, you know." Geraldine recalls playing Dirty Eights and Whist. "We were so poor and I'd have my cousin and her husband come. And a big Saturday night would be us sitting around the card table . . . each one of us would have a quart of beer on each corner." The nights were memorable because of the interaction with guests.[57]

Geraldine describes card parties as the most significant gatherings for social life, that is, prior to the dances of later years. Private social clubs, like the Debonair (men's) Club, began to plan formal dances at the National Guard Armory. Many reminisce about dances at the "Old Armory." Fredine Goodall and Geraldine, in particular, remember how the occasions called for new dresses, sometimes crocheted by their club members. Though the Debonair Club often planned the dances, other men's and women's clubs planned events as well. "But then things got so expensive. The bands joined unions so we couldn't [afford] them. . . . Lots of times we had free drinks, a free bar. You could do that *then*, but you couldn't do that now because everything is so unionized now . . . we used to get a band for a decent price—$125 at one time. And then when they joined the union [the cost was] $250. You know, with only eight girls in the club we couldn't afford that."[58]

The Debonair Social Club dressed for a formal dance in June 1952. Courtesy Archives and Special Collections, Ball State University.

As our conversation continues, Fredine patiently teaches Michelle Johnson—the graduate assistant for our project—to double back, a crochet stitch, while Geraldine guides our dialogue with her wit. Bringing her hook and yarn along, Michelle was eager for this visit. Fredine doesn't crochet anymore, but she hasn't lost her skill.

"Well you see, that's where I miss the girls," Geraldine says, returning to Muncie's nightlife. "We belonged to a club called 'Our Pal.' And we had formals every year." She explains that the women of Our Pal were the same age as the men in the Debonair Club. "And of course when one had a dance you knew you were going to be invited, and so it was just a regular thing to look forward to every year." Geraldine left the table and returned with invitations from 1971. She had kept them all this time as a reminder.[59]

Private clubs not only provided organized leisure for men and women in the black community, they also served as a basis for friendships. As we sat with Geraldine and Fredine—just us girls, laughing the morning away, our watches ticked into class time. They explained their ties to the Debonair Club. Being the girlfriends and wives of members in the club, they often spent time at the Debonair clubhouse.

Geraldine reminds us, "We made our own fun." Fredine's voice, in unison with Geraldine's, allows their friendship to unfold for us. Geraldine's story carries us to the clubhouse of the Debonair Club: "And listen, we would get up there sometimes on Sunday . . . all the girls would cook and fix food. We just made a party out of everything." She glances at Fredine for agreement, "You remember that . . . we all went to church, came home and changed clothes, and we went there to clean the booths and the bar." Geraldine and Fredine's lives have changed, but they embrace their shared memories.[60]

Engrossed in conversation, we are startled by the doorbell. Emma Sue Davis has arrived. "She's in everything," Geraldine promises us. "You *have* to talk to Emma Sue."

Emma Sue apologizes to us. She wanted to bring photographs but didn't get them together in time. But we're grateful that she came, photos or not. Soon after her arrival, she calls a friend, hoping that the friend will stop by too. Emma Sue informs us that in addition to her many commitments, she enjoys working at the post office and is contemplating retirement. She and Geraldine chat about card tournaments that continue today and the clubs that sponsor them. We ask how often they have card tournaments, and Geraldine says, "just whenever you felt like it, no special time. Whenever we hadn't had one in awhile, it was time."

Our conversation leads into the differences between young black women's lives today as opposed to fifty years ago. A member of La Beta, Emma Sue feels like young women don't have the same interest in social clubs today. "There's so many other things, I guess, that black women are into now . . . that when we came along it wasn't available to us."

"You mean careers?" Geraldine asks. They chat together, trying to explain.

"I think they don't have the bond with each other," Emma Sue says regretfully. "They don't have the bond like we had. Most of us had kids. And our kids bonded like we bonded. And so there was this friendship. And they still have it. My kids and all the girls' kids that were in the club." She pursues this thought: "now you don't find that . . . right here in Muncie the kids don't know each other and they don't do things together. We always try to teach our kids that you love one another and you help one another . . . as a black race you stick together."[61]

In the spirit of understanding why the black race "sticks together," we asked Hurley Goodall to respond to a previous draft version of this chapter. The next day he came to a class session to personally give us his input. He was very concerned about getting certain ideas through in this chapter, mainly the reasons that leisurely time in the black community was set apart from the white community. He explains that the division was not because the black community *wanted* to be separated, but because they had no choice—as a result of segregation. It was not that they did not *want* to have functions at the places available to white people. They *had* to have functions at their own homes and churches. These were the only places that were "their own." This way, no one could tell them that they could not have a certain event. It was out of pure necessity.[62]

One evening after attending Bible class with John Young-El at his church, Church of the Living God, we had a chance to talk to him about the skating rinks. He called his friend Radford Jones, one of the church's elders, over to help him out with his memory of the Skate-A-Way. Mr. Jones remembered that it opened in the late 1970s. It was located on East McGalliard, a well-developed area in Muncie just north of Whitely. He said there was also a skating rink called Gibson's, but when blacks wanted to skate to "black music" they would go to the Skate-A-Way. Mr. Jones said sometimes the rink would host "All-Night Skates," where hundreds of black kids would show up. It was like an overnight lock-in and the kids loved it. The rink had a dancing section, with plastic floors that had lights underneath. They also held dancing contests here for children who wanted to compete or just show off their skills. Skate-A-Way closed when a factory bought it. Now blacks go to Gibson's, usually on Thursday nights, if they want to skate, but it's not the same as Skate-A-Way.

The After-Party

After the party is, of course, the after-party. We heard much mention of juke joints like the Chicken Shack and the Pork Chop, but we wanted to know more about them. Talking with Eric, Ralph, Denise, Robert, Robbie, and Viola, we finally got the skinny on these legendary after-hours spots. The Pork Chop was an old two-story house with a basement. All the furniture had been taken out and replaced with a jukebox. A kitchen served fried chicken to nocturnal partygoers who had the munchies. The Pork Chop's main competitor was the Chicken Shack.[63]

The Chicken Shack strikes a chord with Robert "Oh, my God," he says, "the Chicken Shack!" Ralph went on to say, "when everybody gets through partying or whatever they want to do they would wind up out there . . . you'd go and stay there until dawn!!!" Ralph and the others burst into laughter.[64]

"There's places like that depicted in movies," Robert says.

"You remember 'The Color Purple' . . . that little juke joint?" interrupts Eric.

"These clubs were *real* close to that. They might not be that *rustic*-looking," Robert says, "but you're still talking the same atmosphere, you know the dancing. . . ."

"And you can't see the people," Ralph says laughing hysterically, "because of the smoke in there—cooking smoke, cigarette smoke, and *other* kinds of smoke." Ralph continues to laugh. "And inevitably there was a confrontation almost every night."

The Blue Note was also a popular club that hosted several concerts. The Motown Revue was a huge tour that came to Muncie on its way to Indianapolis, the capital city. Robert also remembers acts coming and performing at the Armory, the Skate-A-Way, and the Fieldhouse. These "top" celebrities, they say, were Duke Ellington, the SOS Band, Ike and Tina Turner, the Caravan of Stars, James Brown, Smokey Robinson and the Miracles, and the Temptations. Robert recalled Muncie being referred to as "Little Chicago" in those days. We were astonished to hear that some of these prominent celebrities were not allowed to stay at hotels. They would board in a local black home.

They also brought up a club called the Hole in the Wall. But as they talked amongst themselves we got confused about what exactly this Hole in the Wall was. To our surprise, as they explained it to us, it was not an actual club.

"The Hole in the Wall," Robert explains, "is a name for a club that's *not* a club. It's a house that they rearrange and put a little bar in."

As they talk, we find out that there are *many* Holes in the Wall on different streets and in different houses. Ralph says they were very similar to the Pork Chop and the Chicken Shack.

Bootlegging, they explain, took place at these spots. But there was one legitimate bar called Bob's Tavern, which was not an after-hours spot. Bob Flowers, who owned the place, is something of a legend in this community. He was, it seems, the only black person in the state of Indiana to have a liquor license at the time. He died a millionaire, they say.[65]

Parties, Addiction, and Recovery

"As a young man, I liked to have parties," John Young-El grins good-humoredly. "Invite my friends over. Buy a lot of booze . . . went to smoke-outs on campus."[66] Drinking often coincides with socializing, and John likes to mingle. But his drinking led to other addictions, an experience he openly shares.

"Crack cocaine was the one drug I tried and could not stop using," John states with resolute exactness. "It is highly addictive . . . it is *not* a social drug. After messing around with it for a year I had a traumatic experience and went to the hospital . . . and I've been clean ever since."[67]

"I hope to never feel again the way I felt May 24, 1992," he insists, with his eyes level and locked on us. "I was helpless and hopeless. Helpless is losing self and hopeless is losing God." Things got suddenly serious. We asked John how his life is different now. "I'm a useful and productive citizen in society," John claims. "I try to give back to the community where I live."[68]

John's frankness surprised us; first, because he was up front about his addiction. But further, because his consistent narrative was entrenched in his frame of reference, in his hopes for changes in the city. He advocates rehabilitation for addicts and a personal relationship with God.

"One of the things that you have to do when you stop any addiction, is you have to find something to replace what you gave up. Something to occupy that time. You can't just stop and do nothing," John says as he pauses to reflect. "For me, I stay busy. If I said I never think about doing drugs that would be a lie. The thought pops in my mind occasionally but I never allow it to linger there."[69]

John relies on God and support groups to divert his thoughts from drug use. "I've gotten smart. I pick up the phone and call my sponsor or call somebody, and say, 'Hey, feeling low right now.' You find that when you talk to somebody else that takes all of the power out of that thought . . . and when all else fails I pray."[70] Early in recovery, John spent time with other addicts. Often, he had used previously with people that attended these meetings. Relationships changed, redirected by the stages of recovery. "We are like family. I don't have to say a word and they know if I'm up or down."[71]

The Culture of Leisure in Muncie's African American Community

In *Middletown*, some aspects of leisure mentioned *were* similar to Muncie's African American experience. The Lynds suggest that "the characteristic leisure-time pursuits of the city tend to be things done with others rather than by individuals alone . . . listening to something or talking or playing cards. . . ."[72] Even though the Lynds' study focused primarily on the white community, these simple pastimes are common in the black community as well. "[Muncie] has always delighted in talk."[73]

In earlier years, segregation created racial boundaries that still quietly remain. Within the boundaries of this segregation blacks stuck together in their leisure time—they had to. Now, integration is encouraged. But this same integration leaves some people feeling somewhat threatened that their unique cultures will lose their distinctiveness.

It is said that "there is nothing new under the sun," and this relates to leisure as a whole in Muncie. Muncie isn't particularly different in how people take time out for themselves than any other town or city. There is no one thing that is so distinct that would clearly be a "Muncie thing." Of course, like many cities, Muncie has its own signature events and maybe even pastimes that are identified solely with Muncie, but most likely something similar could be found in another city across the country.

Blacks have almost always had differences in the *way* they handle leisure as compared with whites. But that is true about other issues in other cities, which is an indication to us of why Muncie was deemed the "all-American city" in the 1920s.

One statement Robert made that really stuck in our minds was that Muncie started out as a small town, evolved into a small city, and now it seems to be regressing back to a small town.[74] We could really grasp and understand what he was trying to convey, not because we experienced it ourselves, but because as residents of Muncie, we listen to all these stories and think to ourselves how great it must have been—back then. Now, however, it seems that people are humming a different tune, because the "good times" that they describe with such a sense of longing are immensely gratifying for them to share with us. Things just aren't that way anymore. Events aren't as freeflowing anymore—they rarely "just *happen*" anymore. But what was *it*? Was it the exhilaration of having idle time to do whatever you pleased? Was it the concept of "just *happen*?" *It* was and is anything that anyone considers to be leisure. Pure and unrefined, exclusive to that person or group and to Muncie.

A small town *really is* like a big family. Somehow these people from different walks of life are tied together in some way. Whether it is what they enjoy doing, what activities they engage in, what is important to them, how they have changed personally, or just plain kinship, everyone takes part in this thing we call leisure. Ideas about leisure differ from person to person, but someone is bound to know you or be familiar with what you do or have done for leisure. Through socializing with a number of people, we began to understand that, along with the people we talked to, we enjoyed it. We were socializing, conversing with one another. It's done every day, and is taken for granted as a form of leisure. There is something intimate about sharing with people, letting your guard down, and letting strangers into your life. In this process, strange faces became familiar, the unknown became exposed, and relationships blossomed. We used leisure in the name of research, but we engaged in leisure for the sake of connection.

> This is my story, this is my song,
> Praising my Savior all the day long;
> This is my story, this is my song,
> Praising my Savior all the day long.

"The lyrics of this legendary gospel song best reflect my sentiments as an African American growing up in Muncie," wrote Eric Johnson in a letter to us after he read an early draft of this chapter.

We all have different hopes, and aspirations, likes, dislikes, etc. How-ever, I do think there are certain customs, behavior, and social mores that are associated with a particular ethnic group. . . . Perhaps it was memo-ries of the park shows in McCullough Park, or the dances at the Crosstown YWCA: there is something that bonds us to our community. For the past fifteen years our community has a Back to Muncie reunion. This is largely an Afro-American event. Every four or five years, literally hundreds of folks come to McCullough Park for a weekend of eating, dancing, games, and other social activities. I would like to think these huge gatherings are a result of years of bonding that is prevalent in our community. Or maybe it is the gentle "whisper" expression of love that was conveyed on someone's front porch on a hot July night. Or some-one may recall the prayers for grace and mercy that a loving grand-mother prayed for them during a difficult time in their life. It is my hope that my sentiments will resonate with someone to evoke a fond memory or even a simple smile. More importantly, I would like to convey to oth-ers, especially the next generation of Muncie's Afro-Americans that they are descendants of a nurturing, thriving, and proud community grounded in spirituality. This is indeed my story.[75]

Notes

1. Geraldine Burns, telephone conversation with Sarah Bricker and Mia Fields, February 25, 2003.

2. Ibid.

3. Geraldine Burns, Emma Sue Davis, Fredine Goodall, conversation with Brandy Bounds, Sarah Bricker, Mia Fields, and Michelle Johnson, February 25, 2003.

4. Geraldine Burns, Hurley Goodall, and Ed McNeary, conversation with Brandy Bounds, Sarah Bricker, and Jarrod Dortch, January 29, 2003.

5. Geraldine Burns, Emma Sue Davis, Fredine Goodall conversation, Feb-ruary 25, 2003.

6. Ibid.

7. Geraldine Burns telephone conversation, February 25, 2003.

8. Eric Johnson, conversation with Sarah Bricker and Mia Fields, March 23, 2003.

9. Eric Johnson, conversation with Sarah Bricker and Mia Fields, January 26, 2003.

10. Ibid.

11. Renzie Abram, conversation with Sarah Bricker and Mia Fields, Febru-ary 18, 2003.

12. Viola Boyd, Eric Johnson, Denise Jones, Robert Jones, Robby Jones, and Ralph Vaughn, conversation with Sarah Bricker and Mia Fields, March 2, 2003.

13. Ibid.

14. Ibid.

15. Ibid.

16. Hurley Goodall, conversation with Mia Fields and Sarah Bricker, April 1, 2003.

17. Erica Long, conversation with Mia Fields, March 4, 2003.

18. Ibid.

19. Eric Johnson conversation, January 26, 2003.

20. Eric Johnson conversation, February 9, 2003.

21. Eric Johnson, group conversation with community advisors and students, March 31, 2003.

22. Eric Johnson conversation, January 26, 2003.

23. Hurley Goodall and J. Paul Mitchell, *African Americans in Muncie, 1890–1960* (Muncie, Ind.: Ball State University, 1976), 20–21.

24. Renzie Abram conversation, February 18, 2003.

25. Viola Boyd, Denise Jones, Robert Jones, Robby Jones, Eric Johnson, and Ralph Vaughn conversation, March 2, 2003.

26. Ibid.

27. John Young-El, conversation with Sarah Bricker, Abby Delpha, and Mia Fields, February 4, 2003.

28. Ibid.

29. Ibid.

30. Ibid.

31. John Young-El conversation, February 4, 2003.

32. Ibid.

33. Ibid.

34. Donald Stone, telephone conversation with Mia Fields, March 2, 2003.

35. Ibid.

36. Ed Faulkner, conversation with Sarah Bricker and Mia Fields, February 20, 2003.

37. Ibid.

38. Eric Johnson conversation, January 26, 2003.

39. Ibid.

40. Anonymous contributor, conversation with Sarah Bricker, February 9, 2003.

41. Viola Boyd, Denise Jones, Robert Jones, Robby Jones, Eric Johnson, and Ralph Vaughn conversation, March 2, 2003.

42. Bessie Jordan and Lonnie Jordan, conversation with Sarah Bricker and Mia Fields, January 30, 2003.

43. Ibid.

44. John Young-El conversation, February 4, 2003.

45. Renzie Abram conversation, February 18, 2003.

46. Viola Boyd, Denise Jones, Robert Jones, Robby Jones, Eric Johnson, and Ralph Vaughn conversation, March 2, 2003.

47. Ibid.

48. Ibid.

49. Dan Knott, "Central vs. South: Bragging Rights Up For Grabs." *The Star Press*, January 24, 2003: 1B.

50. Viola Boyd, Denise Jones, Robert Jones, Robby Jones, Eric Johnson, and Ralph Vaughn conversation, March 3, 2003.

51. Ibid.

52. Eric Johnson conversation, January 26, 2003.

53. Ibid.

54. Ibid.

55. Viola Boyd, Denise Jones, Robert Jones, Robby Jones, Eric Johnson, and Ralph Vaughn conversation, March 3, 2003.

56. Ibid.

57. Geraldine Burns, Fredine Goodall, and Emma Sue Davis conversation, February 25, 2003.

58. Ibid.

59. Ibid.

60. Ibid.

61. Geraldine Burns, Fredine Goodall, and Emma Sue Davis conversation, February 25, 2003.

62. Hurley Goodall, conversation with Mia Fields and Sarah Bricker, April 1, 2003.

63. Viola Boyd, Denise Jones, Robert Jones, Robby Jones, Eric Johnson, and Ralph Vaughn conversation, March 3, 2003.

64. Ibid.

65. John Young-El, conversation with Sarah Bricker, Dan Gawlowski, and Mia Fields, January 16, 2003.

66. Ibid.

67. John Young-El conversation, January 16, 2003.

68. John Young-El conversation, February 4, 2003.

69. Ibid.

70. Ibid.

71. John Young-El conversation, February 26, 2003.

72. Lynd and Lynd, *Middletown*, 226.

73. Ibid.

74. Viola Boyd, Denise Jones, Robert Jones, Robby Jones, Eric Johnson, and Ralph Vaughn conversation, March 3, 2003.

75. Letter from Eric Johnson to Sarah Bricker and Mia Fields, April 10, 2003.

7

Engaging in Religious Practices

Jessica Booth and Eric Efaw

(Jessica) I woke up this morning an hour before service. Eric called while I was in the shower. By the time I noticed he had called it was too late to call him back. So I just got ready and drove to church, hoping to see him there.

(Eric) It is now about 10:45. I could crawl into bed and catch some more sleep, or I could go to church like a good Christian boy. I called Jessica earlier but she did not answer. Do I really want to run the risk of going to church by myself? Sitting in a pew alone, the obvious visitor? After a few more moments of indecision, I resolutely hop into the car.

(Jessica) I arrive at Shaffer right at eleven, park on the street, and rush into the church, thinking to myself, "I hope they've just started" and "I hope they are not praying when I walk in." Since the service has already begun, I take the first seat I notice and end up sitting in a pew next to Dolores and Carl Rhinehart. As I sit down, Dolores immediately recognizes me and helps me with my coat. As I settle in and look around, I see Eric sitting across the church.

Upon stepping into the church, any worries either of us had of being among strangers dissipated; most people seated in the pews were somehow connected with *The Other Side of Middletown*. In front of us sat Delores Pryor, Phyllis White, and their families. Dolores and Carl Rhinehart waved and said good morning from across the church. From behind us Geraldine Burns leaned over the pew to whisper hello, and as the service began, Hurley and Fredine Goodall walked in and greeted us as well.

The sanctuary of the church was different from the basement we frequented regularly for class. Settling into our seats, we began to look around and were struck by the small size of the church. Shaffer Chapel played a significant role in Muncie's African American history and somehow we expected the church to be equally as large. Yet we found ourselves in a room that, when filled to capacity, would likely hold no more than a hundred worshippers. For seating purposes, the sanctuary's eighteen red-cushioned pews were arranged nine to a side with one aisle running down the center of the room and another aisle separating the congregation from the altar. Light shining through the six amber stained-glass windows cast a warm glow on the sanctuary's white walls. Three arches separated by square columns divided the pulpit from the congregation. Behind the pulpit were seats for the choir, a drum set, and a piano. Next to the drums stood an American flag. A wooden cross that hung on the front wall declared the room to be a house of God. The sanctuary felt inviting, and we began to feel at home in the small chapel.

Pastor Winburn called on Geraldine Burns and Eric Johnson to give their favorite Bible verses and hymns, which he then incorporated into the service as impromptu inserts. The congregation, about thirty people between the ages of eight and eighty, began to tap their fingers against their bulletins as the choir sang. They gently thumped their hands on the pews, or hit their heels on the ground to the beat of the song. Someone in the crowd began quietly singing along with the choir. Others joined in. We found ourselves singing and tapping, too. The sermon, drawn from John 8:42–45, followed the music. Pastor Winburn explained the sermon's three titles, "Whose Child Are You," "Piggyback Salvation," and "God Imparts His Love through Jesus," by saying, "We didn't know what to call it so we are going to let you choose your own title." Beginning in a soft voice, Pastor Winburn alternated his speech pattern from slow, to regular, to fast, repeating phrases along the way to add significance and tie ideas together. His body language, which flowed with the rhythm of the sermon, added to his dynamic speaking style. Waving his arms in the air and stomping his foot on the ground to accompany the rise and fall of his voice, Pastor Winburn ensured that every member of the congregation paid attention to the sermon and followed his every movement. The congregation, in turn, showed that they were listening by interjecting "mhmm," "hallelujah," and "that's right" throughout. At the end of the service, Pastor Winburn gave the closing prayer while the choir sang in the background. The choir and congregation sang a final song as Pastor Winburn and his wife walked around hand-in-hand greeting everyone and thanking them for coming.

Our experience at Shaffer was the starting point for the rest of our exploration of the church in Muncie's African American community. With the help of our community advisors, Phyllis Bartleson and Pastor Renzie Abram, we were directed to others in the community. Phyllis, as the director of the Human Rights Commission, directed us to Erika Quarles and Sam Long. As a member of the Collective Coalition of Concerned Clergy and pastor of Berea Apostolic Church, Renzie introduced us to Pastor Willie Jackson, Bishop Michael Millben, and Pastor Charlotte Levi. Our conversations with these members of the community and our visits to churches such as Shaffer Chapel helped us to identify common themes and to see the role religion plays in peoples' lives. The church is the bedrock of this community. It provides support, leadership, and hope.

The History of Muncie's African American Churches

In 1868, twelve people met at the home of Mary H. Artist in Muncie to establish a black church. The group had been meeting in the county courthouse, but space was limited. With the urging of three women— Mrs. Artist, Mrs. Booker, and Mrs. Frey—the congregation decided to form their own church.[1] On March 4, 1872, the group purchased property and organized Bethel African Methodist Episcopal (A.M.E.) Church. Reverend Henry White as the first minister then set the congregation to building the church, with "men carrying logs on their shoulders and digging by hand with shovels."[2]

In 1872, shortly after the establishment of Bethel A.M.E., a group of Baptists in town began a new church. Services were first held in the log cabin of William and Sarah Jones. In 1879, the group purchased a plot of land near Bethel A.M.E, and in 1881, Reverend Warren Kimball oversaw the construction of a frame building that became known as Calvary Baptist Church.[3]

Calvary Baptist attempted to meet all the needs of Muncie's black Baptists but could not. So in 1905, Calvary Baptist established a branch church in the neighborhood of Whitely called the Baptist Mission of Whitely.[4] However, members of the neighborhood wanted their own church, so in the same year they made plans to organize a new church. The group became divided on the issue of what the church should be called—with some supporting the name "First Baptist" and others supporting the name "Antioch." Eventually, this debate became so heated that the Baptists of Whitely split into two camps that eventually formed Union Missionary Baptist and Antioch Baptist, both of which were situated in Whitely.[5]

While the Baptist churches were growing and expanding, a group of Methodists decided to start a second Methodist church. In 1895, the group built a one-room frame church that became known as Trinity United Methodist Church and provided the Methodists of Industry with a new place of worship.[6] About twenty-five years later, a group of Methodists in Whitely also seeking to organize their own church met on June 10, 1919.[7] Under the leadership of Thomas Phillips and Presiding Elder Reverend J. P. Wallace, the group began holding church services in the home of a member. They called their new church Shaffer Chapel A.M.E. Church after a national A.M.E. bishop. In 1928, the congregation bought a four-room schoolhouse, moving the church to the location it has held ever since.[8]

Shaffer Chapel congregation, circa 1930. Courtesy Archives and Special Collections, Ball State University.

At around the same time, Christ Temple Church began. When Bishop Oscar Sanders moved to Muncie from Indianapolis, he initially found the town unresponsive to his Pentecostal teachings.[9] He took a job in a local foundry, working during the day and preaching in the streets at night. Determined to establish a new church, Bishop Sanders was described as "the type of minister that did not sugarcoat the Gospel for any person or any certain group of persons and was known from coast to coast . . . as 'Sin-Killing Sanders.'"[10] With such strong convictions and determination, Bishop Sanders soon succeeded in founding Christ Temple in Whitely. As the church grew, it moved and in 1923, finally established a permanent location in 1936 in Industry.[11]

During these early years, members of Muncie's African American community worked to establish churches where they could worship God freely, thank Him for His blessings, and pray for the easing of suffering. Through monetary sacrifice, physical toil, and community action, churches appeared in Muncie's black neighborhoods, and for many years these churches served their congregations—providing a worship center as well as a place for assembly and social life. By the 1940s, Muncie had about ten black churches that served the entire African American population and established the foundation of religion in the community.

Sometime in the 1940s and 1950s, a change began within Muncie's religious community, marked by the slow emergence of many new churches. Phyllis Bartleson remembers that when she was young there were only about ten black churches located in Muncie, but now there are between forty and fifty African American places of worship.[12] This church splintering occurred over many years. "It wasn't as if I went to bed one night and woke up to find forty new churches," says Phyllis.[13] When we asked Phyllis why so many churches began to appear, she offered several explanations. Oftentimes, she says, churches divide as arguments arise among members of the congregation and cause factions to break away from the church and form a new organization. Another common type of contention is what type of service the church should perform—some want a traditional service and others desire a more contemporary, "exciting," service.[14]

Between the 1940s and the 1990s, many of the original black churches in Muncie splintered. Phyllis said, "Trinity used to be *the* church, and then the church split. Word of Life . . . was a splinter of Trinity. The current pastor there and the vast majority of his membership were once members of Trinity. That hurt us."[15] Some church splits may have happened because members felt driven away. Bishop

Michael Millben, who moved to Muncie in the 1980s to become pastor of Christ Temple Church, notes that this was true in the case of his church. Still pastor of Christ Temple, he says about the church he inherited: "I inherited a church that was the premier church that exemplified an exclusive attitude."[16] Animosity in the congregation led to the formation of several splinter groups, which led to new churches. Pastor Renzie Abram recalled that during this period, Pastor Hunt formed Emmanuel Temple Church, Pastor Howard started Greater Grace Apostolic Church, and Pastor Edith Hutchison founded House of Prayer for All People after breaking away from Bishop Sanders of Christ Temple.[17] Again and again, our community consultants told stories of how splintering occurred at many of Muncie's older African American churches as dissatisfied members of the congregation struck out—whether from anger or frustration—and formed their own congregations.

Yet not all of the new churches were formed because of strife and discontent. Individuals who felt compelled to establish entirely new places of worship began other new churches such as Paramount Community Church. "The Lord had given my mother the vision . . . in California, that she would build a church here in Muncie," explains Pastor Charlotte Levi of Paramount about her evangelist mother, Reverend D. M. Russell Levi. "She was just carrying out what the Lord had already shown her. We were just instruments working with her."[18]

The Birth of a Vision

We met Pastor Charlotte Levi on a cold Friday afternoon at Paramount Community Church. Walking into the small building, we stood in a sanctuary accented by blue-cushioned pews and gold-colored light fixtures. Somewhere in the building a hymn played, echoing through the empty room. From the back of the church, a small woman beckoned us to sit down with her in the warmer community room in the rear of the building. Taking our seats, we began conversing with Pastor Levi and quickly found ourselves drawn in by her tenderness and sincerity. Pastor Levi recounted how the Lord had worked wonders in her life and helped her parents begin Paramount.

Pastor D. M. Russell Levi, Pastor Charlotte Levi's mother, realized her dream of founding a church in Muncie in 1944, when five adults and two children met in the home of Brother and Sister Woldridge and began Paramount.[19] The fledgling church purchased an old pottery shop and transported it to a newly purchased vacant lot. Making do with

Pastor Charlotte Levi leads prayer from the front of Paramount Church after a radio service for the elderly and shut-ins—a radio service that has continued since Levi's mother started it in 1953. Photo by Danny Gawlowski.

what they had, Pastor Levi said that they built an altar, placed "old fashioned straight backed chairs" with white covers out for seating, and began picking up children for Sunday School.[20] Pastor D. M. Russell Levi began preaching in the new church and her husband Reverend Lawrence Levi led the music service. Commenting that her parents had made "quite a team," Pastor Levi said that the church soon grew and became known as the "cracker jack and diaper church" and "the orange juice and graham cracker church" because of the large numbers of children who attended.[21]

With more revenue and members, Paramount undertook a building project that greatly expanded the church. As journalist Dick Green wrote in a local newspaper article, "They built a church *inside* a church."[22] Her mother and father led a construction project that built another structure around the pottery shop and used bits of the smaller building to finish a new larger church. "The Lord told her how He wanted it, 40 feet by 60 feet, and when she did 40 feet by 60 feet, He added the other 30 feet to make it 40 feet by 90 feet because He wanted a community room here."[23]

Following the construction plan laid out by God, Paramount continued to grow. When we visited Pastor Charlotte Levi she was still preaching in the church that her parents built. Thinking back on the founding of Paramount, she expressed her feelings about the church and her parents by saying, "Praise the Lord, He gave them wisdom and strength and perseverance. They were able to accomplish much and touch many lives."[24]

As more African American churches like Paramount began to flourish in Muncie, the number of worship centers continued to increase. Our consultants explained this proliferation of churches in different ways. Renzie Abram commented that the majority of the churches he visits have low attendance and attributes this partly to the number of churches in town, saying, "We've divided ourselves. There are so many little churches that you didn't have years ago."[25] Sam Long agreed that "years back, to a certain extent you had pastors trying to outdo other pastors."[26] As the number of churches increased, this competition between churches increased as well. Churchgoers had more and more religious options to choose from, further splintering Muncie's religious community. But while Pastor Jackson agrees that the large number of churches has divided the religious community into many smaller congregations, he also believes that "in some cases, [the divisions] are a good thing." He believes that new churches often emphasize aspects of the ministry differently than established churches and may win souls to Christ that might otherwise remain lost.[27] "The whole idea is to go out and start churches in communities where there aren't churches—although I recognize . . . there are already a lot of churches in Muncie."[28]

Foundations of Unity

"Years ago," says Renzie Abram, "we stayed separated—at least in Muncie—but we're coming together."[29] Pastor Levi agrees: "I have seen a great change as far as the religious community. I've known the time when I would not have been a part of the Collective Coalition of Concerned Clergy (CCCC) because it was all men. You just felt like you weren't accepted, but now that has changed. Women are a part of it now and communication and fellowship is different. . . . Before, there was just no place for us but now, they've accepted women into the group, and two of us are officers."[30]

As Pastors Abram and Levi observe, the religious community has begun to change. In the 1990s, denominations, churches, and individuals began coming together and working to end some of the divisiveness and competition. Through our own attendance at various church services and religious programs, it is evident to us that pastors and congregants in Muncie's black community genuinely enjoy fellowship with Christians from diverse denominations and that, despite apparent divisions, there is a real sense of unity within the religious community today.

Renzie, for example, has preached at Pastor Jerry Bumpus's Holy Ghost Temple Church of God in Christ and Dr. Buddy Kirtz's Shiloh Church of God in Christ. Both of these pastors have in turn preached at Renzie's church.[31] "There are some that are still sort of staying to themselves," Renzie says, "but I believe that if they were invited to one of the churches they would probably go and minister."[32] Another minister who has made attempts to hold services with other churches is Bishop Millben. Several years ago, Bishop Millben took out a full-page ad in Muncie's black paper, the *Muncie Times*, and directed a letter of apology to the black community of Muncie.[33] He wrote: "I apologize for our [Christ Temple's] air of exclusivity and the general aloofness that we've had for our eighty-year history. People have been offended by the way we came off," and the church tended to "demonize" those that left.[34] Because of this letter, Bishop Millben says that a lot of the animosity between Christ Temple and its splinter churches dissipated, and today there is a much better relationship and fellowship among the churches.[35]

Another group that is helping to bring together the churches of Muncie is an organization known as City Wide Church. The concept of City Wide Church began several years ago when Pastor George Saunders of First Baptist Church, a predominantly white church, and Pastor Jackson of Union Missionary Baptist Church decided to trade services. After the first service, however, so many people wanted to become involved that they decided to hold two large services in Worthen Arena at Ball State University. Nearly 5,000 people representing 109 churches from Muncie came to each of the two worship programs.[36] Pastor Saunders and Pastor Jackson each spoke at the events. "It was tremendous," Pastor Jackson says, "There were people everywhere."[37] Out of these services, City Wide Church was born, which now sponsors a yearly event known as Jesus Day. On the first Saturday in June, a parade marches through downtown to Muncie Central High School where a church service comprised of congregations from across Muncie is held on the football field.[38]

Our consultants believe that these events have done much to bring together both the black churches and the white churches of Muncie and foster unity in the religious community. But many believe more needs to be done. There is still a lot of discord among Muncie's African American churches, according to Phyllis. "It is almost like every church has its own little turf," she says. "There is not a lot of interaction."[39] Echoing this sentiment, Sam Long adds: "There are four churches across town that I doubt if each one of them has ten members. Why couldn't they come together? . . . Everybody is talking one Lord, one faith, one baptism. There is only one God and as far as I know, one heaven. We're all trying to get to the same place. If you don't have fellowship down here what makes you think you can have fellowship up there? . . . It is time people pulled together into one church."[40] Pastor Renzie Abram believes that this goal of unifying the churches has begun. "It's not on a large scale," he says. "I'd say it could be—but I see changes. The black churches are coming together."[41] Finally, Pastor Jackson combines elements from all of these comments saying, "I think we might have the foundation there. There was a day when there wasn't a lot of crossing denominational lines. That has changed in the last twenty years and is still changing towards the better. We've got some good stuff going on, but we're trying to make it better. We're celebrating our unity and encouraging greater unity. We've still got some way to go."[42]

More than a Building:
Testimonies of Faith and Salvation

"You have to weather the storm," says John Young-El. "You weather the storm with your faith."[43]

We descended into the basement of Union Missionary Baptist Church looking for Pastor Willie Jackson. His administrative assistant promptly greeted us and showed us to his office. This was our first meeting with Pastor Jackson and since he is such a busy man, we came with direct questions to get the most we could from our time with him. We started the conversation by asking how he defined faith. "The definition of faith really depends on how you are trying to apply it. Faith with regard to salvation is that trusting reliance in what God did through Jesus to provide for our salvation. Faith with regard to my religious orientation is that I am of the Baptist faith. Faith in terms of a working principle in life is just my trust in God that He will provide for all of my needs and take care of me."[44]

Now that we had a working idea of the *word*, the next question we tackled was how faith works in a person's everyday life. We found that faith in Muncie's African American community closely parallels that of the working class described in the original Middletown study.

Finding the Lord: The Road to Salvation

We met with Pastor Renzie Abram for the first time in January 2003. Renzie leads a local Apostolic church and has lived in Muncie almost all of his life, and we felt that a conversation with him might help us understand the role of the church in the African American community of Muncie. Unsure of what to talk about, we made a list of questions so we would have something to start the conversation. As Renzie sat in his chair across the room, looking thoughtfully over the questions, he began to talk about his own road to salvation. "I wasn't ready to turn my life over at that time," he recalled. "I was real young. I didn't know about salvation, turning my life over to the Lord, or getting baptized. But as I got older and heard the word preached, I knew I was a sinner. I knew that I needed to be saved. . . . Being saved is something that Christ has done for us. It is not something I could work for because He paid the price by shedding His blood on Calvary. So when I accepted Christ as my savior and allowed Him to be Lord of my life, I was saved." He adds, "another thing happened: I received the baptism of the Holy Spirit. That gave me power to stop doing some of the wrong I was doing. To be honest with you, I haven't always been saved. I used to lie, I used to steal, and I used to smoke marijuana. When the Lord came into my life it changed my life. I wanted to go to church; I wanted to study His word . . . and in the process of studying His word, praying, and being faithful in the church, He called me into ministry."[45]

Rescue from a life of sin is the promise that Jesus fulfilled when He came to earth and died, our consultants say, and the faith that a person has in that promise is, in turn, the vehicle for salvation. At this level, religious orientation in Muncie's black community is not very diverse. Like the Lynds' study in the late 1920s we found that there are few Muslims or Catholics—for the most part, black people here tend to be rooted in Protestant Christianity.[46] Today the three main denominations in this community are Baptist, Pentecostal, and Methodist.

Renzie Abram. Photo by Danny Gawlowski.

Denominational Differences

Minister Mallory began to speak while the congregation settled into the wooden pews, anxiously awaiting the word. As we sat in the congregation we were struck by how much this church was similar to yet different from all of the others that we had visited in Muncie. Sitting in the second-to-last pew in Union Missionary Baptist Church, we finally realized what was different.

All of the churches had dynamic services, but what we found striking was the degree to which the congregations involved themselves in the service. At Shaffer A.M.E. the congregants occasionally chimed in on what the minister was preaching about with an "amen" or "mhummm," but rarely did anyone get so excited that they would stand or shout. At Christ Temple, it was the total opposite. As believers often say, the "Holy Spirit truly had Its way there." People shouted. Some waved praise flags while others praised the Lord with dance. But now, as we were sitting in Union, we began to notice just how they were interacting and responding to the service. They were not dancing, or "mmm hmming" quietly from their seat, but they were interacting by standing, clapping, and reciting scripture along with the minister as he preached.

Even though everyone has their own way of worship, there seems to be a trend toward more nondenominational or interfaith services. Some Pentecostal churches are giving up their strict dress codes. Events such as revivals and City Wide Church are breaking down denominational barriers.[47] Despite growing unity, however, many people find it hard to let go of their denominational affiliations. "That kind of service just does not jive with my personality," says Erika Quarles, a practicing Roman Catholic, about many Baptist church services in Muncie. Erika grew up in a home with a Catholic mother and a Baptist father who allowed her to choose which church to attend. "Mass is the same as a Baptist church service, just shorter," she jokes. "We do all of the same things, just under a different name. We all have different terminology that we use."[48]

As Erika says, not everyone has the same type of worship style or expects the same thing out of a church service, and Pastor Jackson suggests that although we all want to unite and be one, certain worship styles may not be comfortable for everyone. "The very thing that could bring us together," he says, "is the very thing that keeps us apart."[49]

Believing: The Power of Faith

Phyllis Bartleson had given us Sam Long's name because he was the nephew of Reverend Ivan P. Broaddus, an influential religious leader in Muncie's past. We met with Sam in his home in Whitely to discuss his uncle and to hear his story. Sam had moved from Alabama in his early twenties to Muncie to find work, and in the process he found the Lord. "I went to church to be filled," began Sam Long. When he came to Muncie as a young man, Sam said his uncle, Reverend Broaddus, did not force him to go to church. "I would go to church because I wanted to go to church, because if you force me I'm not going to get anything out of it anyway. . . . I love church. I've got to go there to get filled with the Holy Ghost to carry me through that next week, to get me started off. Especially going off to work in the factory. You're fighting the Devil all the time."[50]

As we continued our conversation in Sam's living room, he went on to say that "God has been good to me and I am willing to serve Him and give Him some of my time, and thank Him for what He did for me this week . . . and to [ask Him to] give me the strength to lead and guide me in the right direction for the next week."

Hearing Sam talk about his perception of God and about his personal faith, we were prompted to ask for an example in his own life where God had moved on his behalf. "I was in the emergency room and the doctors lost me three times, they gave me only hours to live. But I am still here. People were praying for me and I was healed by God. God had the last say, not the doctors."[51] Testimonies like this one, say our consultants, are proof of what faith in God can do, and will do, for His believers.

God's House

For many of our consultants, "church" can refer to a particular place, but in the abstract it can mean just as many different things as "faith" often does. It is a place to learn, socialize, pray, and worship among many other things. Indeed, "it is the hub of our community."[52] When we started this project we knew that attending church would be a must. We started our journey at Christ Temple, where the Martin Luther King Jr. Day celebration was held. Although this was a community event, it was at heart a church service, with prayer, music, and a sermon.

At the service, one minister opened with this prayer:

Thank you for how You've watched over us,
For every way You've made,
For every burden You've lifted,
For every door You've opened Dear God, we just give Your name the

Praise-Honor-and-the-Glory.
Thank You for Jesus Christ,
Thank You for Calvary,
Thank You for the Resurrection,
Thank You for filling us *with your*
Holy
Spirit.

God, You're worthy to be praised. . . .

*Now-Lord-I-**pray*** that Your word is going to go forth and fall on good
   ground tonight.
I *pray* somebody's going to be saved,
That *somebody's* going to be set free and I pray that some *burden* is going
   to be lifted.

Dear God I pray that something *spectacular* and *miraculous* is *going-to*
happen in this place. I *pray **somebody*** is going to be *healed*.
I ***pray*** *somebody* is going to be filled with your Holy Spirit. God, I
   believe in *victory* in this place.
   Right
   Now.
Lord, let the words of my mouth and the meditations of our hearts . . .
let them be *acceptable* in Thy sight.
Lord, You are our *strength* and our redeemer.
In *Jesus* name we pray
Amen (Response: "Amen").[53]

Listening to the prayer, we were reminded that for many of our consultants, prayer is not just a ritual. Indeed, it works in mysterious ways.
Several weeks later, we sat in the fellowship room at Paramount Community Church listening to Pastor Charlotte Levi tell the story of how
her Liberian brother and sister came to America. James was a "mission
baby," which means that he had been sent to the mission when he was
born. Many of the babies who come to the mission had lost their mothers during childbirth. So when Pastor Levi's mother heard of this little
boy, James, she began the process that would lead to his adoption and
travel to the United States. James had a sister, Dorcas, who came to stay
at the mission as well. She was supposed to stay at the mission until
James left, but she decided that she would like to come to America, too.
She had not been part of the adoption but, "the whole mission started
to pray for God to hold up the ship until her paperwork came through.

God gave them two weeks to the day, which was just long enough to get everything taken care of."[54]

Ushering in the Holy Sprit: Music in the Church

Shaffer's service was slowly taking shape. The piano player could hardly talk, but she agreed to sing the solo that the pastor asked of her: "Wrapped Up, Tied Up, and Tangled Up in Jesus," a soulful song that explains the ideal relationship with God. She began the song, playing along on the piano, increasingly getting more and more into the song. Some would say that it was the power of the Holy Sprit that filled her, because as she sang, her voice came back, and she began to shout and praise the Lord even more. "I'm wrapped up, tied up, tangled up in Jesus, and He is all that I need."[55]

Music sung in God's House is like this, our consultants say. "If you have someone sing a solo," says Renzie, "or the choir sings, it tends to electrify the atmosphere."[56] There is no way to describe gospel music other than to call it passionate. Just as prayer takes different forms, so does music. There is congregational music as well as music sung by the choir. Music is used as praise and worship. But it also helps to usher in the Holy Spirit. Through music, man leaves and God takes over.

Viola Boyd leads Shaffer Chapel's congregation in song. Photo by Danny Gawlowski.

The Word

Building a sermon often starts with prayer. "I pray to ask God what I should preach about," says Pastor Jackson. "Once I have a good understanding of God's direction, then it's just studying. I use all of the information I can to understand the subject matter or Scripture."[57] In homiletics, the class that teaches how to build sermons, ministers are taught that sermon preparations should start on Monday, so that you have the entire week to prepare for Sunday. "I usually try and spend some time in preparation each day," says Pastor Jackson, "even if it is only time spent in prayer."[58] Even though you should start on Monday, Renzie reveals "it doesn't always happen that way with me."[59]

"I don't preach my sermon prior to Sunday morning. Every time I preach on Sunday mornings I am sort of honing my skills . . . my practice comes while doing it. Sometimes I preach something totally different than I have prepared," says Pastor Jackson.[60] In our conversation with Bishop Millben, he told us that oftentimes preachers will preach a sermon no matter what is happening, but as far as he is concerned, sometimes God moves and people are ministered to without a sermon. "I'll hold off on the sermon until a later time and let God have his way."[61]

Many sermons in Muncie's black community are delivered in a very animated way. Pastors will often change the level, pitch, or intonation of their voices to get their point across. Some ministers will even leave the pulpit to preach to the congregation. You are not taught any particular style, according to Bishop Millben; you learn and gather techniques from your mentors or as you go along.[62] Although there is no standard style, ministers in this community still find effective ways to deliver their message to the community.

The Religious Community:
Church Is More than Sunday Service

From the porch we could hear loud barking. Phyllis Bartleson answered the door with a bright smile telling us not to be afraid of her puppy. Puppy? As Phyllis locked Cherub, her 100-pound German Shepard, in a bedroom around the corner, we set up our recording equipment, getting ready to start the conversation. Even though this was only our third meeting, we chatted like old friends.

On our initial meeting with Phyllis, she told us a story about the church picnics that the Trinity Sunday School used to take. "I was about seven or eight," she recalled, leaning forward in her chair, as if to get closer to the memory. "There were not many black churches, so we did more things together. I can remember this one time in particular when the churches got together, it was a Sunday School picnic, and we went up to New Castle State Park on State Road Three. I thought that park was so big, and they had ducks that you could feed. I just thought that trip was terrific, riding on the church bus. It was just a good time and there was no distinction between denominations. It is a shame that they don't do those things now."[63]

People remembered that in the past, church doors were always open. You could go in at any time for no other reason than to have a quiet place to talk to God. But that has changed; many people say that the church seems to have less of a community feel than it once did. There was a time when children used to go to the church after school and play. Women were always there baking cookies, cleaning the church, or just talking with each other. Whenever the kids came by, the women would feed them the goodies they had baked. Families would go to church together. Although not all parents came to church with their children, it seems there were far more families attending church together then. "Ten or fifteen years ago most of the parents went to church and their kids went to church," says Sam Long. "We'd walk into church—the wife, the three kids, and me . . . nowadays it's totally different."[64]

Once the church was the community and the community was the church. But that seems to be fading. Pastor Willie Jackson attributes this "shift away from God" to the "world becoming more tilted toward the secular rather than the spiritual, and there is less honest reading—faithful and committed reading—of the Bible. We are not as God-minded as we were."[65]

While the church may have lost some of its old community feeling, it is still a place in the community where people can go. Where the church community was once centered on informal fellowship, now it seems that that the community is recentering around planned events that take place at church like weekly bible study, revivals, and group and auxiliary meetings. Cell ministry groups, for example—like the ones that meet at Bishop Millben's church—are reminiscent of the days when churches met in the homes of believers. The cells are made up of congregational groups that have something in common such as singles, married couples, single mothers, the elderly, and so on. Each cell meets and worships together in different homes. Through ministries such as these, events like Martin Luther King Jr. Day, and City Wide Church, the church is working to re-create its community feel.

Church Leaders, Activists, and Politicians

The African American community's pastors have often doubled as leaders of the community. In Bishop Millben's words, "I think black clergy often get pushed into that position of leadership."[66] Bishop Millben explains that during antebellum times, the church functioned as the only place where African Americans could legally congregate. Through his work with white congregations and pastors, Bishop Millben has noticed that "our congregations have different expectations of us. Most white congregants aren't interested in their pastors getting involved in politics. They don't feel like that is in their purview, and black congregants *expect* their pastors in many cases to get involved."[67] Sam Long adds, "Clergymen should be leaders in a community. They are taken care of by the people. General Motors—they can cut me loose or put so much pressure on me to make me want to quit if I'm fighting for something that benefits someone in the plant. The pastor has a voice and can say what he wants to say anytime he wants to say it, negative or whatever. Politically they can't be touched."[68] The independence of black ministers, and the relationship of that independence to political involvement and agitation cannot be overstated.

Because of these expectations, Bishop Millben believes that "a black pastor has much more influence in his community than do most white pastors."[69] "The black church in black America has always been the voice of the community," adds Pastor Jackson.[70] Renzie Abram further comments that the church has a responsibility to the people of the community, "there are people with needs, and I believe the church should reach out to those that are hungry, homeless, down-and-out, abused, whatever."[71] This black community instills authority and prestige in the office of minister, but expects their pastors to assume a leadership role in the community in return—serving both as a mouthpiece and protector of the people.

Out of the Pulpit: Ministers Take Action

Historically, Muncie's African American community has been led by a number of influential and politically active black pastors who have stepped up during times of hardship and strife. Reverend J. E. Johnson of Shaffer Chapel, who is still revered today, arrived in Muncie shortly after World War I with "little more than a suitcase."[72] He began preaching at Shaffer Chapel and established a mortuary

Reverend John E. Johnson, circa 1930. Courtesy Archives and Special Collections, Ball State University.

nearby. In 1930, a brutal lynching occurred in nearby Marion, Indiana. Three young black men, accused of murdering a white man and raping a white woman, were taken from the county jail—two were dragged through the streets behind cars—and hung from a maple tree in the courthouse square in front of a crowd of thousands. The third man escaped. Deciding that these men deserved a Christian burial, Reverend Johnson drove to Marion and retrieved the bodies, risking his personal safety.[73]

Word of the lynchings had spread fast, far, and wide, and the mood in Muncie's African American community was tense. A rumor began to spread that a white mob planned to descend upon Reverend Johnson's mortuary to steal the bodies and burn them.[74] Because of these concerns, Delaware County's white Sheriff, Fred Puckett, met Reverend Johnson at the Delaware County line and escorted him and the bodies back to Muncie. Anxiety within the black community peaked and many individuals began to arm themselves. With the help of Sheriff Puckett, members of the black community gathered at Shaffer Chapel, the headquarters of the hastily formed militia. African Americans from Muncie and as far away as Indianapolis began to prepare to defend themselves should a mob form.[75] According to one participant in the event, "I will never forget Trooper Orville Taylor [a black veteran of World War I], he was our leader; he was spacing us up and down Highland Avenue, and anybody who came by, especially any white group in a car, would be stopped and questioned. We thought for sure somebody was going to get trigger happy and shoot somebody, but nobody came to get the bodies."[76]

Because of Reverend Johnson's courage, the two murdered young men received a proper burial and Muncie's African American community made a show of strength and solidarity in the face of hostile racism. Throughout the ordeal, Shaffer Chapel played a prominent role as the headquarters of the local militia, and would continue to act as a center of operations during the Civil Rights Era.

During the 1950s, 1960s, and 1970s, a new group of ministers took over as leaders of Muncie's African American community. One of the foremost among these preachers in the minds of our community consultants was Reverend Anthony J. Oliver. "They called him Muncie's Martin Luther King," Renzie says. Oliver helped begin the struggle for equal rights in Delaware County.[77]

Reverend Oliver served as a minister at Shaffer Chapel and, like his predecessor Reverend Johnson, soon assumed a leading role as a community activist. During his tenure at Shaffer, Reverend Oliver sought to integrate businesses across Muncie. He worked to get African Americans hired at Borg-Warner, Pepsi Cola Bottling Co., local banks and lending institutions, and Muncie's utility companies.[78] "I can remember during my high school days," remembers Renzie. "Reverend Oliver would picket Indiana-Michigan Light Company because they didn't have any black employees. I saw he and Mary Dollison picketing, but I was taught we didn't get involved in this. I wish today that I would've helped them out."[79] Hurley Goodall did participate in some of Reverend Oliver's protests and wrote about an incident at the Pepsi Cola Bottling Co.:

> I guess it was sometime around 1962 or 1963 that we were unhappy that there had been several young men who had entered Mr. Gillespie's office and made applications but had been turned down. Mr. Gillespie made various excuses and Reverend Oliver looked at

him in his way with his eyes kind of crossed and his head leaned back and said, "Mr. Gillespie may I use your telephone?" Mr. Gillespie said yes, and Reverend Oliver pulled a paper with a number out of his pocket. The number was for the Pepsi Cola national headquarters in New York City. He dialed the number and got the party on the other end and said, "I'm Reverend A. J. Oliver, a minister in Muncie, Indiana. You have a Pepsi Cola franchise in this city and the people running the plant refuse to hire Negroes and I'm calling to tell you if there are no Negroes hired in this plant by tomorrow morning there will be a picket line around the plant." The person on the other end asked to speak with Mr. Gillespie. Mr. Gillespie spoke with him for several minutes, and his face turned red. When he hung up the phone he turned to Reverend Oliver and said, "Reverend Oliver, if you will have a couple of young Negroes here tomorrow morning at 8:00, I will hire them."[80]

Reverend Oliver also wrote letters and made phone calls to potential employers. On August 2, 1963, for instance, Reverend Oliver wrote a letter to President Emens of Ball State University:

With further reference to our conversation relative to job opportunities to Negroes, I am sending the name of the person. . . . A graduate of Muncie Central High School, Ms. Lisa Cotton is an experienced IBM operator and has a letter of recommendation from her former supervisor. It is my hope that the training and skills of the many fine Negro adults like Ms. Cotton will be utilized. I am happy to send her name to you because of your long record of keen and active interest in employment opportunities for promising Negro people.[81]

Reverend Oliver helped qualified African Americans find jobs, and as a result he helped to integrate Muncie's workforce. Because of his involvement in the economic welfare of the African American community, Reverend Oliver eventually helped to establish the People's Economic Progress Group in 1963, which sought to deal with issues of economic discrimination in Muncie.[82] That same year, Reverend Oliver ran for a spot on the Muncie City Council "so that he could have a wider forum to advocate equality for Negroes." Although he failed to get elected, the minister continued to be involved in politics in Muncie, serving as a voice for the minority community.[83] When Governor George Wallace of Alabama came to Muncie in his 1964 presidential campaign, for instance, Reverend Oliver organized a protest of the event. Hurley Goodall writes that

We built a casket draped in black, put a sign on it, naming the little girls that were blown up in the Birmingham church and the next day proceeded to Ball State with Reverend Oliver at the head of the column, with the sign in both hands protesting Governor Wallace's appearance. . . . There was a picket line with approximately three hundred persons surrounding the building where he spoke, and they picketed continuously all during his talk.[84]

Throughout his tenure as minister at Shaffer, Reverend Oliver remained active in the community—writing, speaking, protesting, and campaigning for equal rights. Yet Reverend Oliver was not alone in his endeavors. He worked closely with other ministers in the community—particularly Reverend Broaddus, who served as pastor of Antioch Baptist Church and Reverend Williams, pastor at Trinity United Methodist Church.

Reverend Ivan P. Broaddus was described by his nephew Sam Long, as a "five-foot, four-inch bunch of dynamite who didn't back down from anything."[85] Sam remembers that "Reverend Broaddus worked with all of them [the other ministers] . . . a lot of them would come to him and follow his leadership. . . . You couldn't get any information pertinent to what was going on from the government downtown, and he'd go down there, get it, and bring it back to the church. In fact, he passed it on to other churches in the city," says Sam.[86] Reverend Broaddus often worked closely with Reverend Williams. According to Sam, "They are the ones who went to City Hall to talk to the mayor and express their feelings about what they're not doing for blacks and what they're not doing for different communities."[87] During his time as pastor of Antioch, Reverend Broaddus helped start the NAACP in Muncie, became involved in community development, and, according to Sam, "participated in anything political that helped improve the city." He served as pastor of Antioch for fifty-three years.[88]

Reverend J. C. Williams, like Reverends Oliver and Broaddus, worked to improve race relations in Muncie and frequently became involved in political and social activism. Phyllis Bartleson remembers that her preacher stressed education. She says that "many of the things I learned about black history and the legacy of my ancestors came through the church."[89] In history classes held at the church, Phyllis remembers, "it was like, 'oh, I didn't know black folks did all that, because we weren't taught that in a regular classroom.'"[90] Through classes such as these, Phyllis says she learned that she could achieve things that, because she was a black woman, she might otherwise have considered impossible. As Phyllis grew older, Reverend Williams encouraged her and others of her generation to get a higher education. "It was almost a given. If you were a member of this church," she says, "you're going to go to school. A lot of our members went on to school and obtained bachelor's or associate's or some even master's degrees."[91]

By stressing education, Reverend Williams sought to ensure that members of his church had both a strong understanding of their cultural heritage and the qualifications to compete in the job market. For those who did not have educational training, however, Reverend Williams and Trinity also implemented Trinity Outreach Programs that taught people in the community skills and ideals. "The Trinity Outreach Program is a grassroots effort to find ways to serve the people of the community in ways that will provide them dignity, education, leadership abilities, and hope," Reverend Williams said in a newspaper interview from 1969.[92] He went on to talk about the Black Bag Shoppe and the Dr. Martin Luther King Black Theater saying, "The Black Bag Shoppe was established to provide a place of employment for young black people and as a venture in business in the ghetto. The Dr. Martin Luther King Black Theater Service Center was established to be more closely related to those who for reason of their own would not come to the church for help in securing employment, family counseling, tutoring, and other services."[93]

Eventually, Reverend Williams's involvement in the community led him to help found the Black Coalition of Muncie following the race riots at Southside High School in the late 1960s. This organization concerned many white members of Muncie. One excerpt from a newspaper of the time is telling. The writer notes: "a number of statements are being made by persons in the community concerning the coalition: One, that you want to be a Dr. Martin Luther King; two, that you want to be a dictator; three, that you encourage black parents to use their children to fight civil rights battles; and four, that you have abandoned your earlier nonmilitant approach."[94] Reverend Williams responded to these accusations by describing the Black Coalition as "an attempt to bring together our people so that we can develop programs which can assist in the alleviation of unnecessary problems that arise in the community because of lack of facts or unity." He went on to say, "In my opinion, if this Black Coalition gets the support of the black community and the white community it can serve as a very effective model for cities the size of Muncie. . . . I think the coalition can be an instrument for reconciliation."[95] Reverend Williams was deeply committed to this sentiment, writing, "I feel that I qualify to be committed to the positive ministry of reconciliation between blacks and whites. My father was murdered by a lynch mob in Alabama while my mother was pregnant with my twin brother and me. . . . I feel strongly that people must be united together in authentic reconciliation, that is, there must come an absolute honesty in the communication between the races."[96]

In 1971, Reverend Williams decided to attempt to take his educational, economic, and social policies to a citywide level by forming the Poor-People's Party and running for mayor. According to the party's Statement of Purpose, "The Poor-People's Party was created out of the desire of many people in seeing that the fundamental aims and purposes of the United States Constitution be made a living and practical reality in the experience of every citizen regardless of their race, sex, or national origin. We define poor as an experience of exclusion in any corporate endeavor which involves other persons in creating mutual benefits for all."[97] The party outlined its major issues of concern as "decent housing, quality education, equal share in decision making in the affairs of government, fair protection of their rights under the law, and in employment. The party will carry out programs to alleviate inequalities which plague the lives of the poor, the disenfranchised, and the members of all minority groups whether they be economically, culturally, or socially disadvantaged."[98]

The formation of this party stirred up controversy around Reverend Williams, but this time it reached into the black community. Sam Long remembers that the African American community had decided to put forth a black man to run for mayor. "That was supposed to be a closed circuit within the black community," he says, "and they were to meet and decide who was the best man to run for mayor. They had one meeting and the next thing you know Reverend Williams went down there and filed for mayor. That just killed his chances. There was no togetherness. It was something he did on his own that should have been voted on. The ministers could have pulled together and said, 'Hey, you'll have the best chance of winning because you have this quality, you did this, you're the person.' But it wasn't done that way, so that was just a name wasted."[99] Despite this criticism, the Poor-People's Party placed candidates in the 1971 race for mayor, city clerk, and city council. But none of the Poor-People's Party's candidates won, and Reverend Williams only garnered 1,194 votes in his bid for the mayor's office.[100] Despite this setback, he spent the remainder of his career as pastor of Trinity fighting for civil rights and acting as a voice of the community.

These men, although at times controversial, served as leaders of Muncie's African American community. They helped to ensure the protection of people's safety and basic rights. In their roles as pastors, they spoke out against injustice and helped to organize the community to action. For many of our community consultants, these men came to represent the ideal pastor and set the standard by which today's pastors are measured. Any time Phyllis spoke about Reverend Williams, her face would light up. As she recounted his various deeds, her voice would quicken with excitement. Likewise, when Sam talked about Reverend Broaddus he would seem to stare into the past, smiling occasionally at the memory of his preacher uncle. The vividness and excitement with which our community consultants talked about Reverends Oliver, Broaddus, and Williams indicated to us the importance of these men to the community.

On the Collective Coalition of Concerned Clergy

As class let out, we got into our cars, checking to make sure we had our field notes and pens. We drove the short distance from Shaffer Chapel to the Union Missionary Baptist Annex where the February meeting of the Collective Coalition of Concerned Clergy (CCCC, or Four Cs) meeting was supposed to be held. Bishop Millben had described the annex as a gray building that sat on the northwest corner of Highland and Macedonia. The large number of cars outside suggested a meeting inside. But nowhere on the structure was there any hint of a cross or other religious icon. In fact, overall, the building slightly resembled a bar.

Undeterred, we pulled into the small parking lot and checked our watches . . . 3:45 P.M. Should we go in? Or should we wait in the car until 4:00, the official meeting time given us by Bishop Millben? As we stepped out of the car, we noticed a man coming down the alley apparently heading from a nearby church to the building behind us. Could our luck be this good? We asked him if he was going to the CCCC meeting. He gave us a smile and said he was. We entered the annex with the man and found ourselves in a large wood-paneled room that looked as if it had indeed been a bar at one time. Set up in the middle of the room was a group of tables arranged into a rectangle around which sat the gathered members of the CCCC. Catching sight of Renzie across the table, we smiled, said hello, and then quietly took seats on a padded cushion that ran the length of the east wall across from the meeting table. Placing our notes on a small round table in front of us, we settled into our seats.

Before us, sitting around the table, were twelve of the pastors of Muncie's African American community. These men and women were intent on doing God's work and on bettering both the black community and Muncie in general. As the conversation began, we started looking around the room, connecting faces to names. Having heard about these pastors from so many other people, we felt as if we had already met most of them, and could name almost every minister and place them with their proper church. In front of us were Pastor Levi of Paramount Community Church, Bishop Millben of Christ Temple, Pastor Jackson of Union Baptist, and Pastor Abram of Berea Apostolic. This made us feel comfortable, and we set about listening to the conversation and taking notes on the interactions among the pastors.

The talk focused on the CCCC-sponsored Martin Luther King Jr. Day events of several weeks ago. Bishop Millben had said that this was the main scheduled topic of conversation for the meeting, and we listened as a thorough report was given on the logistics of the event and how the community perceived the services. Bishop Millben—as the current president—sat at the head of the table and was addressed as Mr. Chairperson, and people often looked to him and Pastor Jackson—the past president—when attempting to arrive at a solution to an issue. Voting was a semiformal affair in which an issue had to be introduced and seconded, and then voted upon with "ayes" and "nays." Aside from the formalities, however, the group spoke to each other in an informal, conversational manner, with joking occasionally overtaking the main line of discussion. What struck us the most was that all the pastors at the meeting seemed to be enjoying themselves and appeared to be friends with everyone else sitting at the table.

As the discussion on Martin Luther King Jr. Day events ended, the talk turned to political and social issues with which the CCCC was currently dealing. First, the group talked about issues related to the city government in Muncie. Recently, an issue of discrimination had arisen in the city, and the CCCC was holding talks with members of the City Council in the hope of correcting the situation. In addition, the CCCC expressed concern over the lack of minorities on the police force, which prompted the mayor to send word to the clergymen to inform them that efforts were underway to increase the recruitment of minority officers. Discussion turned to the CCCC's role as one of several groups seeking to change the name of Broadway Street to Martin Luther King Jr. Boulevard. A letter from the city office expressed approval of this idea and asked the clergymen to organize support for a city meeting dealing with the issue and for a petition to change the name. The gathered members

Bishop Millben speaks at Muncie's City Council to state the Coalition of Concerned Clergy's support for changing the name of Broadway Street to Martin Luther King Jr. Boulevard. Photo by Danny Gawlowski.

of the CCCC elected a delegate to attend the city meeting in order to stir up public support, while other members tried to think of which politicians they knew personally and could petition for assistance. This line of discussion surprised us because we didn't know that the CCCC had such active lobbying tactics. But this kind of direct action turns out to be one of the central roles of the CCCC, to protect the rights of minorities in the city and help to encourage a sense of pride in the African American community by taking issues of workplace and cultural discrimination directly to the mayor and city council.

The degree of power that the CCCC wielded became more apparent during the discussion of the next item on the agenda, a letter from the mayor. In this letter, Mayor Dan Canan expressed a desire to have an open dialogue with the CCCC to keep him abreast of issues facing Muncie's minority and religious communities. Consequently, he proposed the establishment of regular meetings with delegates from the group in order to create a better working relationship between the city office and the clergymen. Agreeing that this would be a positive step, the group elected three of its members to serve as a committee to meet with the mayor.

With the issue resolved, the group prepared to move on when one of the ministers made the point that the CCCC does not work with just black clergymen, but also often relies on the support of their fellow white preachers. Therefore, it was proposed that the committee bring up to the mayor the idea of including white ministers on the committee in order to provide a more diverse perspective and a unified voice of clergymen. This last point struck us as particularly powerful. Here was a letter from the mayor that acknowledged the power and influence of the CCCC in the community by asking them to hold regular meetings with his office. Yet, rather than taking the opportunity and simply establishing themselves, the group sought to include their white colleagues on the committee. To us, this provided evidence of the level of commitment these men and women have to the larger idea of unifying Muncie.

Finally, as the meeting was winding down, one of the pastors brought up the issue of a black man who was about to be sentenced in Muncie for a rather serious crime. However, the sentencing proposed by the court sought to send the man to prison for a term that was much longer than the sentences handed out to several white men who were recently tried and convicted for the same crime. While the pastors stressed that they did not condone the man's actions, they did want to see him treated fairly. One of the ministers suggested that the clergy should go to the man's attorney to show their support for the case, and on the day of the trial they should all try to attend the court session with members of their congregations. This last issue demonstrated to us the willingness of the CCCC to put their reputations on the line in defense of justice. These men and women were prepared to do their best to ensure that the defendant received a fair sentence.

Since the late 1970s, the CCCC has assumed the role of political leadership in Muncie's African American religious community. "We try to be apolitical," says Bishop Millben. "Our purpose is primarily to provide spiritual leadership in the community, but we feel it is incumbent upon us to address any kind of social injustice because we feel it is a spiritual concern and it impacts our congregations."[101] In the past, the CCCC has been involved in social activities such as campaigning to get Dr. Sam Abram hired as the superintendent of Muncie City Schools and even supported one Democratic mayor's bid for reelection by taking out a full-page ad supporting the politician in the *Muncie Times*.[102] "Our level of aggressiveness has been up and down depending upon what issues are out there and who was in the leadership position at the time," comments Bishop Millben.[103]

In order to deal effectively with issues brought to the group, Bishop Millben says, "I try to get a broad support. It is one thing for a bunch of black preachers to say you're not treating us right. The knee-jerk reaction is you've got a vested interest here and you guys've got a chip on your shoulders. Sometimes, you have to be careful about that because we can get a little paranoid, but it's not all paranoia. There are some real problems."[104] In addition to dealing with secular concerns, the CCCC works to maintain the image of the black clergy in Muncie. As Bishop Millben says, "I think that one of the things we are concerned about is ensuring the leadership of the black churches has a certain level of integrity."[105] Finally, the group continues to strive to represent the voice of the black community. As Pastor Jackson says, "Our coalition is a forum through which community issues can get a hearing. We will basically deal with anything that has to do with justice and righteousness."[106]

How Does the Church Still Lead
Muncie's African American Community?

With the CCCC clearly present and acting in the political and social interests of the African American community, the question remains as to what if any leadership role the church holds in Muncie today. Do people still see the church as leaders of the community, and do they still function as the people's voice? As we posed this question to our community consultants, we received a wide variety of answers. Why were we receiving such diverse responses? Were we missing something? Was some clue slipping past us?

When the question of church leadership came up in our conversations, many members of the community expressed the opinion that the clergy were not currently politically and socially active. People gave credit to the CCCC for sponsoring the various events on Martin Luther King Jr. Day, but believed that other than their involvement in this one event, the group remained relatively inactive. Because of this perceived lack of community involvement, a number of our consultants expressed frustration with today's clergymen. They felt that in the past pastors in the city were more active in community affairs.

But Pastor Renzie Abram's perspective is that his church is more politically active and involved in the community today than it was in the past. "I was taught we didn't get involved in politics . . . it was the teaching of my Pentecostal church that we stayed away from such things," says Renzie. "I think that at that time a lot of people did not get involved. We were taught not to vote, to pray for the leaders. We didn't get involved, now we do."[107] As pastor of an Apostolic Church, Renzie encourages his congregation to participate in the political process, and he is personally involved in the CCCC.[108] He told us that he believed ministers have a responsibility to become active in the community: "As ministers, if we don't help people in need what are we good for? I think we should speak up for justice as well as preach the gospel . . . we should hear the concerns of people in our city who have been hurt and mistreated and do something about it."[109]

Bishop Millben adds to this sentiment: "Politics is a practical thing you get pulled into all of the time because it affects so many of your people."[110] But, this can be complicated, trying to perform a leadership role straddling both the religious and secular worlds. The two interests may conflict and compete with each other for time and effort. He admits that he is often uncomfortable with his role as a leader in the community, saying, "I am always struggling with balance in that whole area . . . I am first and foremost a minister of the gospel. . . . I don't want to get to the place where I am just trying to be a social activist and that is it."[111]

Pastor Jackson has a slightly different take: "I want to be involved and I want Union Church involved in anything that is meaningful and significant in our community, and it doesn't have to be religious. I don't think the leadership role of the church has changed much. The voice of the church is as highly regarded now as it formerly was. I think that is because there are a number of other voices that are respected that did not exist forty or fifty years ago, not on equal planes in terms of respect."[112] Pastor Jackson also comments that he believes the church is still an important body within the community: "It is only able to mobilize the community because of its stance for what is right . . . anybody who wants to be right and just, whether they are saved or unsaved, will often give a hearing to the words of the Church."[113]

When we asked Pastor Jackson why he thought the leadership style of the church had changed, he said, "I think it is the size of the issues. I think in the King, Abernathy, and Jesse Jackson era, the issues were so national. They were large issues. They were issues that superceded local affairs and community and neighborhood matters. They were issues that even superceded blacks. . . . One of the reasons that explains the differences is just the size of the issues."[114] He went on to say, "I don't know, for example, to get the merit commission to look at how it does testing and how it does selecting—I'm not sure that is an issue to march down Main Street on. But it might be. . . . Back in that day, when you were talking about denying people voting rights and you were talking about siccing German shepherd police dogs on people, and lynching, that battle was going on all over the country. I just think those were issues of such national importance that it took that kind of up-front, out-front movement. And I even think in some cases what you saw in the local communities was motivated in the national community. So you might see your local pastor march down Main Street, but in some of these cases the motivations for what happened on the local level came from dealing with national cases."[115]

Erika Quarles, a young woman in her midtwenties, provided a voice from the next generation: "I think church leadership is good, but I think . . . you have to be sensitive about faith and religion these days. A lot of people are just automatically turned off by the church. Yes, that's the core of the African American community, but we can't just work with the African American community because that is not realistic."[116] Continuing, she says, "I think it can get us to a certain point. It's not going to get us where we need to be. I think that a lot of times when you say 'faith' people have misconceptions of pastors." When asked who she saw as today's leaders, Erika responded, "It has to be someone who can adapt," and added, "we need someone who can talk on the Whitely community level, and be able to talk to the kids, and be able to talk to the people on the street corner. . . . In our generation, we don't have a dominant religious figure."[117]

The role of the clergy in the black community appears to be in transition. In the past, the pulpit represented both a religious and political office. But it seems that today the religious and secular roles of ministers are two separate identities. Bishop Millben's struggle with the responsibility he feels to function as both a minister and a secular leader makes this point clear. As he puts it: "I am always struggling with balance in that area."[118] The ambivalence in how pastors should fulfill their roles in the community and how active of a political stance they should take resulted in many of the conflicting beliefs seen above. Older generations seek ministers who function as social and political activists, pastors attempt to find a balance between religious and secular concerns, and younger generations want community leaders who are not bound to religious beliefs.

In addition to the influence of these ideals of what the clergy should represent, Pastor Jackson brought up the changing nature of the issues that leaders in the black community must deal with. He pointed out that during the Civil Rights Era, pastors spoke out about issues of national concern. But many of today's issues are less obvious and more complex. Because of the changing nature of the issues being confronted, Pastor Jackson suggests that new tactics might prove more effective than marches and protests.[119] As we witnessed at the CCCC meeting, today's pastors may spend time meeting with the mayor behind closed doors, writing letters to various politicians, and supporting issues through more subtle means. Those accustomed to ministers like Reverends Oliver, Broaddus, and Williams, who actively picketed, protested, and marched on various institutions of power in the city, expect a truly "involved" minister to engage in such activities. Add to this that members of younger generations, such as Erika, feel less of an attachment to religious authority, and the issue becomes increasingly complex. The community is left with two vaguely defined groups: one that thinks the church does nothing and another that believes the church is working to make things better. In order to adapt to these new situations, the CCCC appears to have largely abandoned the traditional tactics of the last generation's activist ministers. Rather than attempting to rally the community to visible action, this generation combats discrimination and injustice behind the scenes and through political channels.

Notes

1. Hurley Goodall, "Practicing Religion," personal papers, 1.
2. Ibid.
3. Ibid.
4. James R. Clark, "History of Black Churches in Delaware County," 1976, 4 (Ball State University, ASC).
5. Goodall, "Practicing Religion," 3.
6. Clark, "History of Black Churches," 3.
7. Goodall, "Practicing Religion," 3.
8. Ibid.
9. Clark, "History of Black Churches," 7.
10. Ibid.
11. Ibid.
12. Phyllis Bartleson, conversation with Jessica Booth and Eric Efaw, January 15, 2003.
13. Phyllis Bartleson, conversation with Jessica Booth and Eric Efaw, January 29, 2003.
14. Ibid.
15. Phyllis Bartleson, conversation with Jessica Booth and Eric Efaw, February 4, 2003.

16. Bishop Michael Millben, conversation with Jessica Booth, Eric Efaw, and Danny Gawlowski, February 11, 2003.

17. Pastor Renzie Abram, conversation with Jessica Booth, Eric Efaw, and Danny Gawlowski, January 17, 2003.

18. Pastor Charlotte Levi, conversation with Jessica Booth and Eric Efaw, February 21, 2003.

19. Anonymous, "History of Paramount Community Gospel Church," unpublished manuscript, 1.

20. Pastor Charlotte Levi conversation, February 21, 2003.

21. Ibid.

22. Ibid.

23. Ibid.

24. Pastor Charlotte Levi conversation, February 21, 2003.

25. Pastor Renzie Abram conversation, January 17, 2003.

26. Sam Long, conversation with Jessica Booth, Eric Efaw, and Danny Gawlowski, February 19, 2003.

27. Pastor Willie Jackson, conversation with Jessica Booth and Eric Efaw, February 26, 2003.

28. Ibid.

29. Pastor Renzie Abram conversation, January 17, 2003.

30. Pastor Charlotte Levi conversation, February 21, 2003.

31. Pastor Renzie Abram conversation, January 17, 2003.

32. Ibid.

33. Bishop Michael Millben conversation, February 11, 2003.

34. Ibid.

35. Ibid.

36. Pastor Willie Jackson conversation, February 26, 2003.

37. Ibid.

38. Bishop Michael Millben conversation, February 11, 2003.

39. Phyllis Bartleson conversation, February 4, 2003.

40. Sam Long conversation, February 19, 2003.

41. Pastor Renzie Abram conversation, January 17, 2003.

42. Pastor Willie Jackson conversation, February 26, 2003.

43. John Young-El, conversation with Sara Bricker and Mia Fields, January 16, 2003.

44. Pastor Willie Jackson conversation, February 26, 2003.

45. Pastor Renzie Abram conversation, January 17, 2003.

46. Robert S. Lynd and Helen Merrell Lynd, *Middletown: A Study in Contemporary Culture* (New York: Harcourt Brace & Company, 1929), 346.

47. Bishop Michael Millben conversation, February 11, 2003.

48. Erika Quarles, conversation with Jessica Booth and Eric Efaw, February 20, 2003.

49. Pastor Willie Jackson conversation, February 26, 2003.

50. Sam Long conversation, February 19, 2003.

51. Ibid.

52. Erika Quarles conversation, February 20, 2003.

53. Martin Luther King Day service at Christ Temple, opening prayer delivered by Pastor Jeffery Johnson, January 20, 2003.

54. Pastor Charlotte Levi conversation, February 21, 2003.

55. Church service at Shaffer Chapel, February 9, 2003.

56. Pastor Renzie Abram conversation, January 17, 2003.

57. Pastor Willie Jackson conversation, February 26, 2003.

58. Ibid.

59. Pastor Renzie Abram conversation, January 17, 2003.

60. Pastor Willie Jackson conversation, February 26, 2003.

61. Bishop Michael Millben conversation, February 11, 2003.

62. Ibid.

63. Phyllis Bartleson conversation, February 4, 2003.

64. Sam Long conversation, February 19, 2003.

65. Pastor Willie Jackson conversation, February 26, 2003.

66. Bishop Michael Millben conversation, February 11, 2003.

67. Ibid.

68. Sam Long conversation, February 19, 2003.

69. Bishop Michael Millben conversation, February 11, 2003.

70. Pastor Willie Jackson conversation, February 26, 2003.

71. Pastor Renzie Abram conversation, January 17, 2003.

72. Hurley Goodall and J. Paul Mitchell, *African Americans in Muncie, 1890–1960* (Muncie, Ind.: Ball State University, 1976), 27.

73. Ibid., 25.

74. Ibid.

75. Ibid.

76. Goodall and Mitchell, *A History of Negroes*, 25.

77. Pastor Renzie Abram conversation, January 17, 2003.

78. Hurley Goodall, "Reverend Anthony J. Oliver Sr., May 1978" (Ball State University, ASC, Black Muncie History Project 1880–1978, Mss. 33, Box 2, Folder 8), 9.

79. Pastor Renzie Abram conversation, January 17, 2003.

80. Goodall, "Reverend Anthony J. Oliver Sr., May 1978," 9–10.

81. Ibid., 16.

82. Ibid., 20.

83. Ibid., 17.

84. Goodall, "Reverend Anthony J. Oliver Sr., May 1978," 28.

85. Sam Long conversation, February 19, 2003.

86. Ibid.

87. Ibid.

88. Ibid.

89. Phyllis Bartleson conversation, February 4, 2003.

90. Ibid.

91. Ibid.

92. "The Black Coalition: Its Chairman, Its Goals, and Its Plans," *Muncie Star*, November 9, 1969 (Ball State University, ASC, Black Muncie History Project, Mss. 33, Box 1, Folder 6).

93. Ibid.

94. Ibid.

95. Ibid.

96. "The Black Coalition: Its Chairman, Its Goals, Ind. and Its Plans."

97. Anonymous, *The Poor-People's Part of Muncie Indiana, 1971* (Muncie,: The Poor-People's Party, 1971), 1.

98. Ibid.

99. Sam Long conversation, February 19, 2003.

100. Bob Cunningham, *The History of Muncie City Elections, 1905–1986* (Muncie, Ind.: B. Cunningham, 1986).

101. Ibid.

102. Ibid.

103. Ibid.

104. Bishop Michael Millben conversation, February 11, 2003.

105. Ibid.

106. Pastor Willie Jackson conversation, February 26, 2003.

107. Pastor Renzie Abram conversation, January 17, 2003.

108. Ibid.

109. Ibid.

110. Bishop Michael Millben conversation, February 11, 2003.

111. Ibid.

112. Pastor Willie Jackson conversation, February 11, 2003.

113. Ibid.

114. Ibid.

115. Pastor Willie Jackson conversation, February 11, 2003.

116. Erika Quarles conversation, February 20, 2003.

117. Ibid.

118. Bishop Michael Millben conversation, February 11, 2003.

119. Pastor Willie Jackson conversation, February 11, 2003.

8

Engaging in Community Activities

Elizabeth Campbell and Jarrod Dortch, with Michelle Anderson, Sarah Bricker, Mia Fields, Danny Gawlowski, Anne Kraemer, and Ashley Moore[1]

The night was bitter cold, and those of us who had joined the short march from Muncie Central High School to Christ Temple Apostolic Church were glad to see the church, shining bright in the night like a beacon, only a short distance away. Today had been Martin Luther King Jr. Day and we had spent nearly all of it engaged in community activities, from breakfast this morning right through to the community-wide service and celebration that would take place here tonight. Approaching the church steps, we joined a tide of humanity that washed us through the church doors and into the bright lobby. This was, by Muncie standards, an unusually large crowd. Five hundred? Six hundred? Seven hundred? It was also, by the same standards, unusually diverse—the sanctuary, the lobby, and the streets outside teemed with people young and old, male and female, black and white.

Once inside, we gathered near the back of the lobby and talked about our initial impressions of this day, this church, and about the different Martin Luther King Jr. Day activities in which we had participated. Each of us chattered excitedly about the people we'd met, about those we hoped to meet, and about what we would do next. As we talked, we watched the front doors where the sea of people flowed unabated.

As the time for the service to start drew near, we rejoined the crowd. Moving toward the sanctuary, the crowd slowed as it passed through the four single doors and into the temple's large sanctuary. Inside, the crowd suddenly dispersed as everyone headed for different places. Some went toward the very front, some to the middle, some left or right, some to the large old Anglican church-style boxes in the very back of the church. People wandered slowly up and down the aisles, looking for an available red-cushioned seat in the crowded wooden pews, or perhaps for someone they'd intended to meet here.

We, in our overly casual college attire, could not help but notice that nearly everyone else in the church was well dressed. Women wore suits or slacks, skirts and crisply pressed blouses, dresses, high heels, and, in some cases, hats. Men wore suits, mostly conservative, though some suits here and there were bright or shiny, or both—deep purple, rich maroon, a green or golden glow. Men without suits wore sport coats. All had worn dress overcoats into the church, though most had hung their coats on the racks in the lobby.

An usher, dressed in a white blouse and black skirt, guided us to a spot on the sanctuary's far right side, just a few rows from the front. A table, littered with multicolored streamers, banners, and ribbons, stood just in front of the first pew on our side. All of the floors—sanctuary, apse, and altar—were covered in the same deep red carpet. Warm wood panels lined the back of the altar, and on those panels hung several large banners, decorated with bright colors, gold accents, and deep words. On the front of a single large podium in the center of the altar was a gold-trimmed, deep blue banner, decorated with the powerfully Christian symbols of a dove and fire. Behind the podium, a series of wide, stepped choir pews ran the length of the back wall. In front of the pews and to the left, a low-key group of musicians were gathered. Some practiced, some joked, some gazed out at the sanctuary as it filled. To the right, a small line of chairs faced the podium. Bishop Millben, pastor of Christ Temple and host of the evening's service, sat in one of the chairs and faced the podium. His chair looked like a throne.

Another man stepped to the podium and welcomed everyone with prayer. He read from the Scriptures, and then introduced the Collective Coalition of Concerned Clergy (CCCC, or Four Cs), sponsors for all of the day's events, and the Citywide Choir. The formerly low-key band suddenly jumped into an upbeat gospel song, as the members of the CCCC, all dressed in dark, conservative suits, walked down the aisle toward the altar and seated themselves in the front-most pews. Behind the clergy marched the two hundred or so members of the Citywide Choir, who all wore "uniforms" of black and red, though each member of the choir interpreted his or her uniform a bit differently. Some wore black bottoms and red tops. Others wore all black underneath, topped with a red vest, sweater, or jacket. Still others wore red bottoms and black tops. Some dressed all in black. A very few dressed all in red. One woman wore a great, flowing black caftan. An equally great flowing red silk scarf trailed behind her as she walked with the choir across the altar and into the choir pews. The choir sang all the way from the back of the church to their pews, making a raucous and joyful noise. They turned to face the congregation as they reached their seats.

The song finished, another minister came to the podium. A wide smile played across his face as he surveyed us. "Look to your left," he happily announced, "and say, 'Neighbor, I'm in the right place at the right time.'" "Neighbor," we all said, "I'm in the right place at the right time." The minister continued, still smiling. "Glory be to God." "Now tell your right hand neighbors, 'I'm breaking down barriers, and building bridges.'" We did as instructed, a little louder this time. By the time we finished, we were all smiling. "Amen," the minister finished. The praise and worship part of the service had begun, and everyone's spirits started to rise. Ministers from across the community came up to the podium to make brief statements about the nature of a day devoted to Dr. Martin Luther King Jr., to offer praises, and to thank the organizers of today's events. Each minister built on the good feelings created by the minister who had gone before him or her, and the sanctuary soon filled with gladness.

The African Connection, a group of African Christians, came onto the altar and performed a Zulu Christian hymn, moving the service from preaching back to song. The singers wore the clothes of their homelands: ornately decorated dashikis, brightly colored and patterned dresses, intricately tied headwraps. The African Connection swayed as they sang. Some members of the Citywide Choir swayed as well, and joined in the Zulu hymn's chorus.

After the Africans finished, they filed off the altar. The Citywide Choir stopped singing and swaying and stood tall, their shoulders back. The choir director, who had positioned herself directly in front of the choir, faced them. She lifted her arms straight up into the air, paused for just a few seconds, then threw both arms open wide. Two hundred voices rang out as sudden and loud as thunder as the Citywide Choir burst again into joyous song.

The Choir brought the good feelings that had been building to a peak. Many got "into the Spirit." People stood up in their pews clapping, tapping their feet, and dancing. The Spirit soon filled some, who then took the many colored ribbons and streamers from the front table and began to wave them over their heads. The feeling in the church was very good and very strong—an upbeat, lively song rang out, happy people sang and danced, and streamers of all colors flew through the air. A young man seated behind us jumped up and ran down to the front of the church. There he picked up a very large flag, a flag nearly as tall as he was, and ran across the front of the church. As he ran, the bright yellow flag flared in the air behind him. Its message, "Jesus" in huge, bright red letters, was now plainly visible to all of us.

Overcome, the young man ran through the church: up the right aisle, across the back, down the left aisle, across the front again, and up the middle aisle. He circled the church several times in this way, the "Jesus" flag following in his wake. One of the members of the choir, also taken by the Spirit, danced in his place, then danced down the steps and onto and around the altar, his body kept mostly straight and unmoving, his feet a flurry of slides, steps, and stomps.

With the Spirit fully among us now, Pastor Willie Jackson introduced our special guest for the evening, Pastor Jeffrey Johnson of Indianapolis. Pastor Johnson, who had also been overtaken by the Spirit, took the podium and told us of his great desire to preach, to "really, PREACH" tonight. Martin Luther King Jr. Day, he said, was the day that we celebrate the life, works, and legacy of Dr. King. And Dr. King was a great civil rights leader. But he was also a preacher. Dr. King knew and loved the word of God. And preaching would be a fitting way to honor Martin Luther King Jr. And so Pastor Johnson preached, powerfully and passionately, on the difficulties of trying to live well, of always keeping the goodness of God foremost in our minds, of the difficulties of life on this earth. He reminded us of the sinfulness and treachery of others and especially of the times in our lives when it seems God does not hear our prayers.

There ARE no **E-*MER*-*gen-cies*** with *God*
Don't thinK because **God** **H***As***n't** done anything, that He *CAN* **not** do anything
There are no **E-*MER*-*gen-cies*** with **Him**
God is noT up in **H***eaven*
  w*R*inging His *H*ands
    wondering—
    HOW-am-I-Going-to-Get-Jeffrey-Johnson-out-of-THIS-one?
God is noT *up* there
  *pac*ing the floor
    in the *GOLD*en *streets* in **H***eaven*
      wondering—
        HOW-am-I-Going-to-Bring-him-through-THIS-Time?
        —y'all?—
God does **NOT** *get* in a **H***UR*-*ry*
  over **ST**uff that up**S***ets* Us.

Pastor Jeffrey Johnson preaching the gospel at Christ Temple during Martin Luther King Jr. Day. Photo by Danny Gawlowski.

We talked back to Pastor Johnson, filling his pauses. "**Al***right*," we said. "**A***men*." "**Uh**-*uh*, no He **D***on't*." "**Y***e***SS**." "**Hal***l*e*lujah*." We looked at all of those around us, at all of the faces we already knew. Dr. Lassiter sat in the back, earphones on, recording the service. Community advisors Dolores and Carl Rhinehart sat near him, listening attentively, smiling, and nodding. All of our community advisors were there: Dolores and Carl, Pastor Renzie Abram, Julius Anderson, Phyllis Bartleson, Geraldine Burns, Ed Faulkner, Hurley and Fredine Goodall, Eric Johnson, Ed McNeary, Delores Pryor, and Phyllis White. John Young-El, another community advisor and member of the Citywide Choir, stood with the choir behind Pastor Johnson. As we looked around at all of these faces, we were struck by how familiar they had become. For many of us, this was the day that opened us to the community, and opened the community to us.

What Is the Black Community?

What does "community" mean here? Is it a place around which we can draw clear borders? Is it an intangible thing, an idea dependent on cultural, social, or cognitive constructs? Is it merely a collection of individuals? Is it a code word for "black"? And what are this community's activities? The Lynds broke community activities—thus we might say the idea of community—into five main areas: government, health, caring for the unable, getting information, and group solidarity. In truth, we could have written an entire chapter on any one of these aspects of community. But the areas that rose for us, the topics our community advisors and consultants visited and revisited, were primarily the Lynds' first and last categories—government (or politics) and group solidarity, which most often revolved around racial identity.

Before we explore this much further, it seems we must define community first. Hurley Goodall, one of our community advisors for this chapter, begins his discussion of community by raising the topic of race. "Community here in Muncie consists of two totally different communities," says Hurley. "One white, with distinct geographic, economic, and religious boundaries; and another black, with the same structures that meet and interact when mutual survival requires it."[2]

So, community here is partly (and perhaps primarily) about race.[3] In fact, the ideas of race and community are so deeply intertwined here that talk about community almost always leads to talk about race. But community is not only about color, nor does color automatically create a community. Contrary to the commonly held ideas about a unified and monolithic African American (or colored, or Negro, or black, or Afro-American) community, the ties that bind here do not end with color. Just as the African American community is a "subcommunity" of Muncie, there are also subcommunities within the African American community itself. These subcommunities are made of groups that are younger or older; members of different families; those who do or do not go to church. The subcommunities can be broken down into even smaller units. Within the community of churchgoers, for example, are sub-subcommunities based on denomination, degree of affiliation, and level of involvement. There are communities, and subcommunities (and sub-subcommunities) of school-age children, of parents, of politicians and local leaders, and of those who go to the university. The black community here is many communities, fluid groups of people that come together around different ideas and experiences.

Community, of course, is a product of culture, of those things that we do together that bind us. It is also a product of the mind, of the ways that we think about ourselves in relationship to others. But community can also be a tangible thing, a place on the ground. Hurley

Goodall further defines Muncie's "black community" as "primarily the two distinct areas of the city inhabited by a population that is predominantly African American."[4]

Hurley refers to Whitely and Industry, the city's two dominantly black neighborhoods. Most of Delaware County's African Americans live in two census tracts, each of which correspond to one of the city's two black neighborhoods. These neighborhoods are especially interesting because of their degree of "blackness." Nationally, the average predominantly African American census tract (like those that correspond with Whitely and Industry) has a population that is 67 percent black. But Muncie's black neighborhoods are more segregated than the nation's average black neighborhoods. In 2000, city census tract no. 12, which includes much of Whitely, was a little more than 71 percent African American. Census tract three, which incorporates much of Industry was even more segregated. African Americans made up nearly 84 percent of the tract's population in 2000, making Industry's degree of racial segregation more than 15 percent above the national average. Both Whitely and Industry then are significantly "black" neighborhoods, places we can point to when we talk about Muncie's black community.[5]

When people talk about the black community here, they refer to its places, to its institutions and ideas. Above, Hurley refers to Muncie's two distinctly black neighborhoods, but he goes on to refer to something else, something that shapes the way that community is further articulated in Muncie. When he talks about the community's economic, governmental, and educational structures, he notes that they are "highly dependent on" structures dominated by the majority (or white) population. Therefore, the black community, in addition to everything we have said so far, is also a thing that exists in concert with, or in opposition to, the city's white, or majority, community. Conversations about the black community must thus inevitably touch on its relationship to the majority community.

Its relationship to the majority community calls up a powerful and unifying history and experience for Muncie's African Americans, a history and experience that they share with African Americans across the nation. In reflecting on Muncie's African American consciousness of race and awareness of its implications, Hurley compares the city's black experience to its white experience: "Why does Middletown's African American population have such an obsession with racism in Middletown? Because black people will talk to you about it just about anytime you want to talk to them about it. The white community is just the opposite. They have so much difficulty admitting racism is a serious problem in the community."[6]

As in every other American community, race matters in Muncie. And the race consciousness that springs from the black experience here, especially in the face of white ignorance or outright denial of that experience, leads members of the community to, among other things, seek unity, to reach out and try to bring community members together.

Black Community Events

The Muncie Homecoming Festival, formerly known as "Back to Muncie," is one of the black community's most important and anticipated events. Held every four years, the festival follows in the tradition of black homecomings throughout the country by setting aside a time when those who have moved away are encouraged to come home for a visit. Families often hold reunions during Homecoming, and the days are filled with informal visits, games, and meals, along with organized events, worship services, and performances. Homecoming, as a way of also celebrating the ongoing successes of the community, often brings back and highlights prominent figures who were born and raised in Muncie. Although the event is not limited to African Americans, it remains almost entirely black. Most of the nonblack individuals who actively participate in Homecoming are those who have married into the black community.

In its racial separateness, Muncie Homecoming exemplifies the split nature of Muncie's events. Ren-á Wagner and Yolanda Jones, primary organizers of Muncie Homecoming 2003, reflect much and often on the distinctly divided nature of the city's events. There are very few events or places that attract a varied crowd, they say. They, along with many of our consultants, point out a hidden code that conveys the blackness or whiteness of an event, a code based in tradition, neighborhood, and familiarity. Events that have always been "black," like Homecoming and Black Expo (another dominantly black event), remain black partly because whites and blacks know which events belong to whom. Part of that separateness stems from a long tradition of not crossing perceived racial lines. But sometimes those lines are guarded. "This is an African American event," says Yolanda. "This is something for us."[7]

Perhaps the most common way of determining whether an event is "white" or "black" is through place. Events held at any black church, for example, rarely bring in whites beyond those related to African

Americans (the Martin Luther King Jr. celebration is an exception). Conversely, events at public places like the Minnetrista Cultural Center (a local museum) or Ball State University will almost always draw white crowds, unless they specifically include African Americans in both the program and outreach efforts.

The relationship between the location and racial composition of an event is best illustrated by the Muncie Rib Fest, which began at the South Madison Street Multi-Service Center (the "Multi"). The Multi is a place deeply tied to the city's African American community, and in its early years at the Multi, Rib Fest was an almost entirely black event. But the event was moved to downtown Muncie, a location perceived as race-neutral by some, white by others. Once moved, Rib Fest began to draw a mixed crowd, and some African Americans stopped attending. For them, moving the event out of a black space was akin to turning it into a white event.

Another important factor that helps to determine the "blackness" or "whiteness" of an event has to do with how and where the event is advertised. Most things announced in black churches or church bulletins are aimed at the black community, as are most things advertised in the *Muncie Times*, a locally owned newspaper that serves the African

A contestant in the Rib Fest competition winces as he builds up his fire. Photo by Danny Gawlowski.

American communities of Muncie and surrounding small cities. "We're using the *Muncie Times*," say Ren-á and Yolanda about their efforts to keep people informed as plans for Homecoming progress. "And we have a mailing list. We're starting with that, and word of mouth is getting out fast." It's important to use those methods with which African Americans are familiar, they say, for many reasons. First of all, that's how people are kept informed. But staying within that network is important for other reasons as well. It's important that people understand that an event is aimed at them. Ren-á echoes her earlier observation, suggesting that the way they choose to communicate with the community is very important. "If we went outside the African American community," she says, "the African Americans would stop coming. They're looking for something for us [African Americans]. That is what happened to the Rib Fest."[8]

Black Networks

The events that both divide and link citizens of Muncie are visible manifestations of something less tangible but just as clear—the network of political, professional, social, and familial relationships that weave through Muncie's African American community and bind people to one another. Muncie's African Americans have experienced prejudice, both large and small, throughout their lives. Because of this experience they (and perhaps African Americans in general) recognize that America's dominant ideology—that dedication and hard work will always bring success—is closer to a myth than a promise. People here understand deeply that success is partly about what you do, but it is mostly about who you know. In order to succeed, you need to work hard. But in order to start that hard work, you need opportunity. And opportunity almost always boils down to access. Hurley puts it this way: "It's always who you know. If you know the right people, it opens doors. If you don't know the right people, you don't know the opportunity ever existed. It's not fair, but that's the way it happens."[9]

Phyllis Bartleson agrees. "Oh, honey," she chuckles. "You always get help. You know just like the job here, the commissioner . . . told me to apply, otherwise I would not have known there was a vacancy. So you always get help, whether it's directly or indirectly."[10]

These kinds of professional networks do create opportunities for African Americans. But owing to years of institutionalized racism, and its resulting de facto professional and social segregation, many African Americans do not hold the kinds of high-ranking positions that would enable them to provide opportunities to others. This lack of contacts in high places, especially in the more profitable corporate sectors of the economy, limits African Americans who seek these kinds of positions. The kinds of contacts that today's middle-aged whites were developing thirty years ago, when blacks were just beginning to break away from generations of professional and political oppression, have repercussions today. Hurley proposes an example: "If a guy graduated from IU (Indiana University) and he went to school with John Jones and John Jones is now the Dean, he'd say 'Hey John, this is Joe, I'm sending Junior down there, I want you to take care of him.' . . . But, we [blacks] don't have any Johns to call and say 'I'm sending Junior down.' So we have to jump twice as high to even get the opportunity because there is no relationship between our community and the people running these institutions. That makes it doubly hard."[11]

In a company town like Muncie, where powerful industrialists and their families held sway over the city for many years, a very particular kind of affirmative action handed opportunities to the city's elite. Hurley tells another story. When Edmund Ball (son of one of the five Ball brothers, all scions of Muncie) graduated from Yale, the family created a space for him right out of college—a vice president's position at Ball Brothers Glass. "That's white affirmative action," Hurley says. "If daddy had the money he made a place for you. They were in a position to do that."[12]

Hurley, who had to work his way up through the ranks, finds the kind of affirmative action associated with wealth and privilege particularly distasteful. "It's like they [elite whites] never had to look for a job in their lives. They have no idea what it's like to be out there looking for a job when no one will hire you."[13] This harsh reality confronts many black youths who want to have a fair chance in the job market.

Networks are particularly important in the face of pervasive job discrimination, which continues today. Human Rights Commission Director Phyllis Bartleson, curious about the degree to which skin color still affected employment practices in Muncie, conducted an experiment several years ago. She sent two young women out into the community to apply for jobs. The young women had much in common—college experience, age, appearance, grades, and extracurricular activities. But there was one crucial difference. One was black and one was white. The result of this test in Muncie was predictable—the young white woman got called back for interviews and was even offered on-the-spot interviews in several cases. The young black woman was not offered interviews, and in many places (some of the same places that offered the white woman an interview) she was not even offered an application.

Pervasive, institutionalized racism also led to constant rejections for loan requests—which prevented many in the community from opening businesses or buying homes. As in the case of employment, for many years there were not established relationships between the black community and the people running lending institutions. The justifications for declining to loan in the black community were many (redlining, lower property values, perceived higher risk of default), but the effect was simple: blacks who wanted to establish businesses faced obstacles to capital that whites seldom did. Moreover, when blacks were able to get loans for businesses, it was most often because they knew someone in the white community who would advocate on their behalf. Dolores Rhinehart vividly remembers that when she and Carl decided to move their barbershop, they had a very difficult time getting a loan. "But because the woman across the street worked for the president of the bank . . . we were able to get the loan." Carl interjects, underlining the importance of networks and personal connections in this small, small city. "She introduced me to the president of the bank," Carl says, and continues emphatically, "You have to know somebody."

The same kind of discrimination played out in residential housing as well.[14] Vida Burton, Dolores's sister, remembers, "We, too, had a difficult time trying to get a loan. . . . We were going to buy the house Dolores and Carl were moving out of. We had to put up $3,000 to finance the $10,000 loan . . . if it hadn't been for Mrs. Rhinehart talking to them, we wouldn't have gotten the loan. She went down there wanting to know why we weren't getting the loan. It was a mess."[15] Without networks or personal connections to people in power, neither Dolores and Carl nor Vida would have been able to finance their business or homes.

Politics

Even more than the networks that determine job opportunities, politics is all about the people you know. Take, for example, the city's firehouses, which have long been the centers of Democratic Party politics, and in turn, of opportunities provided to (especially black) political hopefuls.

Muncie's fire department is so closely linked to the Democratic Party, in fact, that many of the city's most prominent leaders have been "Firehouse Democrats." Current and former State Representatives Tiny Adams and Hurley Goodall, respectively, have roots in the city's firehouses, as do local Democratic leaders like Monte Murphy—an African American firefighter and city councilman.

Monte Murphy (middle), Muncie's only African American City Council member, looks over primary election results with his father and mother at the Muncie Democratic Headquarters. Photo by Danny Gawlowski.

Monte came to the fire department after his political career had already started. Although it usually happens the other way around, Monte agrees that the city's firehouses have become important political institutions for several reasons. First, firefighters know the conditions, character, and issues of the city's neighborhoods. As such, they have important political and social insights into the overall community. Second, the nature of firehouse life and work seems to breed politicians. Much of a firefighter's life is spent gathered with others and waiting. Talk fills that waiting, and in Muncie there is a long tradition of political talk at the firehouses. Mentoring can happen here too, and younger men can gain important knowledge during the course of these long conversations. Many report that their first political involvements came after a firehouse discussion.

Monte's entrance into politics came a little differently, through his family. Both of his parents were politically active in the local Democratic Party. His father rose to power as a Democratic precinct committeeman. Both father and mother helped to register voters and run polling places, and Monte's father was also a firefighter.

Monte's district, the Sixth, includes Whitely and Industry, the city's two predominantly black neighborhoods. But the district's overall population is 60 percent white. Although Monte represents most of the city's African Americans, he must also represent his district's nonblack population if he is to remain a viable candidate and an effective councilman.

After sixteen years in office, Monte has come to notice differences between his black and white constituents, differences that relate to the themes we have so far identified and discussed—community and the networks that run through communities. Although generalizations don't always hold true, Monte has found that when his black constituents talk to him about community problems, they most often refer to larger, overall issues like crime, the city's streets and infrastructure, or the condition of city housing. But whites talk more about individual problems, conflicts with neighbors, barking dogs, and so on.

He has also noticed patterns in local hiring practices. Returning to the earlier theme of networking, Monte often works to secure employment for individuals, especially for African Americans in his district. He is committed to desegregating local factories and offices, and considers it an important part of his work. Breaking down racial barriers in the workplace is important to Monte because of his personal experience. When he returned to Muncie after college at South Carolina State University, he sought work in vain. His primary obstacle to employment seemed to rest in his inexperience, a lack of training. But he noticed that the same places that wouldn't hire an inexperienced African American and train him or her for a particular job *would* hire and train an inexperienced white. He attributes this partly to a mixture of racism and partly to a lack of connections. There weren't enough African Americans already in those places to pave the way for others. Echoing the thoughts of so many in this community, Monte chuckles. "After all," he says, "that's what really matters. It's not what you know, it's who you know."[16]

Black Leaders

Almost from the time they arrived in Muncie, the city's African Americans have participated in the political life of the city. African American men gained the vote in 1867, and in the 1870s and the 1880s political clubs provided opportunities for political activity to the city's blacks.[17] These early clubs, like the Garfield and Porter Club, or Blaine and Logan Club, were usually affiliated with political parties—nearly always Republican. President Abraham Lincoln's Republican Party, whose nineteenth-century stance against slavery gave Republicanism quite a boost among African Americans, was the party of choice for

African Americans. The nineteenth-century Democratic Party, identified as it was with white supremacy and the slaveholding south, held little appeal for local blacks.

Affiliation with the Republican Party began to shift after World War I, when Muncie's black soldiers returned home from fighting in Europe to find renewed enforcement of Jim Crow laws and a growing Ku Klux Klan. The Klan controlled Indiana's Republican Party during the early and mid-1920s, and as Klansmen held grand camp meetings, spouted their nativist rhetoric, and marched through the streets of Muncie, the city's African Americans began to identify themselves more and more as Democrats. During the Depression of the 1930s, Democratic President Franklin Delano Roosevelt's New Deal gave public works jobs to African Americans as well as whites. This shift in the Democratic Party further challenged and changed the political loyalties of African Americans, though not entirely. When black dentist Dr. A. Wayne Brooks ran for an at-large seat on the Muncie City Council in 1934 (and came in second), he did so as a Republican. Members of what can loosely be termed Muncie's "black elite" (like Dr. Brooks) were more likely to remain loyal to the Republican Party.

Ed McNeary, former president of Muncie's NAACP, has studied local politics, both black and white, for many years. He sums up the allegiances of the city's African Americans today in this way: "Basically Afro-Americans voted Democrat in Muncie. There is a small portion of blacks that would vote Republican . . . but there are just a handful of those. They have a tendency to feel that the Democrats do more for them, that the Democratic Party is mostly for the masses of people. I think when Roosevelt came into office we were in a major Depression and he was able to get us out of that and get us on the road to recovery. We lived in Memphis, Tennessee . . . [and] my Dad worked on a thing called a CCC Camp; they built dams and things of that sort. I think with blacks it was an information hand-down, the father told the sons or daughter 'don't vote Republican' because [Republicans] are for the rich man."[18]

In 1952, Ray Armstrong became the first African American to win a seat on the Muncie City Council. In 1967, Daniel Kelley Jr., a U.S. Workers International Representative, became the second African American to win that seat. This seat—the sixth district seat—has been held by a member of Muncie's black community ever since.

Although Muncie's African Americans have been solidly Democratic since the 1930s, there have been occasional forays into issue-oriented third-party affiliations. Reverend J. C. Williams, who ran for mayor in 1971 on the Poor-People's Party (PPP) ticket, was a very influential member of the Muncie community. His campaign highlighted differences of opinion in the black community, and in many ways it still does. Anthony Conley, grandson of revered community activist Vivian Conley, was only twelve or thirteen when Reverend Williams ran for mayor, but he remembers it well. His grandmother was very active in the PPP and in Reverend Williams's campaign. In remembering that time, Anthony points out the many political complexities within the African American community: "The Poor-People's Party was a typical third-party movement that sought to provide Muncie residents with an alternative to the established political positions. Based at Trinity United Methodist Church, and led by Trinity's charismatic minister, Rev. J. C. Williams, the PPP's supporters were diverse in terms of age, race, gender, and class. . . . The forces against them in a small town—where people were deeply concerned about their employment positions—were virtually insurmountable. . . . It should be noted that numerous blacks in Muncie strongly opposed the PPP. They saw it as a "mongrel" group. Trinity was one of the painfully few churches in Muncie to have a seriously integrated congregation, and some blacks and whites did not like that."[19]

Anthony's observations raise a number of other issues as well. Although Muncie was as active as any community during the Civil Rights Era of the late 1950s, 1960s, and early 1970s, the city was no hotbed of radicalism. Reverend Williams's platform met with stiff resistance not because of his stance on the issues per se, but because some believed that his candidacy would split the black vote. With the black vote being divided between two black candidates, yet another member of the majority community would win the mayoral election. The winning white candidate would, in all likelihood, ignore issues that affected the African American community. And during that time, plenty of issues affected the African American community.

Even as Reverend Williams stirred up his troops, another leader was emerging who would prove to be a dominant force in the community for many years. Hurley Charles Goodall was born May 23, 1927, in Muncie's Whitely community, the youngest of Hurley and Dorene Goodall's three sons. When Hurley was three his father died, a potentially catastrophic event for a family at that time, especially coming as it did at the very beginnings of the Depression. But the Goodalls were buoyed by Dorene's hard work and by the help of the uncles, aunts, and neighbors who surrounded their Wolf Street home.

Hurley's mother, Dorene, was more than a good provider—she was also a union leader at Ball Brothers Glass, where she worked for many years, and a woman of keen political sensibilities. She passed those sensibilities, wrapped around the ideas of fairness and equity, on to Hurley, who expressed his own desire for fairness as a very young man. As a Central High School student, Hurley challenged the coach of his school's all-white basketball team by comparing the team's performance to the "Bingo Five," a black intramural team: "In high school we had an intramural team known as the 'Bingo Five.' They defeated the junior varsity team in a scrimmage. I sent a letter to the sports editor of the city paper and posed the question: 'Why is there an intramural team that could beat the JV, but couldn't play on the team?' The gym teacher at the time, Art Beckner, was also the basketball coach and had me stand in the corner during gym class for a week."[20]

Hurley joined the army after his 1945 graduation from Muncie Central and was sent off to Japan. He went back to work at Muncie Malleable when his army time was over. He and Fredine Wynn married shortly after he returned. Hurley's time at the Malleable was important because it was there that he became involved in the leadership of the United Auto Workers Union (UAW). He laughs about his first elected office: "I was twenty and just back from the army and I was nominated to be the recording secretary and won. The reason they elected me was because the older men didn't want to write and keep the minutes. This introduced me into the officer ranks where I went to board meetings and executive meetings. After that I was a shop steward, then on the bargaining committee, and eventually elected president at around age twenty-five."[21]

The experience and training Hurley received as a union leader laid the groundwork for his future political successes. This union leadership experience would prove to be important in training many of Muncie's twentieth-century Democratic leaders, both black and white.

In 1958 Hurley became one of the city's first two (twentieth century) African American firefighters, and soon thereafter was appointed to the Muncie Human Rights Commission. In 1970, after he, Fredine, and fifteen others tried unsuccessfully to stop the city school board from building a third (and unnecessary) high school, Hurley ran for a seat on the Muncie Board of Education. He won, becoming the first black ever to hold that office. He went on to the Indiana State Legislature in 1978, the first black ever to represent his district, where he helped to organize the Indiana Black Legislative Caucus and was a house sponsor of the Martin Luther King Jr. holiday bill in 1986. Hurley served in the state legislature until

Hurley Goodall speaks at the UAW National Convention in Atlantic City, April 1957. President of Local 532, he was twenty-nine at the time. Courtesy of Hurley and Fredine Goodall.

1992, retiring at the age of sixty-five. It was time, he says, to step aside and let someone else lead the way.

Hurley came out of a particular time and place, and it is difficult to imagine someone coming to power in the early twenty-first century in the same way that he did during the late twentieth century. He got his political training at a time when industrial jobs were plentiful and unions were strong. The industrial union today, the place where many of his generation acquired and honed their leadership skills, is all but gone.

So where will the new leaders come from? Anthony Conley, who has chosen to live in Indianapolis rather than Muncie, doesn't see Muncie's next generation of black leadership. Although he recognizes the impact that the loss of industrial jobs and unions has had on the black community, he adds that part of the reason for the lack of young leaders today is that "there has been virtually no effort to identify, develop, and mentor young black talent in Muncie."[22] Some suggest that older leaders are partly responsible for the lack of young leaders, believing that past generations have stifled the newer generations. "Part of the problem," one woman succinctly says, "is that some people need to step out of the way. You have served your time and it is time for you to let someone else do the work, allow some younger people to come in and assist."[23]

Hurley, part of the older generation to whom younger people might be referring, thinks that unwillingness to let go of power might have some bearing on the lack of black leaders. But it runs much deeper than that, he says. The issues have changed significantly since he was young. It was easy then to point to a problem and demonstrate the workings of racism within it. No blacks on the fire department, no blacks in the swimming pools, no blacks in citywide offices—all of that was easy to see. But the issues that confront African Americans today are so much more complex, so much more difficult to trace. In many ways, the easy work has been done. The work that lies ahead will be as hard to do as it is sometimes hard to define. Hurley muses on the current state of Muncie's African American political affairs: "For the most part, the current leadership is restricted to specific areas such as education, politics, civil rights, neighborhood associations, and youth leaders. There is no overriding leader who leads by example, by charisma, or by anger. I believe that leaders are created by issues and there are no issues that tend to unite everyone and by themselves create a climate where leaders emerge who can energize the community to act. I don't think there is a rift between young and old. I think there is a frustration based on a lack of progress over the past few years in the area of race relations in Muncie. The easy changes have been made. The right to vote, the right to equal housing opportunities, to live where one can afford to live, better promotional opportunities on the job, and fair treatment from those in positions of power, such as the police. The tough issues are those where change will cost something such as affirmative action, a share of the economic pie, and reparations for past injustices."[24]

In Hurley's time it was easier to see progress, easier to point to victories and losses. "Young people also don't see the progress that's been made. We can see it, it's easy looking back over our lives, but it's been different for them. . . ."[25]

But there is one clear issue around which a leader is emerging today: the controversial push to rename a city street in honor of the late Dr. Martin Luther King Jr. Muncie currently has a Dr. Martin Luther King Boulevard, but it's an odd street in an even odder place. Unlike most Martin Luther King boulevards, which in many cities lead into a black neighborhood, Muncie's Martin Luther King Boulevard is a short, little-used overpass that runs near Shed Town, which has the reputation of being the city's most notoriously antiblack neighborhood. When an image of Dr. King along the boulevard was defaced (again) earlier this year, Randall Sims, president of the Whitely Neighborhood Association, decided to push for a change. He wanted to "move" Martin Luther King Boulevard by renaming one of the city's busier thoroughfares in honor of the slain civil rights leader. Broadway Avenue, a north–south street that leads into and borders the Whitely neighborhood has become the street of choice for those who favor renaming. It is associated with one of the city's black neighborhoods, a connection that makes intuitive sense to many involved in the push to rename. Broadway is also a much busier street than the current Martin Luther King Boulevard, and many believe, probably correctly, that signs that honor Dr. King are less likely to be defaced or otherwise vandalized on a better-traveled street. But those who seek to rename Broadway have met with stiff opposition. The primary opposition comes from the many white business owners who worry about the expense of converting all of their letterhead, invoices, cards, and other materials to read "Dr. Martin Luther King Jr. Boulevard" instead of Broadway Avenue. Many in the black community see this as a smokescreen. They believe that the true opposition is based in the fear that the name change will negatively impact business. Martin Luther King boulevards across the country are associated with black neighborhoods, and many of the city's African Americans believe that the real opposition from Broadway business owners is that they don't want potential customers to think they're in a black neighborhood.

The push to rename Broadway Avenue is Randall Sims's first issue. But Sims is receiving broad-based support on this issue from members of the CCCC, and from several of the city's established black political figures. It is too soon to know whether or not Sims will emerge as a solid, long-term leader, but many are watching.

This issue of future leadership is very important to many. Anthony Conley offers several ideas about what could change the perceived direction of Muncie's black leadership, ideas that are echoed by others throughout the community: "First, the will must exist; the community must want to attract and retain young leaders. I do not see this happening to any measurable degree. Second, there must be something here to attract and retain them. Career opportunities must exist. The local school system must be first-rate to attract first-rate talent: Muncie's public school system is woeful at best—visit the state of Indiana's website to view the ISTEP scores for black kids in this city. Finally, there must be venues for legitimate and productive socialization among blacks in the city, gambling houses and juke joints not withstanding. As you know, with the exception of the churches, these institutions are all but nonexistent: almost no black restaurants, no spots for blacks who do not like a lot of drinking and cigarette smoking, no meaningful black social clubs, no meaningful black athletic leagues are operating from the local community centers or through the city's parks system, no group of dedicated black men and women who are working to identify the ongoing political, social, and economic status of blacks in the city."

So there is much that must be done; still many see the opportunity for growth and positive action in the near future. Many have also acknowledged that you have to know that there is a problem, acknowledge it, and from there proceed to work as a community to better the situation.

On January 20, 2003, we all arose early for the Martin Luther King Jr. breakfast, held downtown at First Merchants Bank. We were amazed at the turnout, not only of the African American community, but also of the entire Muncie community. A presence of so many people from so many different backgrounds was indeed a fitting tribute to a man who preached racial harmony and understanding.

Leaders from the Muncie community spoke about the day's various events; the Mayor gave his blessings; there were prayers; and Stefan Anderson—chairman of the board at First Merchants Bank—gave the keynote. When Anderson stood up to deliver his talk, it struck many of us as a bit odd that a European American had been asked to deliver the day's opening talk—at first, that is. As we listened, we were so struck by his sentiments—about race and racism, about how far Muncie had come and how far it had to go, and about white privilege—that we all decided (as first suggested by Hurley) that his talk would be a powerful and fitting conclusion to this chapter and for this book. Indeed, Hurley said, "this is the first time I've ever heard anyone from the white community of his stature say these things publicly in Muncie." We close this chapter with Anderson's remarks, which follow, with his blessings:

> It is an unearned privilege which you have accorded me to be a part of this morning's activities.
>
> As I reflected on this opportunity, it occurred to me that in celebrating the life of Martin Luther King, we should also remember that there was another "D" word which marked Dr. King's life. That word was "dare." His example says to us that we must both dream and dare. Unless we dare, we will never realize the dream.
>
> This thought came to me in blazing clarity as I read Dr. King's letter written in April 1963 from the Birmingham jail. Reading that classic letter, I was also struck by the parallels to St. Paul's epistles. Paul's four letters written from prison speak of many of the same concepts found in Dr. King's Birmingham letter. Both men had been counseled to slow down or stop their work. Both had suffered and had demonstrated their willingness to suffer for the rightness of their cause. Both faced overwhelming antagonism from the established structures of their day.
>
> Both were sustained by clear visions of a world which assured man's dignity and salvation. But above all, both were risk takers; they *dared*. Both dared with an unshakable faith in the future they sought.
>
> Dr. King's Nobel Prize acceptance speech of 1968 was in one sense a declaration of faith that rightness and goodwill would prevail. He said in Oslo: "Our faith can give us courage to face the uncertainties of the future. It will give our tired feet new strength as we continue our stride forward toward the city of freedom."
>
> But as he strode toward the city of freedom, he dared to challenge complacency and lip service. From that Birmingham jail he wrote: "We will have to repent . . . not merely for the hateful words and actions of bad people but for the appalling silence of good people."

The Jewish writer Elie Wiesel, reflecting on his experience in Nazi death camps, said it somewhat differently: our most compelling commandment, he said, is "Do not stand idly by."

If we are not to stand idly by, we must dare and take risks. Voices call to us to "wait," but in Dr. King's words, "the time is always right to do right."

I am one who believes we share a common *desire* to "do right" to fulfill the dream.

So today in Muncie, Indiana, can we ask, "What are the barriers we must address to build bridges of understanding?" In this one person's view, there are several: First, an unwillingness on the part of many of us to talk frankly and openly about the issues and to confront the reality of racism. Second, a recurring fear of leaving our own individual comfort zones. Third, racial isolation in our churches. Fourth, frequently failing to understand that the most insidious forms of racism are sometimes invisible to whites. And fifth, using rose-colored glasses to look at the issues: that is, to say look how far we have come when we should be looking at how far we have to go.

Having said these things, however, I believe nonetheless that we shouldn't ignore the progress made. If you haven't read Hurley Goodall's book, *African Americans in Muncie, 1890–1960*, you should do so. In the epilogue of that book, are these words: "From the shrouded beginnings in escape from slavery, Muncie's black community has come a long way. Through individual acts of personal bravery, patience in the face of heartbreak, and persistence it has overcome a significant number of barriers."

Indeed the community has made progress. As late as 1952, the first black teacher taught in our schools. As late as 1957, the first black fireman; 1967, the first black on the City Council; and as late as 1970, the first black on the school board. As Hurley says, we have come a distance. And I believe the trend-line is up.

For example, the number of organizations now undertaking work to foster racial understanding and valuing diversity is increasing. The activity of the Human Rights Commission, the work of the TEAM-work for Quality Living Racism Committee, the Social Justice Committee of Christian Ministries, a new diversity program getting underway at the Chamber of Commerce, the mayor's quiet encouragement of programs in city government, the remarkable and stimulating high school program of last week called "Embracing Cultures," the *Star Press* leadership in starting employee programs to produce racial understanding, and interest on the part of the Community Foundation to provide funding for programs which encourage interracial understanding. And I could go on.

But if the trend-line is up, the question we all must ask is "Is it up enough?" I think the answer to that question is "No." And it is important to ask the question, because we all know in our hearts that disparate opportunity based on race or skin color or any other factor robs communities of their vitality. And ultimately undermines economic and social progress.

The biblical directives to us are clear. St. Paul wrote from his prison cell to the Phillipians (2:1): "Remember we are brothers, love one another." Or, in his letter to the Romans, who would later place him in prison, he said very simply, "May we live in harmony and praise God with one voice" (Romans 15:5)—words remarkably comparable to those of Martin Luther King in Birmingham in 1963.

So what must we do? If we must dare, what do we dare do to build bridges and break barriers?

Proclaiming our shared values is a start, but talking about the things we all agree on is not going to move that trend-line up very fast. To do that, we need to do several things now:

First, recognize that the greater one's capacity to affect positive social change, the greater is one's responsibility to do so. St. Paul talks about our obligation to use our "God-given gifts." Today, we talk about our leaders using their "political capital." But all of us have "personal capital" and what I call "position capital." In communities, leaders and managers—especially people who head institutions and organizations—usually have position capital. Position capital brings both capacity and responsibility to influence constructive change. Are we using this position capital to promote equal opportunity and social justice? Not in the abstract, but in our immediate world of work. Are we really monitoring what's happening in our own organizations?

Second, working together, organizations of this community need to identify the *tools* which institutions can use to change attitudes, promote diversity and racial understanding. I think there is a lot of feeling in this community of this kind: "I want to do something, but what?" We need to answer that question, and remove that issue as an excuse for inaction. Doing something is better than doing nothing.

Third, we need to be intentional and disciplined in creating meaningful interaction between persons of different races and cultures. Working together builds relationships. Real working relationships cut through racial barriers, a fact that Dr. Sam Abram has been so helpful in helping me understand. Martin Luther King in his Nobel acceptance speech said this in another way: "I am convinced that Negroes and white men in increasing numbers can create alliances to overcome their common problems."

Fourth, we must work to retain our most educated young people of all races in our community. They can only do so if they see opportunity.

Fifth, we have to be willing to use the "R" word—racism—and quit using polite euphemisms for it. This is a core problem present in every community of America. We all know that racism manifests itself in several ways—but its most insidious form is institutional: systems or procedures which confer unearned privilege based on skin color or gender. I believe that it can exist without consciously ill intent. If I am right about this then we need to work together openly and honestly to help each other see it, understand it, and eliminate it.

And finally, we need to more consciously build on the spiritual heritage which we share. Those of us who are Christians have spiritual guidelines that unequivocally provide us an action plan. But whatever our religious heritage, we all subscribe to a simple maxim: do the right thing.

I believe we can do the right thing if we are willing to dare to action, to realize our dreams. I know that I have too often shared the dream but failed to dare. Martin Luther King dared. He took risks and so must we. Let us then dare, and as a beacon for our work together, remember the closing words in that letter from the Birmingham jail. He said: "Let us all hope that the dark clouds of racial prejudice will soon pass away and the deep fog of misunderstanding will be lifted and in some not too distant tomorrow, the radiant stars of love and brotherhood will shine over our great nation with all their scintillating beauty."

We can join hands: we can build bridges and we will seek those radiant stars.[26]

Notes

1. The original composition of this research and writing team was Jarrod Dortch and Brandy Bounds. But due to medical problems, Brandy Bounds had to pull out of the class after about a month into the seminar. Several students stepped forward to help Jarrod complete the research and writing for the chapter (hence this chapter's large number of authors). Elizabeth Campbell, in particular, volunteered to take a leadership role in this effort, and helped to define the chapter's trajectory.

2. Hurley Goodall, conversation with Jarrod Dortch, March 21, 2003.

3. Recognizing the fallacy of the biological construct of race, we understand "race" to be a powerful cultural construct around which people build community. See Luke Eric Lassiter, *Invitation to Anthropology* (Walnut Creek, Calif.: AltaMira Press, 2002), 9–35.

4. Hurley Goodall conversation, March 21, 2003.

5. The reasons for this segregation have not been determined, although they might be linked to attrition, the process of population loss that has taken hold of Muncie in recent decades. Proportionately speaking, whites have left Muncie in greater numbers. Working-class whites have moved away in search of work. Middle, upper middle, and professional class whites often move into the better funded and higher scoring school districts of nearby Yorktown and Delta. This could account for the increase in percentage of African Americans in the city (from 9.6 percent in 1970 to 11 percent in 2000). This is an area ripe for significant demographic analysis.

6. Geraldine Burns, Hurley Goodall, and Ed McNeary, conversation with Brandy Bounds, Jarrod Dortch, and Danny Gawlowski, January 22, 2003.

7. Ren-á Wagner and Yolanda Jones, conversation with Brandy Bounds, Sara Bricker, and Mia Fields, February 19, 2003.

8. Ren-á Wagner and Yolanda Jones conversation, February 19, 2003.

9. Hurley and Fredine Goodall, conversation with Michelle Anderson, Anne Kraemer, and Ashley Moore, February 11, 2003.

10. Ibid.

11. Hurley and Fredine Goodall conversation, February 11, 2003

12. Ibid.

13. Ibid.

14. Dolores and Carl Rhinehart, conversation with Michelle Anderson, Anne Kraemer, and Ashley Moore, January 16, 2003.

15. Vida Burton and Ruth Robinson, conversation with Anne Kraemer and Ashley Moore, February 2, 2003.

16. Danny Gawlowski, conversation with Monte Murphy, March 29, 2003.

17. African American women, of course, did not get the vote until the Nineteenth Amendment, passed by Congress in 1919 and ratified by the states in 1920.

18. Ed McNeary, conversation with Jarrod Dortch, March 5, 2003.

19. Anthony Conley, conversation with Jarrod Dortch, March 27, 2003.

20. Hurley Goodall conversation, March 21, 2003.

21. Ibid.

22. Anthony Conley conversation, March 27, 2003.

23. Ren-á Wagner and Yolanda Jones conversation, February 19, 2003.

24. Hurley Goodall conversation, March 21, 2003.

25. Ibid.

26. Stefan S. Anderson, "Remarks for the MLK Breakfast," January 20, 2003.

Conclusion

Lessons Learned about Muncie, Race, and Ethnography

Luke Eric Lassiter

On January 21—the day after Muncie's Martin Luther King Jr. celebrations—we met for class. We immediately began talking about the previous day's events. We started by discussing the various messages we had heard, from Pastor Johnson's inspiring sermon to the afternoon workshop speakers. Given this, however, some of the black students expressed their frustration with hearing the same speeches—King's "I Have a Dream" speech, for example—every year. But one speech stood out.

"I think the most realistic and forthright speech of the day," said Jarrod Dortch, "was given by the banker that morning at First Merchants. His speech was the best. It was heartfelt. He was honest about it. He said, 'I'm not there yet. I am trying. I'm making progress. These are things that I have found that I need to do.' I think he did a *really* good job."

We talked about how Anderson had brought the complexities of structural racism to the forefront, and how he had talked about white privilege in a day and time when few businessmen of his stature are unable or unwilling to admit such complicated subtleties of race and racism.

"A lot of black people looked over him," continued Jarrod, "but he did a *really* good job. His message was probably the most profound of the whole day."

"You said earlier that it's the same message every year," said Danny Gawlowski, addressing Jarrod and harkening back to an earlier point in our conversation. "I've been pondering that. Yeah, it may be the same issues every year, but I still don't think that that message is getting out. I mean, it's a *really* good message; I think it should be repeated over and over again. Maybe that's because it's the first time *I've* really heard it; it's the first time I've *really* gone to all of the events. But there are still *lots* of people who never have been. . . . Like on Friday, all *The Daily News* [Ball State's newspaper] reported was 'a debate' about whether the university should really have the day off. *They* clearly don't get it. I mean, people like Anderson and others' messages are really good, because I think the message is, maybe, *starting* to get out. Maybe we just have to think about who we're talking *to*. . . ."

"Yeah, I had to work yesterday morning," said Cari Peterson after awhile. "I work at a preschool on the south side, and we have an equal number of black and white children. So we went to the Children's Museum in Indianapolis; it was free admission in honor of the holiday. . . . I work with three other white teachers, and they were like 'Well, 'these people' need the day off because it's a 'black holiday.' And then we got to the Children's Museum and the black people were like 'Why are *you* here? It's Martin Luther King Day. You're white.' This really upset me, because Martin Luther King Jr. is a leader for everyone—not just black or white people. It made me mad that people thought like that."

"That's the ignorance that we're still facing," said Carla Burke.

"It's like people look at it as if all of Martin Luther King's intentions were just for the black race," added Mia Fields.

"And that's not true at all . . ." said Cari. "Maybe that's why white people haven't ever been to any of the MLK events; it's a 'black holiday.'"

"Has anybody's perspective changed since going to the MLK events?" asked Michelle Johnson, changing the subject slightly.

"Michelle Anderson pointed this out last night," said Anne Kraemer. "And it's been in my head ever since. She said, 'I feel like I've been so much more accepted by the black community here than I feel that many blacks have ever been accepted by the white community.' I feel this way, too. It's made such an impact on me that I can't even put it into words."

"This from people, of course, who have been fed by the Rhineharts," joked Beth Campbell. Everyone burst out in laughter, no doubt remembering their own experiences with the Rhineharts' warm hospitality.

"Yeah," continued Anne. "And the lady I sat with at church last night. She was just amazing. When we sang the Black National Anthem together, she leaned over to me and said, 'Now learn that song.' As I left she was up by the door. She grabbed me and said, 'God bless.' You know, I had never met her before. She didn't have to do that. She was very open."

"I had the same kind of experience you had," said Jessica Booth after awhile, "except I sat next to a white lady during the service. Well, I got there late because I couldn't find a place to park. The usher led me to the seat. There really wasn't a seat, but the lady moved her coat and she was like 'Oh, it's so cold out there. Are you cold?' She was moving my coat and helping me. And I was like 'Oh, thanks.' But, you know, it kind of made me feel good. Because she was an older lady, and I totally didn't expect that. I didn't know who she was. We talked during the whole service. She was just really nice. When we got ready to leave, she said 'Now, be careful; and good luck getting back to your car, because I know you parked really far away.' She was just really nice. It was a good experience."

Some time passed as we discussed how surprisingly diverse and integrated the Martin Luther King Jr. events were. "Okay, I was like 'This is a blessed day,'" said Carla. "Everyone is going to be nice to one another. Everybody is coming to these Martin Luther King Jr. events. But is this what 'reality' is like? No."

"This *classroom* is not what reality is about," interjected Jarrod, "to be perfectly honest."

"Yeah, I can be honest," said Brandy Bounds, "and say I have never had this kind of conversation about race with *anybody*. Be them all black, be them half black and half white, whatever—this is not indicative of casual conversation if I was to say 'Well, yeah, you're uncomfortable because you're white' and it not offend somebody. I think that our conversations are not realistic; but it's *good* that we have these conversations in here, because we can use each other as soundboards. And conversations will leave this room and start somewhere else."

"Yeah," said Anne. "I discuss race at home now all the time. And my roommates are like. . . ." Anne conjured up a surprised look as everyone laughed. "They are! I'll talk about race and I'll say something like 'blacks' and they'll be like 'What? You said the "B" word!' . . . My roommates are really amazed, actually. They're like 'Wow.' You know, I'm really passionate about it now; it's become very open and very safe to talk about race in here."

Doing and Writing Collaborative Ethnography in Muncie

An important lesson of doing and writing ethnography is that it teaches us about ourselves as we learn about others. This is not just a one-way process, however, restricted only to the "ethnographer." Because doing

ethnography engenders cross-cultural understandings—through conversation, for example—both ethnographers and consultants learn
about each other as they work to coconstruct a collaborative ethnographic text.

The Students: Conversations about Race and Racism

For the students, an important part of the class had to do with
learning to talk openly and regularly about race in the classroom (six of
the students were black; eight were white). Race and racism was important to our consultants for obvious reasons: it structured their experiences, memories, stories, communities, businesses, and leisure.
And because it was so central to understanding both the historical and
contemporary African American community in Muncie, we spent
much time talking about how well we were understanding race from
the viewpoint of our community advisors and other consultants. But
the process also helped all of us to better understand the role of race in
our own lives (both faculty and students, both black and white).

Many of the white students (and faculty) came to understand
more deeply how the experience of institutional racism affected the
everyday life of not only their consultants but of their fellow students—the kind of institutional racism that Stefan Anderson spoke of

A class discussion inside the Virginia B. Ball Center for Creative Inquiry. Photo by
Danny Gawlowski.

in his Martin Luther King Jr. breakfast remarks. Their eyes were opened several times throughout the semester as the black students told story after story about, on the one hand, their own experiences with the kind of racism they had themselves faced at work, in the community, and in the university; and, on the other hand, how this was similar to and different from the kinds of racism that their consultants talked about. This was brought home most powerfully when a white Ball State University faculty member complained to several of the white students that our research team was ignoring the "real" black community—the "real" black community, that is, of criminals and drug dealers, who were the same age, the faculty pointedly said, as one of the black students in the class. The students, most of whom were exactly the same age as the black student in question, immediately picked up on the significance of this association. They were hurt and angry, mainly because they believed that the faculty member had included them in a commentary that was insensitive at best. Through class discussion about incidents such as these, the white students, perhaps for the first time, felt what it was like to experience the kind of subtle assumptions of race that their consultants talked about in their field conversations.

Near the semester's end (April 2003), the students organized a public presentation for the Muncie community at large, which we held at Union Baptist Church in Whitely. The students prepared short presentations about what they had learned for each of their respective areas, but they also wanted the community to know how this project had changed them, too. One of the white students, Eric Efaw, had been radicalized by the semester's experiences. He included in his remarks a call to action:

> Through my interaction with my community advisors and classmates I have learned a lot of powerful lessons that I will keep with me as I leave Muncie and Ball State. Foremost among these lessons, however, is the idea that in order for our society to truly be united and multicultural we *all* must *work* at it. As many of my advisors have expressed to me, minorities have to interact with the Euro-American majority community on a daily basis, but whites are able to more or less isolate themselves from other ethnicities if they so choose. Therefore, in order to build a multicultural society we as individuals, as a university, and as a nation must stop expecting minorities to bear the sole burden of multiculturalism. The majority community must take the initiative to participate in, understand, and appreciate other peoples' ways of life. It is more than having black friends, more than

studying black topics, and more than expressing one's support of "black events" in public. To be multicultural we must question how we feel about others when we are alone and there is no one to hear our thoughts. Being multicultural involves going to events where we might be a minority and at times might feel out of place. But by attending these events and learning from other cultures, eventually we will develop a feeling of ease and acceptance. More importantly, there will be understanding and hopefully friendships. This is a lesson I will take with me from this project and with any luck will impart to others in my life.[1]

Learning about race and racism was not limited to the white students. Many of the black students came to understand their own experience of being African American differently. At that same presentation, Ashley Moore, one of the black students, reflected on the deeper understandings she had gained:

After the first meeting with the community advisors, I knew that our class was taking on a big role and fulfilling one of Hurley's dreams, and to actually accomplish it is an amazing feeling. Hurley taught me a lot: not only factual information, but information on the kind of person who I want to be. I want to be able to give back to my community the way he has and to just be a positive example to the community overall. This class that I have participated in—if I can really call it a class; I would rather say *experience* that I have had—has changed me as a person. I never valued all the things that I have in my life right now. After talking to people like Hurley, Ruth Redd, and everyone else around the community, I know the things I have I should not take for granted because they were not always available to people like me. I no longer take things like education for granted, and I am more determined to succeed with the education that I am blessed with, so that I can give back to My People. Even the little things, such as eating in a restaurant with my class or drinking from the same water fountain as the girls in my group, are all things that my ancestors before me had to fight and die for. I never really thought about it until now, and it seems as if I enjoy those things a little more. I relax in the restaurants; I take my time at that water fountain; things like that. I am happy to be able to complete this book for the community, but even happier for the knowledge that I have gained from them.[2]

In the end, the students were not just a group of "black students" and "white students." They were a team, an extraordinary team, I must say, that far exceeded our expectations.

Community Collaborators: Conversations about the University, Students, and Young People

Our students were changed through this process, but so too were our collaborators. "It was quite an experience for me to work with these young people on such a worthy project—a project that I think was long overdue . . . " says Phyllis Bartleson. "I think there's a better understanding—particularly from the white students—about what goes on in the black community. You mentioned earlier the stereotypes [about the black community], and I think this is a way to dispel some of those falsities that we have. And I think it works both ways, too. As an older person in the community, we have our own minds set about young people—regardless of what color—and about college students: they party all the time. It's not true. We all have false perceptions."[3]

Hurley agrees: "I don't think I've *ever* met a finer group of young people. . . . They've always been on time, they've been where they said they would be. They're very respectful. And that's something you don't see all the time with young people. I'm not saying this because I'm trying to blow smoke. I'm saying it because I really feel that way."[4]

Students and Community Advisors discuss what they have learned from each other during a community meeting at Shaffer Chapel. Photo by Danny Gawlowski.

The mutual respect and trust that developed between the collaborators and students did much to increase better understandings between these two groups about one another, and in the process, the gap between the "researchers" and "subjects" was narrowed. But it also narrowed the larger gap between the university and the community. In a letter to the students at the end of the semester, Hurley put it most eloquently:

> Hopefully Ball State University has learned a lot from this experience and will support more efforts in the future to reach outside the borders of the campus and learn about and understand the community in which it sits.
> The best thing about this experience is that we all learned we are in this community together whether we like it or not, and the sooner we learn to reach out to each other and care for each other, the stronger and better our community will be for all who reside here.[5]

To be sure, many universities besides Ball State could well benefit from taking Hurley's comments to heart. I, for one, believe that collaborative ethnography—directed by an ethical commitment to local constituencies and uninhibited by the academic impulse to privilege academe over local audiences—is among the most powerful ways "to reach outside the borders of the campus and learn about and understand the community in which it sits."

On the University's Mythology of Muncie

Along these lines, we (particularly the faculty and students) found ourselves wondering about the myth of "averageness" in Middletown. Muncie is representative in some ways. It has certainly experienced many of the same trends as so many other communities that have moved from an industrial to service economy. In that sense, Muncie is certainly a "microcosm" of America. But that "representativeness" for which Muncie is so well known may also blind us to the actual complexities of real peoples' individual experiences in working through these now-universal challenges. Many small communities like Muncie, for example, have experienced out-migration of their young (and others) in search of jobs. This is, to be sure, a widespread experience of our postindustrial economy, not only in America, but also increasingly throughout the world. We are all on the move; we are all following jobs—often at incredible costs to our families and our communities. Yet individual experience, memory, and story give life to the challenges that we all face today, making these challenges real and tangible. In this particular case, the experiences, memories, and stories of people like the Rhineharts, Hurley Goodall, and Phyllis Bartleson *also* make the distinctive experience of Muncie more real and tangible. When we generalize and typify, essentially averaging out individual experience, we can miss the struggles, the frustrations, and the solutions of individual people and their communities. These people and places offer insight, not only into larger trends, but also into the various and diverse ways that people are making a difference, one person and one community at a time.

This insight profoundly affected the faculty and students involved in this project: the experiences, memories, and stories shared with us by our community collaborators made Muncie real and tangible for us. As Anne Kramer put it in our presentation to the Muncie community at Union Baptist, "One of the best parts [of this project] is now I don't feel like just a Ball State student, I am a member of the Muncie community. I can drive around town and point out the homes and businesses of friends and advisors."[6] In that it made Muncie real and tangible for us, it also challenged a powerful "story" of Muncie told and retold on our campus (which is similar, I'm sure, to the stories that are told and retold on campuses all over this country). When I, for one, came to Ball State University, I was repeatedly told how "average" the community was, how "average" the university was, and how "average" the students were. The students know this story, and its variants, all too well.

Perhaps this story is driven, in part, by the overall Middletown literature that assures us, over and over again, that we just may be right. But I think it is most probably an artifact of a larger mythology that many universities (particularly those that are not first-tier) tell and retell about themselves and, more to the point, about the communities in which they reside. I use "mythology" here in the sense that many anthropologists use it: mythology represents a truth for its believers, a truth that is engaged and reengaged through story, and that helps believers rationalize their thinking and behavior in accordance with these stories. Simply put, it allows many of those in the university to evade an engagement with the surrounding community in all of its complexities: "There's nothing here; so there's no reason for me to venture out into it."

All of this is to say that contrary to the story that is told and retold on our campus about the "averageness" of Muncie, we discovered a very different place, full of interesting experiences, memories, and stories; and in turn, our collaborators also found that the students weren't "average" in any sense of the word: they were, indeed, extraordinary young people with the ability to listen, emphasize, and translate experience through ethnography.

On Teaching Ethnography

Finally, a brief note on what I, personally, have learned about *teaching* ethnography.

When I was a senior in college at Radford University, I enrolled in a seminar in which I worked intensively with a group of recovering drug addicts to collaboratively research and write an ethnography of drug addiction and recovery. It was the first time I felt that I was doing "real" anthropology. But most importantly, it was the first time that my education really felt immediately relevant and fully engaged: I wrote, with my collaborators, a text that my consultants would use for "the still-suffering addict." I left college for graduate school with a whole new appreciation for the power of collaborative, project-driven, and community-based projects.

Ever since I began teaching my own undergraduate students, I have sought ways to reproduce a similar educational experience for them, but I have never had that opportunity until now. The Virginia B. Ball Center allowed me to practice a very rare kind of engaged pedagogy. Personally, I can think of no more powerful way to practice and teach the life of the mind.

Notes

1. Eric Efaw, comments at "Writing Muncie's African American Community: How We Wrote *The Other Side of Middletown*," Union Baptist Church, Muncie, Indiana, April 17, 2003.

2. Ashley Moore, comments at "Writing Muncie's African American Community: How We Wrote *The Other Side of Middletown*," Union Baptist Church, Muncie, Indiana, April 17, 2003.

3. Phyllis Bartleson, comments at public forum on *The Other Side of Middletown*, Shaffer A.M.E. Church, Muncie, Indiana, March 31, 2003.

4. Hurley Goodall, comments at public forum on *The Other Side of Middletown*, Shaffer A.M.E. Church, Muncie, Indiana, March 31, 2003.

5. Open letter from Hurley Goodall to the students, April 18, 2003.

6. Anne Kraemer, comments at "Writing Muncie's African American Community: How We Wrote *The Other Side of Middletown*," Union Baptist Church, Muncie, Indiana, April 17, 2003.

Epilogue

Elizabeth Campbell and Luke Eric Lassiter

> Injustice anywhere is a threat to justice everywhere. We are caught in an inescapable network of mutuality, tied in a single garment of destiny. Whatever affects one directly, affects all indirectly.
>
> —Martin Luther King Jr.,
> Letter from a Birmingham Jail

In their follow-up study, *Middletown in Transition*, the Lynds wrote, "the cleft between the white and Negro populations of Middletown is the deepest and most blindly followed line of division in the community."[1] Muncie, like many American communities, saw this cleft gradually narrow during the twentieth century. Today, the Ku Klux Klan does not have the hold on local politics it once did, blacks are no longer prohibited from all-white swimming pools, and African Americans have assumed some positions of power. Still, despite assertions to the contrary, the cleft about which the Lynds wrote is still here. It may not be quite as deep now, but in many ways, it is even more blindly followed. As in communities across America, ideas about race and the practice of racism have become much more insidious. When blacks were denied services, homes, and opportunities outright, injustices were easier to identify and address. But as Stefan Anderson pointed out in his Martin Luther King Jr. speech, the racism against which many struggle today is fundamental to the very structure of our system. In Muncie, racism runs so deep and has become so much a part of daily life that most citizens now disguise their racism in very sophisticated ways. And they usually get away with it.

But sometimes even that which runs deep is revealed. As this book entered production a series of events took place that pointed out the deep and powerful hold racism still has on this community.

In April 2003, with overwhelming support from the African American community, Randall Sims—president of the Whitely Neighborhood Association—collaborated with City Council member Monte Murphy—the chairman of the council's land and traffic committee—to propose that Muncie change the name of Broadway Avenue to Martin Luther King Jr. Boulevard. Murphy brought the idea before City Council in late April 2003. Immediately, several Broadway Avenue business owners clamored that the change would compromise their business. One establishment, Ed's Warehouse, even went so far as to forcefully claim that the name change would unequivocally put them *out* of business.[2] Even though "the city council has made no fewer than seventy-one name changes of streets in the past one hundred years" (with no evidence of any company having been put out of business by the change); even though Monte Murphy proposed that the name change be put off until 2005 to allow time for changing letterheads (the major complaint); even though several individuals and community organizations promised to help defray costs—still, local businesses continued their fight unabated to keep things just as they were: to keep Broadway Avenue just as it was, and to make sure that Martin Luther King Jr. Boulevard remained a bypass (literally and figuratively).[3]

As if by default, the Lynds's observations found renewed significance in the months of April, May, and June when the Martin Luther King Jr. Boulevard name change issue suddenly took hold. The city divided into two camps. Either you were absolutely for the change, or you were absolutely against it. Citizens chose sides and lined up, and barely a week went by without commentaries, articles, and letters to the editor in Muncie's *Star Press*. Many in the African American community suggested that opponents were hiding their true racist sentiments—racist sentiments that had been seen before when, in the 1970s, an attempt to change the name of another street (Kirby Street) to Martin Luther King Jr. Boulevard was also met with intractable opposition (a committee appointed by the City Council defiantly declared, in the end, that "it wouldn't change the name of *any* Muncie street to honor King").[4] Despite the community's long history with this issue, opponents of the name change held fast to their claim that their opposition was not about race; it was about economics, plain and simple.

Opponents of the Martin Luther King Jr. name change were almost able to keep their argument entirely in the realm of the subtle and metaphorical. But events unfolded to reveal that these divisions were about much more than just business expenses. At a City Council meeting held at the end of May, emotions climaxed when an employee of the Delaware County Engineer's Office called a group of young black girls (which included Randall Sims's daughter) "niggers." The woman later admitted to a reporter that she had said about the girls, "those people are acting like niggers." The meeting, which had been adjourned, descended into near chaos. Called to explain the slur, Adams unapologetically defended her actions, placing the blame for all that had happened on Randall Sims. It was he, she said, who had made the name change a "racial issue."[5] She was subsequently disciplined by the county commissioners and suspended for two days without pay; but within a week, the same commissioners decided they had acted in the heat of the moment and rescinded Adams's punishment, reinstating her lost pay.[6]

Adding insult to injury, just a few days after the city council meeting, the Martin Luther King Jr. Boulevard signs on the bypass were, once again, defaced. This time, vandals superimposed "Koon," spelled out in large black letters, over "King."[7] And through all of this, name change opponents continued to confidently claim that changing Broadway to Martin Luther King Jr. Boulevard was, still, not about race.

But for many in Muncie, both black and white, it most certainly was about race. How could it *not* be—especially now, several argued. Indeed, even the Muncie–Delaware County Chamber of Commerce had stated that most business owners (outside those vocal few on Broadway) were in favor of the name change.[8]

In a packed City Council meeting in early June, Monte Murphy called for the final vote to change the name of Broadway Avenue to Martin Luther King Jr. Boulevard. Surprisingly, the motion passed 5–4, and jubilation quickly spread among the some three hundred people in attendance. But within minutes of the vote, several council members expressed confusion as to the nature of their votes. Apparently, they did not realize what they had been voting on. Council member Mary Jo Barton said that she thought she had been voting on an amendment, and demanded that the council reconsider the vote. The council revoted, rejecting the name change 7-2 on the second vote.[9] Here was a strange and surreal turn of events; for several minutes, confusion reigned and few could explain what had just happened. For example, when asked why he voted against the name change, council member Jack Isenbarger told a reporter that he voted against the measure because "I wanted to."[10]

City Council member Monte Murphy (center) reflects silently immediately after the bill he introduced to rename Broadway to Martin Luther King Jr. Memorial was defeated. Photo by Daniel Gawlowski.

In the next several weeks, anger and disappointment spread throughout the African American community. It was just as Martin Luther King Jr. had written over fifty years ago from a Birmingham jail: African Americans were *still* "living constantly at tiptoe stance, never quite knowing what to expect next."[11] Yet some black leaders were not surprised by this turn of events. Hurley, for one, anticipated that the measure might not pass. "I've lived in this community all of my life. And some things seem like they just *won't* change. To be absolutely honest, I'm glad that my kids are gone. They don't have to put up with this backward place anymore. I mean, after all, what serious business would come here and employ narrow-minded people like this? That's the real damage, to me."[12]

Despite the bitterness that has risen around this issue, young leaders like Randall Sims and Monte Murphy are not giving up. Neither are organizations like the Human Rights Commission, the CCCC, the Martin Luther King Jr. Dream Team, nor Muncie's TEAMwork for Quality Living (who have an active community forum on race relations in Muncie). As we write this, these organizations and others are discussing ways to resolve the deep divides that this issue has so forcefully articulated. To be sure, the "cleft between the white and Negro populations of Middletown" is still very real and tangible here—as it is in the rest of our nation. While some wonder if substantive change in race relations will ever come Muncie's way, others are more hopeful that Munsonians can find their way across the racial divide.

It was a sobering way to end this project. But it certainly pointed out the challenges ahead. This project has been as much about the relationships built between and among students, community members, and faculty as it has been about the story we have told. And perhaps therein lies its value. If we want things to change, as one Muncie resident put it: "We have to get to know each other. When we do, we begin to understand there's a whole lot more we have in common than we have different."[13]

Notes

1. Robert S. Lynd and Helen Merrell Lynd, *Middletown in Transition: A Study in Cultural Conflicts* (New York: Harcourt Brace & Company, 1937), 463.

2. Rick Yencer, "Name Change Divides Community," *The Star Press*, April 29, 2003.

3. Ibid.; Larry Riley, "Broadway Just Asphalt, So Why the Fuss?" *The Star Press*, May 25, 2003.

4. Riley, "Broadway Just Asphalt," emphasis in original.

5. Danny Gawlowski, personal communication.

6. Keith Roysdon, "County Employee Disciplined," *The Star Press*, May 29, 2003; idem, "Commissioners Rescind Penalty for Ethnic Slur," *The Star Press*, June 4, 2003.

7. Rick Yencer, "MLK Signs Defaced," *The Star Press*, May 31, 2003.

8. Yencer, "Name Change."

9. Council members who voted for the name change were Monte Murphy and William Shroyer. Voting against the measure were Mary Jo Barton, James Carey, Jack Isenbarger, Charles Leonard, Sam Marshall, David Taylor, and Bruce Wiemer.

10. Rick Yencer, "Name Change Rejected: Several Council Members Change Votes after Initial Confusion," *The Star Press*, June 3, 2003.

11. Martin Luther King Jr., "Letter from a Birmingham Jail," April 16, 1963.

12. Hurley Goodall, conversation with Elizabeth Campbell, Fredine Goodall, Michelle Johnson, and Luke Eric Lassiter, June 26, 2003.

13. H. Royce Mitchell, quoted in Keith Roysdon, "To Fight Racism, We Must 'Get to Know Each Other,'" *The Star Press*, June 30, 2002.

Afterword

Theodore Caplow

This exceptional project began with the collaboration between two exceptional men—Hurley Goodall and Luke Eric Lassiter. They attracted many other people, Ball State University students and local citizens, who worked together with extraordinary devotion to complete the entire project, including the preparation of this book, within the space of a single academic term.

Goodall has long been the presiding elder of Muncie's African American community, its most prominent political figure, and the principal custodian of its history. As a production worker, union leader, firefighter, civil rights activist, and elected official, he has walked the walk and talked the talk depicted here.

Lassiter is an anthropologist with a reforming mission. Conventional ethnographic research, which was generally practiced in simple societies in remote places, set unbridgeable inequalities between the ethnographer and his subjects. Traditionally, the ethnographer, who was extremely rich by tribal standards, master of unknown technologies, and protected by the colonial authorities, had no obligation to share his findings with the people his research concerned.

Lassiter, along with many of his contemporaries, rejects this condescension in favor of an egalitarian approach, whereby the people being studied have voice and vote at every stage of the research process. This process has the obvious merit of assuring continuous clarification and the obvious defect of permitting the suppression of unwelcome information. From a scientific standpoint, the results may be mixed, but on the humanistic level, the collaborative ethnographer is a much more attractive figure than his conventional predecessor—not to mention the great benefits to the students and their consultants.

Also, on the humanistic level, this project rights a long-standing wrong—the systematic neglect of African Americans in the vast literature of Muncie as Middletown. It goes back to a decision made by the Lynds in the first Middletown study when, reporting their social surveys, they remarked without explanation, "No answers from negroes were included in the tabulation."[1] Elsewhere, they did explain that, having chosen Muncie for its high proportion of native-born whites, their focus remained on that large segment of the population. Their second Middletown study was more informative about the black population, but presented no survey data.

When we undertook to replicate the 1924–1925 questionnaires in 1977–1978, as part of the study called "Middletown III," we again (mistakenly, I now believe) set aside the questionnaires of black respondents, because we had no baseline data to which to compare them. This was a particularly serious omission for the high school survey, the most informative of them all, because African American representation in the high school population had risen from less than 3 percent in 1924 to 11 percent in 1977. That particular omission will finally be remedied in a forthcoming paper in the *Public Opinion Quarterly*, which includes the 1977 and 1999 attitudes and opinions of Middletown's African American high school students in abundant detail.[2]

In the early 1980s, several of us participated in another effort to fill in the blank by helping to design a comprehensive study of "Black Middletown," funded by the National Institutes of Health and directed by two African American scholars. The innovative element of that project was an effort to create the missing 1924–1925 baselines for the black community by interviewing African Americans who had been eighteen or older and living in Muncie in 1924, and who were still available to report their recollections of that era. Although the "Black Middletown" project eventually foundered due to personal issues, the retrospective interview transcripts it collected twenty years ago have been very useful in this collaborative project.

Still another attempt to recreate the missing baseline information is a work in progress by three members of the "Middletown IV" research team—Howard M. Bahr, Mindy Judd Pearson, and Leif G. Elder—who are using census data and documentary materials to expand the profile of Muncie's black community between 1924 and 1977.[3]

These investigations will provide a better statistical framework than has hitherto been available, but they will not bring us closer to the living experience of men, women, and children. For that purpose, Goodall and Mitchell's *African Americans in Muncie, 1890–1960* remains the primary source for the earlier years, as *The Other Side of Middletown* will now be for more recent decades.[4]

The material in this volume is too rich to be easily summarized, but one or two points stand out.

The status gap between whites and blacks in Middletown has been significantly narrowed but not eliminated. Blacks now have equal access to the production and clerical jobs from which they were formerly excluded and easy access to secondary and higher education. But they have not entered the local elite in significant numbers. There are no families of great wealth among the black population and no professionals who command a national audience. The young African American men and women who want to rise in the world take their college degrees and migrate to one of the great metropolitan centers where race counts for less.

But the status gap has narrowed enough to deprive the segregated institutions of the black community of their raison d'etre and—with only the partial exception of the churches—they have withered away. When the older members of Middletown's black community look back to their youthful years, they see a much livelier social scene, more elaborate leisure patterns, more participation in voluntary associations, and far more family solidarity than today. Whites in Middletown have suffered some of the same deprivations, as television has replaced sociability, but they started with a stronger institutional structure and more of it has survived.

But there remains amidst the institutional wreckage that surrounds African Americans in Muncie much human grace, a measure of material prosperity, some collective solidarity, and a strong sense of place. With these substantial assets, Middletown's black community is certain to endure.

Notes

1. Robert S. Lynd and Helen Merrell Lynd, *Middletown: A Study in Modern American Culture* (New York: Harcourt Brace & Company, 1929), 511.

2. Theodore Caplow, Howard M. Bahr, and Vaught R. A. Call, "The Middletown Replications: 75 Years of Change in Adolescent Attitudes 1924–1979," *Public Opinion Quarterly* (forthcoming).

3. Howard M. Bahr, Mindy Judd Pearson, and Leif G. Elder, "Erasure, Convergence, and the Great Divide: Observations on Middletown's Black Population" (in progress).

4. See Hurley Goodall and J. Paul Mitchell, *African Americans in Muncie, 1890–1960* (Muncie, Ind.: Ball State University, 1976).

Appendix A

Notes on the Collaborative Process

Michelle Natasya Johnson

Anthropologist and folklorist Glenn Hinson writes that:

> True collaboration entails a sharing of authority and sharing of vi-
> sions. This means more than just asking for consultant commentary,
> more than inviting contributions that deepen but don't detail, more
> than the kind of community tokenism that invites contributions to the
> opening but not to the planning sessions. Sharing authority and vi-
> sions contributes to shape and form, text, and intended audience. It
> also means directing the collaborative work toward multiple ends,
> ends that speak to different needs and different constituencies, ends
> that might be so different as to have never been considered by one or
> more of the collaborating parties.[1]

Like dialogic ethnography (that is, ethnography that places dialogue at the center of an ethnographic representation), collaborative
ethnography shifts the dominant author or voice to multiple voices.
But the addition of a dialogue with consultants about written representation further shifts ethnographic representation to a shared process
whereby both authority and the representation itself are shared. The vision and audience of the ethnography is negotiated through a dialectic
process from the conception of the research to the finished product, the
published ethnography.[2]

As the graduate assistant for this project, my role was to document
a collaborative process through which fieldwork dialogues not only
shaped the students' understandings but also their ethnographic text.
As such, two forms of collaboration developed: the collaboration between students and the collaboration between students and community advisors. First, the collaboration between students took many

forms, both between groups and within groups. This collaboration did not happen overnight, of course. It slowly progressed during the first three to four weeks of the project. For the most part, the students grouped together were meeting for the first time through this class project. Even the students who were already familiar with each other had never conducted ethnographic research together. Furthermore, the groundwork required for the project during the first few weeks did not mandate or encourage any kind of collaboration between students outside of informing group members of work and extracurricular schedules. Nevertheless, as the project wore on and became more time- and thought-consuming, it was evident that the only way to manage this enormous task was to collaborate.

Within groups, students divided various tasks amongst themselves such as scheduling and conducting interviews, recording conversations, tape logging, taking field notes, and writing and rewriting their final chapters. This type of collaboration formed relatively smoothly for a few groups and was like pulling teeth for others. Particularly in groups with one or both members obligated to extracurricular student activities, the collaboration on this level was much slower to develop and typically resulted in one student doing the majority of the work. Confrontation and gossip helped to balance workloads and initiate cohesiveness. A few times it took more than one confrontation. One student put it this way: "Looking back at the collaborative process, I have had to look myself in the mirror and question my work ethic and my ability to work with others. I have had to reshape my thinking when dealing with collaborative projects and group work. Oftentimes when paired with a partner or a group who you are not familiar with, you tend to lean on your past history and how you have dealt with these situations before. I have found that you have to adapt your abilities to those of the people you are working with in order to create the best possible makeup of skills and ability. You also should treat it as a marriage of sorts, with neither partner carrying too much of the burden and equally sharing responsibility and work. These are important factors, but I think the most important one is communication, either with your partner, classmates, or consultants. If you communicate well you will have a more productive and successful product, and you will have a good working relationship with them in the future and it opens opportunities later."[3]

During one occasion, I observed collaborative writing strategies within a group as well. For example, the Getting a Living group rotated writing paragraphs on a topic until they generated a basic theme or had a feel for what they were trying to accomplish. In one instance, Anne Kraemer wrote the first paragraph, and Michelle Anderson wrote the next paragraph. Once Michelle was done, Ashley Moore similarly added to the text, provided questions for clarification, and listed avenues for further research and writing. On the same occasion, this group had conducted an interview very late in the project and wanted to incorporate the conversation into the chapter. They did so collaboratively, with Michelle managing the Marantz recorder, playing the tape back and forth, while Ashley interpreted some of the heavily accented words and colloquialisms and Anne transcribed the conversation from the tape.

Collaboration *between* the groups started to take shape after first or second community interviews were conducted. Listening to the community advisors' life experiences, the students quickly realized that the chapters' themes blended together. As a result, many times during class conversation elements of all of the chapter themes would interweave with each other. Consequently, students readily exchanged consultant contact information and life experience stories that pertained to each other's chapters. As a matter of fact, for over a month the first thirty minutes to an hour of each class (which met for at least three four-hour sessions each week) was spent relating consultant experiences and contact information. Thus many groups—such as Using Leisure and Engaging in Community Activities—conducted some of their interviews together.

The student groups did not just collaborate by sharing personal and consultant experiences and conducting interviews together. They also collaborated to help piece together the final chapter of the book. The initial group of two responsible for the final chapter, Engaging in Community Activities, suddenly became a group of one a little under halfway into the project. In response, fellow students helped conduct interviews, search through old interviews for relevant information, and write the final chapter.

Collaboration between groups was also challenging at times. In particular, the student photographer Danny Gawlowski was, by default, in a peculiar situation. His contributions to the book are the chapter photographs. Because the student portion of the book drastically changed several times throughout the writing and rewriting process, the accompanying chapter photos were relevant one week and inappropriate the next. Needless to say, the photographer's work was never done, and attempts to remedy the mismatch of photos and text included suggestions to incorporate text according to the photos he had already shot. Of course, these suggestions did not go over well with the student authors.

Similar to the multifaceted collaboration of the students, collaborations between student and community advisors also took place on several levels: personally, critically, and professionally. First and foremost, however, collaboration between students and community advisors was on a personal level. Students and advisors both engaged in relaxed conversation, sharing experiences from their respective lives; their conversations were never one-way. This personal collaboration laid the groundwork for trust and relationship building, which led to deeper levels of collaboration as the project progressed.

As the fieldwork continued, students began writing the ethnography. After a few hefty edits—you put this in, you take this out, you shake it all about—the resulting text engaged the students and community advisors in the second—and most critical—level of collaboration. One of the most important processes of this whole project was the negotiation of the text as it developed.

The reflective conversation between students and advisors about the text began with minor clarifications. One afternoon when students gathered for lunch, for example, Jessica Booth relayed to Eric Efaw (the Engaging in Religious Practices group) that Sam Abram had called her to clarify a point in the text. In a similar manner, community advisors also responded to the text through letters to the students. Writing to the Making a Home group, Hurley Goodall stated, "Freddie and I have had a chance to read and discuss your paper and other than a few typo's and an error in whose mother lived with us, it was my mother not Fredine's, we think you did an excellent job in capturing the essence of your topic."[4]

Many of the community advisors, like the students, had never taken part in a collaborative process like this. Some of the earliest conversations about changes were hesitant. During the public forum about the developing text, for example, Daidra Pryor leaned across the table and whispered to me, "The girls got the number wrong." I looked at the excerpt as she pointed it out, quickly swallowed a cookie, and responded in the same hushed voice, "Oh yeah, look at that. Well tell them so they can fix it." "Now?" she questioned. "Of course, that is what we are here for," I said. Looking uneasy Daidra replied, "But I don't want to embarrass them." "Embarrass, them!? That is an easy mistake. You won't embarrass them." After a few more moments of hesitation, Daidra quietly walked over to the other table where the Making a Home group sat and pointed out the correction.[5]

Daidra Pryor and Jayné Carey review Michelle Johnson's notes as she interviews them about their reactions after a community-student meeting at Shaffer Chapel. Photo by Danny Gawlowski.

Most edits and criticisms of the chapters generally proceeded in this manner—not always this hesitant, but placidly. For example, upon reading the "Using Leisure" chapter, community advisor Eric Johnson felt more information needed to be provided. In effect, he wrote a letter clarifying his residency in Muncie and how he is still involved in the community. He sent this information to Sarah Bricker and Mia Fields, and they incorporated it back into their developing chapter. Not hesitant by any means, Julius Anderson responded to the "Training the Young" chapter that Carla Burke and Carrie Kissel had authored. Commenting on the flavor of the developing chapter, he suggested that the students work harder to bring "out the aroma of spending time with people, reflecting on the intensity of the community's experience." Together, the group reformatted the chapter to do as he advised.

Whether deciding to include, rearrange, omit, revise, or clean up, the students and community advisors worked together collaboratively to author and shape the text as they envisioned it to represent the life experiences of the community members who participated in the project. This is especially important because, as Hurley says, "the people who write determine what it is, and it has always been somebody else writing about us."[6] Collaboration, although not always perfect, helps to address these inequities in ethnographic writing, allowing for a more ethically responsible ethnography.

Ethics has played a major role in all stages of this ethnography, from the selection of consultants and funding to field research methods and even to considering the ramifications of the published work. Today, researchers are held accountable for their research more often, generally by professional codes of ethics, and more importantly by their consultants. This means that scholarship of this kind should contribute to the communities and the consultants with whom the research is conducted.

Notes

1. Glenn D. Hinson, "'You've Got to Include an Invitation': Engaged Reciprocity and Negotiated Purpose in Collaborative Ethnography." Paper presented at the ninety-eighth annual meetings of the American Anthropological Association, Chicago, Illinois, 1999.

2. See Luke Eric Lassiter, "Authoritative Texts, Collaborative Ethnography, and Native American Studies," *American Indian Quarterly* 24 (2000): 601–14; Luke Eric Lassiter, "From 'Reading Over the Shoulders of Natives' to 'Reading Alongside Natives,' Literally: Toward a Collaborative and Reciprocal Ethnography," *Journal of Anthropological Research* 57 (2001): 137–49.

3. Jarrod Dortch, comments at "Writing Muncie's African American Community: How We Wrote the Other Side of Middletown," Union Baptist Church, Muncie, Indiana, April 17, 2003.

4. Letter from Hurley and Fredine Goodall to Abigail Delpha and Cari Peterson, April 1, 2003.

5. Daidra Pryor, conversation with Michelle Natasya Johnson, March 31, 2003.

6. Hurley Goodall, conversation with Michelle Natasya Johnson, February 13, 2003.

Appendix B

House Concurrent Resolution 33

State of Indiana

Indiana General Assembly

HOUSE CONCURRENT RESOLUTION NO. 33

Introduced by Representatives:

R. Tiny Adams, Charlie Brown, William A. Crawford, Mae Dickinson, Earl Harris, Carolene Mays, Gregory W. Porter, Vernon G. Smith, Vanessa Summers

Sponsored by Senator:

Allie V. Craycraft, Jr.

Adopted by voice vote on March 17, 2003, during the First Regular Session of the 113th General Assembly.

A HOUSE CONCURRENT RESOLUTION honoring the Virginia B. Ball Center for Creative Inquiry, a division of Ball State University.

WHEREAS, The Virginia B. Ball Center for Creative Inquiry is the host of a unique project entitled "The Other Side of Middletown" created to study Muncie's African American community, which was deliberately omitted from the widely cited "Middletown: A Study in Modern American Culture" by Robert S. and Helen Merrell Lynd first published in 1929;

WHEREAS, The Virginia B. Ball Center for Creative Inquiry, a division of Ball State University, has commissioned a unique project that will bring the best and brightest students at the University into the homes, churches, and businesses of the African American community to listen, observe, talk, study, and publish a book on the African American experiences in Middletown (Muncie, Indiana);

WHEREAS, The findings of this project will then be compared to the findings of the original Lynd study;

WHEREAS, "The Other Side of Middletown" will be under the supervision of Dr. Luke Eric Lassiter of the Ball State University Department of Anthropology;

WHEREAS, After careful screening of possible participants, students Michelle Anderson, Jessica Booth, Brandy Bounds, Sarah Bricker, Carla Burk, Abigail (Abby) Delpha, Jarrod Dortch, Eric Efaw, Mia Fields, Daniel Gawlowski, Carrie Kissel, Ann Kramer, Ashley Moore, and Cari Peterson were selected to participate in the new study;

WHEREAS, Leadership for the project will be provided by Dr. Eric Lassiter, project director, Elizabeth (Beth) Cambell, assistant project director, Michelle Johnson, graduate assistant, and Hurley C. Goodall, community advisor and former state representative;

WHEREAS, Team advisors are community advisors Julius Anderson, Reverend Renzie Abram, Phyllis Bartleson, Geraldine Burns, Edgar Faulkner, Jr., Eric Johnson, Ed McNeary, Carl Rhinehart, Delores Rhinehart, and John Young El who will provide community input and guidance, helping to open Middletown homes, businesses, and institutions to the students and will critique their work;

WHEREAS, Dr. Joseph Trimmer, director of the Virginia B. Ball Center for Creative Inquiry, John Straw, director of Ball State University Archives, Michael Doyle, assistant professor, Department of History at Ball State University, and Dr. Bruce Geelhoed, director of the Center for Middletown Studies at Ball State University, gave the project support in their respective fields of expertise;

WHEREAS, Community organizations such as the Muncie Commission on the Social Status of Black Males, the Community Foundation of Muncie and Delaware County, and the Minnetrista Cultural Center gave their resources, expertise, and support to the project;

WHEREAS, Shaffer Chapel African American Episcopal Church, an institution with a long involvement in the struggles of the African American community in Middletown, opened its doors and its arms to the students to help them immerse themselves in the African American community with all its contradictions and struggles;

WHEREAS, Many of the students involved in the project had never entered an African American home, church, or business;

WHEREAS, The Virginia B. Ball Center for Creative Inquiry is to be highly commended for providing such a cutting edge educational opportunity for its students; and

WHEREAS, Ball State University is to be highly commended for giving its blessing to such a unique opportunity for some of its best students and for providing other institutions with a model that gives students opportunities to stretch themselves and explore new ways to interact with their environment;

THEREFORE, Be it resolved by the House of Representatives
of the General Assembly of the State of Indiana,
the Senate concurring:

SECTION 1. That the Indiana General Assembly wishes to acknowledge its support and encouragement of such unique programs as "The Other Side of Middletown" that bring students and the communities in which they live during their college careers closer together.

SECTION 2. That the Indiana General Assembly wishes to commend Ball State University for this innovative approach to learning and the benefits it brings to the students.

SECTION 3. That the Indiana General Assembly urges other state universities to look at and consider similar innovative ways to give new meaningful learning opportunities to their students.

SECTION 4. That the Principal Clerk of the House of Representatives shall transmit a copy of this resolution to the Virginia B. Ball Center for Creative Inquiry and Dr. Blaine A. Brownell, President of Ball State University.

R. Tiny Adams
State Representative

Mae Dickinson
State Representative

Carolene Mays
State Representative

Gregory Porter
State Representative

Charlie Brown
State Representative

William A. Crawford
State Representative

Vernon Smith
State Representative

Vanessa Summers
State Representative

B. Patrick Bauer
Speaker of the House

Diane Masariu Carter
Clerk of the House

Selected Bibliography

Engaged Anthropology and Collaborative, Community-Based Ethnography

Basch, Linda G., Lucie Wood Saunders, Jagna Wojcicka Sharff, and James Peacock, eds. 1999. *Transforming Academia: Challenges and Opportunities for an Engaged Anthropology.* Arlington, Va.: American Anthropological Association.

Brettell, Caroline B., ed. 1996. *When They Read What We Write: The Politics of Ethnography.* Westport, Conn.: Bergin & Garvey.

Clifford, James. 1988. *The Predicament of Culture: Twentieth-Century Ethnography, Literature, and Art.* Cambridge, Mass.: Harvard University Press.

Clifford, James, and George E. Marcus, eds. 1986. *Writing Culture: The Poetics and Politics of Ethnography.* Berkeley: University of California Press.

Fluehr-Lobban, Carolyn, ed. 2003. *Ethics and the Profession of Anthropology: Dialogue for Ethically Conscious Practice,* 2d ed. Walnut Creek, Calif.: AltaMira Press.

Fox, Richard G., ed. 1991. *Recapturing Anthropology: Working in the Present.* Sante Fe, N.M.: School of American Research Press.

Grindall, Bruce, and Frank Salamone, eds. 1995. *Bridges to Humanity: Narratives on Anthropology and Friendship.* Prospect Heights, Ill.: Waveland Press.

Hymes, Dell, ed. 1969. *Reinventing Anthropology.* New York: Pantheon.

Jaarsma, Sjoerd, ed. 2002. *Handle with Care: Ownership and Control of Ethnographic Materials.* Pittsburgh: University of Pittsburgh Press.

Kemmis, Stephen, and Robin McTaggart. 2000. Participatory Action Research. In *Handbook of Qualitative Research,* 2d ed., Eds. Norman K. Denzin and Yvonna S. Lincoln, 567–605. Thousand Oaks, Calif.: Sage Publications.

Lassiter, Luke Eric. 1999. "We Keep What We Have by Giving It Away." *Anthropology News* 40(1): 3, 7.

———. 2001. "From 'Reading Over the Shoulders of Natives' to 'Reading Alongside Natives,' Literally: Toward a Collaborative and Reciprocal Ethnography." *Journal of Anthropological Research* 57(2): 137–49.

Lawless, Elaine. 1992. 'I Was Afraid Someone Like You . . . an Outsider . . . Would Misunderstand': Negotiating Interpretive Difference between Ethnographers and Subjects." *Journal of American Folklore* 105: 301–14.

LeCompte, Margaret D., Jean Schensul, Margaret R. Weeks, and Merrill Singer. 1999. *Researcher Roles and Research Partnerships*. Walnut Creek, Calif.: AltaMira Press.

Marcus, George E. 1998. *Ethnography through Thick and Thin*. Princeton, N.J.: Princeton University Press.

———, ed. 1999. *Critical Anthropology Now: Unexpected Contexts, Shifting Constituencies, Changing Agendas*. Sante Fe, N.M.: School of American Research Press.

Marcus, George E., and Michael M. J. Fischer. 1986. *Anthropology as Cultural Critique: An Experimental Moment in the Human Sciences*. Chicago: University of Chicago Press.

Peacock, James L. 1997. "The Future of Anthropology." *American Anthropologist* 99(1): 9–29.

Preston, Dennis R. 1982. "'Ritin' Fowklower Daun Rong: Folklorists Failures in Phonology." *Journal of American Folklore* 95: 304–26.

Rosaldo, Renato. 1993. *Culture and Truth: The Remaking of Social Analysis*. Boston: Beacon Press.

Sanday, Peggy Reeves, ed. 1976. *Anthropology and the Public Interest*. New York: Academic Press.

Sanjek, Roger, ed. 1990. *Fieldnotes: The Makings of Anthropology*. Ithaca, N.Y.: Cornell University Press.

Stringer, Ernie, Mary Fances Agnello, Shelia Conant Baldwin, Lois McFadyen Christensen, Deana Lee Philbrook Henry, Kenneth Ivan Henry, Terresa Payne Katt, Patricia Gathman Nason, Vicky Newman, Rhonda Petty, and Patsy S. Tinsley-Batson. 1997. *Community-Based Ethnography: Breaking Traditional Boundaries of Research, Teaching, and Learning*. London: Lawrence Erlbaum Associates, Publishers.

Stull, Donald D., and Jean Schensul. 1987. *Collaborative Research and Social Change: Applied Anthropology in Action*. Boulder, Colo.: Westview Press.

Tedlock, Barbara. 1991. "From Participant Observation to the Observation of Participation: The Emergence of Narrative Ethnography." *Journal of Anthropological Research* 47: 69–94.

Tedlock, Dennis. 1983. *The Spoken Word and the Work of Interpretation*. Philadelphia: University of Pennsylvania Press.

Tedlock, Dennis, and Bruce Mannheim, eds. 1995. *The Dialogic Emergence of Culture*. Urbana: University of Illinois Press.

Student-Centered Ethnography

Angrosino, Michael V. 2002. *Doing Cultural Anthropology: Projects for Ethnographic Data Collection*. Prospect Heights, Ill.: Waveland Press.

Crane, Julia G., and Michael V. Angrosino. 1984. *Field Projects in Anthropology: A Student Handbook*. Prospect Heights, Ill.: Waveland Press.

Emerson, Robert M., Rachel I. Fretz, and Linda L. Shaw. 1995. *Writing Ethnographic Fieldnotes*. Chicago: University of Chicago Press.

Kutsche, Paul. 1998. *Field Ethnography: A Manual for Doing Cultural Anthropology*. Upper Saddle River, N.J.: Prentice Hall.

LaLone, Mary, ed. 1997. *Appalachian Coal Mining Memories: Life in the Coal Fields of Virginia's New River Valley*. Blacksburg, Va.: Pocahontas Press.

Michrina, Barry P., and Cherylanne Richards. 1996. *Person to Person: Fieldwork, Dialogue, and the Hermeneutic Method*. Albany: State University of New York Press.

Papa, Lee, and Luke Eric Lassiter. 2003. "The Muncie Race Riots of 1967, Representing Community Memory through Public Performance, and Collaborative Ethnography between Faculty, Students, and the Local Community." *Journal of Contemporary Ethnography* 32: 147–66.

Selig, Ruth Osterweis. 1998. "Doing Ethnography at Macalester College: From the Inside Out." In *Anthropology Explored: The Best of Smithsonian AnthroNotes*, 250–58. Washington, D.C.: Smithsonian Institution Press.

Spradley, James P., and David W. McCurdy. 1972. *The Cultural Experience: Ethnography in Complex Society*. Chicago: Science Research Associates.

Sunstein, Bonnie Stone, and Elizabeth Chiseri-Strater. 2002. *Fieldworking: Reading and Writing Research*, 2d ed. Boston: Bedford/St. Martin's.

Middletown and African American Muncie

Bahr, Howard M. 1978. Changes in Family Life in Middletown, 1924–1977. *Public Opinion Quarterly* 44(1): 35–52.

Bahr, Howard M., and Bruce A. Chadwick. "Religion and Family in Middletown, USA." *Journal of Marriage and the Family* 47(2): 407–14.

Ball State University. 2003. Middletown Studies Collection and Digital Archives. Electronic Document, www.bsu.edu/library/collections/archives/arcmiddstudiesc, accessed December 7, 2003.

Blocker, Jack S. 1996. "Black Migration to Muncie, 1860–1930." *Indiana Magazine of History* 92: 297–320.

Bourke-White, Margaret. 1937. "Muncie Ind. Is the Great US Middletown." *Life* 2 (May 10): 15–26.

Caccamo, Rita. 2000. *Back to Middletown: Three Generations of Sociological Reflections*. Stanford, Calif.: Stanford University Press.

Caplow, Theodore H. 1979. "The Measurement of Social Change in Middletown." *Indiana Magazine of History* 75: 344–57.

———. 2001. *The First Measured Century*. Washington, D.C.: AEI Press.

Caplow, Theodore H., and Howard M. Bahr. 1979. "Half a Century of Change in Adolescent Attitudes: Replication of a Middletown Survey by the Lynds." *Public Opinion Quarterly* 43(1): 1–17.

Caplow, Theodore H., and Bruce A. Chadwick. 1979. "Inequality and Life Style in Middletown, 1920–1978." *Social Science Quarterly* 60(3): 367–86.

Caplow, Theodore H., Howard M. Bahr, and Bruce A. Chadwick. 1983. *All Faithful People: Change and Continuity in Middletown's Religion*. Minneapolis: University of Minnesota Press.

Caplow, Theodore H., Howard M. Bahr, Bruce A. Chadwick, Reuben Hill, and Margaret Holmes Williamson. 1982. *Middletown Families: Fifty Years of Change and Continuity*. Minneapolis: University of Minnesota Press.

Condran, John G. 1976. *Working in Middletown: Getting a Living in Muncie*. Muncie, Ind.: Indiana Committee for the Humanities.

Creighton Zollar, Ann, and Julie A. Honnold. 1991. "Marital Status and Life Satisfaction in Black Middletown." *Research in Race and Ethnic Relations* 6: 49–62.

Dennis, Rutledge M. 1991. "Dual Marginality and Discontent among Black Middletown Youth." *Research in Race and Ethnic Relations* 6: 3–25.

Edmonds, Anthony O., and E. Bruce Geelhoed. 2001. *Ball State University: An Interpretive History*. Bloomington: Indiana University Press.

Fox, Richard Wightman. 1983. "Epitaph for Middletown: Robert S. Lynd and the Analysis of Consumer Culture." In *The Culture of Consumption: Critical Essays in American History, 1880–1980*, eds. Richard Wightman Fox and T. J. Jackson Lears, 101–41. New York: Pantheon Books.

Frank, Carrolyle M. 1979. "Who Governed Middletown? Community Power in Muncie, Indiana, in the 1930s." *Indiana Magazine of History* 75: 321–42.

Geelhoed, E. Bruce. 2000. *Muncie: The Middletown of America*. Chicago: Arcadia Publishing.

Gibbs, Wilma L. 1996. *Selected African-American History Collections*. Indianapolis: Indiana Historical Society.

Goodall, Hurley, and J. Paul Mitchell. 1976. *African Americans in Muncie, 1890–1960*. Muncie, Ind.: Ball State University.

Gordon, Whitney H. 1964. *A Community in Stress*. New York: Living Books.

Hoover, Dwight W. 1989. Changing Views of Community Studies: Middletown as a Case Study. *Journal of the History of the Behavioral-Sciences* 25(2): 111–24.

———. 1991a. *Middletown Revisited*. Muncie, Ind.: Ball State University.

———. 1991b. "Middletown: A Case Study of Religious Development, 1827–1982." *Social Compass* 38(3): 273–84.

———. 1992. *Middletown: The Making of a Documentary Film Series*. Philadelphia: Harwood Academic Publishers.

Huang, Xiaozhao. 2000. *A Study of African-American Vernacular English in America's "Middletown": Evidence of Linguistic Convergence*. Lewiston, N.Y.: E. Mellen Press.

Jensen, Richard. 1979. "The Lynds Revisited." *Indiana Magazine of History* 75(4): 303–19.

Jones, Carmel L. 1978. "Migration, Religion, and Occupational Mobility of Southern Appalachians in Muncie, Indiana." Ph.D. dissertation, Ball State University.

Lutholtz, M. William. 1991. *Grand Dragon: D. C. Stephenson and the Ku Klux Klan in Indiana*. West Lafayette: Purdue University Press.

Lynd, Robert S., and Helen Merrell Lynd. 1929. *Middletown: A Study in Contemporary American Culture*. New York: Harcourt Brace & Company.

———. 1937. *Middletown in Transition: A Study in Cultural Conflicts*. New York: Harcourt Brace & Company.

Madison, James H. *A Lynching in the Heartland: Race and Memory in America*. New York: Palgrave.

Martin, John Bartlow. 1944. "Is Muncie Still Middletown? *Harper's*" 189 (July): 97–109.

———. 1946. "Middletown Revisited." *Harper's* 193 (August): 111–19.

———. 1947. *Indiana: An Interpretation*. New York: A. A. Knopf.

Polsby, Nelson W. 1960. "Power in Middletown: Facts and Values in Community Research." *Canadian Journal of Economics and Political Science* 26(4): 592–603.

Rottenberg, Dan, ed. 1997. *Middletown Jews: The Tenuous Survival of an American Jewish Community*. Bloomington: Indiana University Press.

Sargent, Thomas A., ed. 1984. *The Middletown Photographs*. Muncie, Ind.: Ball State University Center for Middletown Studies.

Spurgeon, Wiley W. Jr. 1984. *Muncie and Delaware County: An Illustrated Retrospective*. Woodland Hills, Calif.: Windsor Publications.

Straw, John B. 2000. *Dick Greene's Neighborhood: Muncie, Indiana*. St. Louis, Mo.: G. Bradley Publishing.

Tambo, David C., Dwight W. Hoover, and John D. Hewitt. 1988. *Middletown: An Annotated Bibliography*. New York: Garland Publishers.

Thornbrough, Emma Lou. 1993. *The Negro in Indiana before 1900: A Study of a Minority*. Bloomington: Indiana University Press.

Vander Hill, C. Warren. 1980. "Middletown: The Most Studied Community in America." *Indiana Social Studies Quarterly* 33(2): 47–57.

Vincent, Stephen A. 2002. *Southern Seed, Northern Soil: African-American Farm Communities in the Midwest, 1765–1900*. Bloomington: Indiana University Press.

Williams, Gregory H. 1995. *Life on the Color Line: The True Story of a White Boy Who Discovered He Was Black*. New York: Dutton.

WQED/PBS-TV. 1982. The Middletown Film Series: "The Campaign," "The Big Game," "A Community of Praise," "Family Business," "Second Time Around." Pittsburgh, Pa.: WQED/PBS-TV.

Index

Abram, Judith, 140
Abram, Michael, 140
Abram, Millie, 140
Abram, Renzie, Jr., 7, 133, 199, 202, 231; and Berea Apostolic Church, 193, 199, 201, 217; on church activism, 220–21; on church divisions, 196, 198, 200; as community advisor to the "Engaging in Religious Practices" chapter team, 193; on ghost stories, 159–60; on McCulloch Park, 173; on military service, 92; on music in the church, 206; on out-migration of youth, 94; religious education of, 79; on recreation/leisure, 164; on respect, 146; on Reverend Anthony J. Oliver, 211; on salvation, 201; on work, 77, 78–79, 83
Abram, Sam, 70, 152, 219, 250; on education, 133–34, 149; education of, 140, 151; on out-migration of youth, 139
Abram, Sherri, 140

activists, church. *See* Engaging in Religious Practices, and civil rights in Muncie
Adams, Tiny, 238
advisors, community, 7, 8–10, 95–96, 131–33, 231, 259–60. *See also individual names of*
African Americans: and civil rights, 3, 10, 63–71, 82, 209–23; and desegregation, 65–67; and factory work, 52, 54, 56–57, 64; and farming, 4, *48*, 52–53; and firefighting, 53; history of, 9, 15, 47–71; and the Indiana State Constitution, 49–50, 71n4, 72n11, 134; lynching of, 61–62, 210–11; and Muncie, ix, 1–3, 4, 16, 41, 51–71, 232–34, 263–67, 269–71; out-migration of, 93–95; pioneers to/settlers in Indiana, 4, 47–51, 71n2, 71n3; population of, in Muncie, 2–3, 52, 53–54, 55–58, 64, 70, 71n3, 74n52, 74n53, 233, 252n5; segregation of, 50–51, 56–65, 66–67, 164–65, 170–74, 178, 182, 183–84, 241, 252n5;

About the Authors and Community Advisors

The community advisors, students, and professors who worked on The Other Side of Middletown *project stand outside of Shaffer Chapel before a public presentation to Muncie at large.*

Renzie Abram Jr. is pastor of Berea Apostolic in Muncie, Indiana. In addition to receiving his Ph.D. in religion and doctorate in ministry, he worked for General Motors and Delphi for a combination of thirty-seven years.

Julius Anderson is a supervisor for residence hall maintenance at Ball State University. Originally from Arizona, he attended both middle and high school in Muncie, and soon after enlisted in the U.S. Navy. Retiring after twenty years of service, he returned to Muncie.

Michelle Anderson graduated from Ball State University in 2003 with a degree in anthropology. She has interests in both biological and cultural anthropology, and is currently seeking employment as an applied anthropologist.

Phyllis Bartleson is the director of Muncie's Human Rights Commission. A native of Muncie, she became interested in the plight of Muncie's black community at an early age and has spent many years advancing civil rights for *all* people.

Jessica Booth is currently a Ball State University junior with a major in journalism. After graduation she plans to pursue a career in layout and design for newspapers and/or magazines.

Sarah Bricker graduated from Ball State University in 2003 with a degree in anthropology and Spanish. She is currently working for the Teach for America program, teaching in the Mississippi Delta.

Carla Burke is currently a Ball State University senior with a major in secondary education, focusing in English, and with a minor in multiculturalism studies. After graduation she plans to teach high school and pursue her love of writing.

Geraldine Burns, a native of Muncie, worked in politics for thirty years, during which time she was both a precinct vice-committeeman and committeeman. She retired as a purchasing agent from the city of Muncie in 1991.

Elizabeth Campbell is a public folklorist. She has organized a number of collaborative projects, including the Indiana State Museum exhibit on east Indiana's African American pioneers, *Our Land, Our Souls, Our Freedom*.

Theodore Caplow is Commonwealth Professor of Sociology at the University of Virginia. He has been studying Muncie as Middletown since 1976 and is the author or coauthor of two books and dozens of papers on that inexhaustible topic.

Abigail Delpha is currently a Ball State University senior with majors in sociology and Spanish, and a minor in interpersonal relations. After graduation she hopes to work either in the nonprofit industry or in education as a teacher, administrator, or counselor.

Jarrod Dortch graduated from Ball State University in 2003 with a degree in history and a minor in multicultural studies. He is currently a graduate student in Ball State's communications program.

Eric Efaw graduated from Ball State University in 2003 with majors in anthropology and history. After a short respite he plans to attend graduate school in either history or anthropology.

Edgar Faulkner, a native of Muncie, is the owner and operator of Faulkner's Mortuary, which his parents opened in 1952. He also works as a supervisor for Borg-Warner.

Mia Fields is currently a senior at Ball State University with a major in English (emphasis on creative writing) and minors in Spanish, theater, and interpersonal relations. After graduation, she plans to attend graduate school and either pursue a career as a writer or run a center for inner-city youth.

Danny Gawlowski is currently a senior at Ball State University with majors in anthropology and photojournalism. After this project was completed, he continued to work on a series of photo essays that are now featured on www.bsu.edu/vbc/middletown.

E. Bruce Geelhoed is a professor of history at Ball State University and the director of the Center for Middletown studies. He is the coauthor, with Anthony O. Edmonds, of two recent studies, *Ball State University: An Interpretive History* and *Eisenhower, Macmillan, and Allied Unity, 1957–1961*.

Fredine Goodall, originally from Alabama, moved to Muncie in 1943. She was a member of Muncie's first School of Practical Nursing class in 1952. As an LPN, she worked at Ball Memorial Hospital for thirty-one years, retiring in 1991.

Hurley Goodall is a retired Indiana State Representative. A native of Muncie, he has collected materials and written on Muncie's African American community for more than three decades. He is the author of numerous essays and monographs, including *Inside the House: My Years in the Indiana Legislature, 1978–1992*, and, with J. Paul Mitchell, *African Americans in Muncie, 1890–1960.*

Eric Johnson, a native and resident of Muncie, commutes to Indianapolis every day where he works for the Marion County Division of Family and Children Services.

Michelle Natasya Johnson is currently a Ball State University anthropology graduate student. She has interests in African American culture and the history of anthropology (particularly the history of African Americans in the field). After finishing her master of arts at Ball State, she has her sights set on a Ph.D.

Carrie Kissel graduated from Ball State University in 2003 with a degree in anthropology. After a short respite she plans to attend graduate school in either applied anthropology or archaeology.

Anne Kraemer graduated from Ball State University in 2003 with a degree in anthropology and history. She is currently an anthropology graduate student at the University of Kansas.

Luke Eric Lassiter is an associate professor of anthropology at Ball State University. He has authored/coauthored/coedited several books, including, most recently, *Invitation to Anthropology* and, with Celeste Ray, *Signifying Serpents and Mardi Gras Runners.*

Edward McNeary is a former president of Muncie's NAACP, a capacity in which he served for ten years. He recently retired from Delco Battery, where he was also the chair of the Fair Employment Practices Committee.

Ashley Moore is currently a sophomore at Ball State University with majors in telecommunications and Spanish. She has a lifelong dream of becoming an MTV VJ (really). So look for her on television (really).

Cari Peterson is currently a junior at Ball State University with majors in philosophy and organization communication, and with minors in studio photography, public health, and fashion design. After graduation, she plans to work for an events planning organization.

Delores Pryor grew up in Muncie and currently teaches at Wilson Middle School, where she has worked for twenty-seven years.

Carl Rhinehart, originally from Connersville, Indiana, opened Rhinehart's Barber Shop, which is still in business, with his wife, Dolores, in 1954. Carl is officially retired, but keeps on working.

Dolores Rhinehart is a native of Muncie. With her husband, Carl, she opened Rhinehart's Barber Shop in 1954 and started doing hair herself after she graduated from the Poro Barber and Beauty College in 1959. Like Carl, she's officially retired, but keeps on working.

Phyllis Joanne White, a native of Muncie, retired from General Motors as a supervisor–office coordinator in 2000. She now works as a receptionist for Action Inc. in Muncie.

John Young-El, a native of Muncie, is the director of the Muncie Commission on the Social Status of Black Males. He also works as a water pollution control facility operator.